When I Was a Photographer

When I Was a Photographer

Félix Nadar

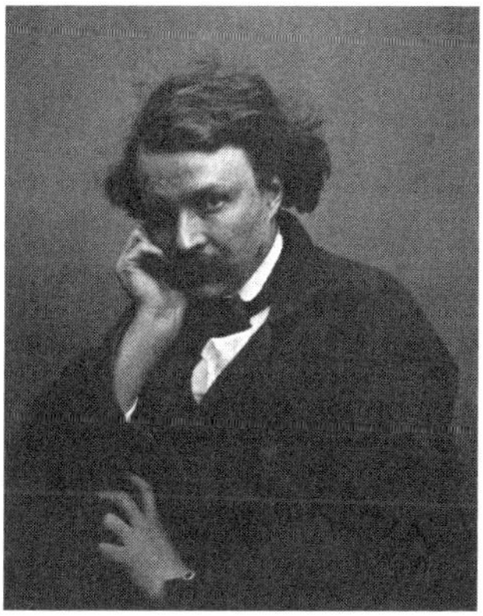

TRANSLATED BY

EDUARDO CADAVA AND LIANA THEODORATOU

THE MIT PRESS
CAMBRIDGE, MASSACHUSETTS
LONDON, ENGLAND

Originally published in French as *Quand j'étais photographe* by E. Flammarion, Paris, in 1900.

This book was set in Century Schoolbook Pro by The MIT Press. Printed and bound in the United States of America.

Library of Congress Cataloging-in-Publication Data
Nadar, Félix, 1820–1910.
[Quand j'étais photographe. English]
When I was a photographer / Félix Nadar ; translated
by Eduardo Cadava and Liana Theodoratou.
pages cm
Translation of: Quand j'étais photographe.
Includes bibliographical references and index.
ISBN 978-0-262-02945-2 (hardcover : alk. paper)
1. Nadar, Félix, 1820–1910—Anecdotes.
2. Photography—France—Anecdotes.
3. Photographers—France—Anecdotes.
I. Cadava, Eduardo. II. Theodoratou, Liana.
III. Title.
TR149.N2713 2015
770.92—dc23
[B]

2015001894

10 9 8 7 6 5 4 3 2 1

Contents

Acknowledgments vii
Introduction: Nadar's Photographopolis ix
Translators' Note xlix

Balzac and the Daguerreotype	1
Gazebon Avenged	9
The Blind Princess	29
Homicidal Photography	39
The First Attempt at Aerostatic Photography	57
Subterranean Paris	75
Female and Male Clients	97
The Professional Secret	111
Doctor Van Monckhoven	119
Obsidional Photography	131
The Primitives of Photography	141
The New President of the French Society of Photography	179
The Bee Tamer	193
1830 and Thereabouts	203

Chronology 227
Notes 237
Index 265

Acknowledgments

One of the great pleasures of finishing a project, and especially one that has taken a number of years to accomplish, is the opportunity to extend a gesture of gratitude to all the friends, colleagues, and supporters who made its realization possible.

Nevertheless, like a translation that seeks to remember its debts to the original it inevitably transforms—even as it must acknowledge its incapacity to preserve everything—the memory of acknowledgments can never remember well enough the numerous gifts to be acknowledged. Even if we can never entirely express the gratitude and indebtedness from which this work has been born, though, we wish to acknowledge the wonderful community that has enabled it to come to light.

We first want to thank Roger Conover, executive editor at the MIT Press, for embracing the possibility of translating Nadar's memoirs in the first place and for his enthusiastic support throughout the project. His consistent patience, kindness, and scrupulousness have been greatly appreciated and, indeed, this project would not have been realized without his sense of its importance and his dedication to it. We wish to thank Matthew Abbate, senior editor, who was particularly helpful and supportive in the later stages of the book's production and who so kindly helped with our index. We thank Margarita Encomienda, senior designer, for her lovely design of the book, and Justin Kehoe, assistant acquisitions editor, for his early help with the manuscript's preparation.

We are grateful to the many friends and colleagues who expressed an interest in this project and who talked with us about it, often in wildly different contexts. We especially wish to thank Branka Arsic, Ariella Azoulay, Jennifer Bajorek, Melina Bálcazar, Benjamin Buchloh, Esther Cohen, Andrew Dechet, Marie de Testa, Hannah Feldman, David Ferris, Mia Fineman, Hal Foster, Nathalie Froloff, Carlos Gollonet Carnicero, Anjuli Gunaratne, Michael Jennings, Branden Joseph, Tom Levin, Aaron Levy, Mauricio Lissovsky, Susan Meiselas, Rosalind Morris, Elena Peregrina, Avital Ronell, Lidia Santarelli, Fazal Sheikh, Kaja Silverman, Joel Smith, Federica Soletta, Gayatri Chakravorty Spivak, Peter Szendy, and David Wills.

We would like to thank Zakir Paul for his help with the "Professional Secret" vignette, Lidia Santarelli for her assistance with part of the "Primitives of Photography" section, and David Wills for his generous and precise help with particularly intransigent passages. We especially wish to thank Gillian Beaumont, who graciously read through our entire manuscript and made innumerable small suggestions that helped make the translation more graceful and elegant throughout. We are grateful to the kindness of each of these richly inventive translators.

We wish to thank Gwen Roginsky from the Editorial Department of the Metropolitan Museum of Art for kindly permitting us to reproduce part of the wonderfully helpful "Chronology" that was prepared by Maria Morris Hambourg and others for the Museum's 1995 catalog *Nadar*. We also thank *Grey Room* and the MIT Press for allowing us to incorporate the first, shorter version of "Nadar's Photographopolis"—published by them in 2012—into this edition's longer introduction.

We thank everyone who helped make this book possible. Its existence confirms that nothing can ever be produced alone, and this is particularly fitting, it seems to us, in a project about a photographer and writer whose fame is so associated with the richness of his friendships and relations. Like Nadar, we have been blessed with such friendships and relations and we owe a felt debt for the remarkable and sustaining world that they enable us to inhabit.

Introduction: Nadar's Photographopolis

EDUARDO CADAVA

The world itself has taken on a "photographic face"; it can be photographed because it strives to be completely reducible to the spatial continuum that yields to snapshots. ... What the photographs by their sheer accumulation attempt to banish is the recollection of death, which is part and parcel of every memory-image ... the world has become a photographable present, and the photographed present has been entirely eternalized. Seemingly ripped from the clutch of death, in reality it has succumbed to it all the more.
Siegfried Kracauer, "Photography" (1927)[1]

I

In a fragment belonging to the posthumous text "On the Concept of History"—a fragment entitled "The Dialectical Image" that cites a passage from André Monglond—Walter Benjamin writes:

> If one looks upon history as a text, then what is valuable in it is what a recent author says of literary texts: the past has left in them images which can be compared to those held fast in a light sensitive plate. "Only the future has developers at its disposal that are strong enough to allow the image to come to light in all its details. Many a page in Marivaux or Rousseau reveals a secret sense, which the contemporary reader cannot have deciphered completely." This historical method is a philological one, whose foundation is the book of life. "To read what was never written," says Hofmannsthal. The reader to be thought of here is the true historian.[2]

Although Monglond suggests that history can be likened to the process wherein a photograph is produced in order to hold a memory fast, Benjamin complicates the comparison by introducing a series of comparisons into it. As David Ferris notes, if we include the opening conditional phrase—"If one looks upon history as a text"—the sentence makes three comparisons: "The first, hypothetical, makes history and a text equivalent to one another. The second compares a text to a photographic plate. The third, by accepting the terms of the first hypothetical comparison, would offer knowledge of the initial subject of this whole sequence: history." "[T]he logic enacted by these comparisons," he goes on to suggest, "takes the form of a syllogism that can be expressed as follows: if history is comparable to a text and a text is comparable to a photographic plate, then history is comparable to that same photographic plate."[3]

But what is properly historical here only reveals itself to a future generation capable of recognizing it; that is, a generation possessing developers strong enough to fix an image never seen before. This is what is so difficult to understand in Benjamin's account: because the image that emerges was already there but could not be seen either when it was taken or in the intervening time, these images offer different degrees of detail. This is why there can be no image that does not involve a deviation or swerve. In the second entry to Convolute N of his *Arcades Project*, Benjamin underlines the critical importance of this deviation to the historical aim of this project, while attributing its cause to time. He writes: "What for others are deviations are, for me, the data which determine my course—I base my reckoning on the differentials of time (which, for others, disturb the 'main lines' of inquiry)."[4] To "read what was never written" therefore involves reading the deviations introduced by these "differentials of time," something that Benjamin had already suggested when, in one of his earliest comments on Baudelaire, he wrote:

> Let us compare time to a photographer—earthly time to a photographer who photographs the essence of things. But because of the nature of earthly time and its apparatus, the photographer manages only to register the negative of that essence on his photographic plates. No one can read these plates; no one can deduce from the negative, on which time records the objects, the true essence of things as they really are. Moreover, the elixir that might act as a developing agent is unknown.[5]

If we remain unable to develop these negatives, however, we still may be able to have, as Benjamin says Baudelaire can, a "presentiment of its real picture" (*ML*, 27), by registering that the dialectical image is to be read in language. What is legible in a dialectical image is a constellation of the then and now, but it is not a matter of the now reading the then; it is a matter of reading the then in the now, or, more precisely, of reading the then now, which is what I wish to do now, here.

I have begun with Benjamin not simply because I wish to put what I will say about Félix Nadar's memoirs, *Quand j'étais photographe* (When I Was a Photographer), under the sign of his name, nor simply because he has been one of Nadar's greatest readers (Benjamin repeatedly cites the memoirs in his writings on Baudelaire and in his *Arcades Project*), but in order to suggest that, if we have scarcely ever read Nadar's text, it is perhaps because we have had to wait to be able do so. What would be required for such a reading, Benjamin suggests, is a labor of reading that seeks to trace what has never been written or read, and to follow the wandering, deviating quality of the text, especially because this wandering character has often been what has dissuaded readers from it. As Rosalind Krauss has noted, the memoirs are

> structured like a set of old wives' tales, as though a community had entrusted its archives to the local gossip. Of its fourteen chapters, only one, "The Primitives of Photography," really settles down to producing anything like a historical account. And although this is the longest chapter in the book, it comes nearly at the end, after an almost maddening array of peculiarly personal reminiscences, some of which bear a relationship to the presumed subject that is tangential at best.

"Perhaps it is this quality of rambling anecdote," she adds, "of arbitrary elaboration of what seem like irrelevant details, of a constant wandering away from what would seem to be the point, that accounts for the book's relative obscurity."[6]

I would like to suggest that, if the book has remained obscure and largely unread, it is because it is difficult, and this despite its seemingly conversational style. What has remained unread because of this difficulty is the book's wildly performative character, a feature that makes it at times more important to register what the text is doing than what it is saying. In addition, the itinerant range of Nadar's many activities—photographer, writer, actor, caricaturist, and inventor—has encouraged us to think of him as an artist and inventor rather than as a rigorous thinker.[7] Even in writings that sometimes seem gossipy and capricious, however, we still can register an analytic power that makes this text one of the most exciting, precise, and rich writings on photography we have. Presented in fourteen vignettes, the text comes to us as a series of snapshots-in-prose, each of which offers us an allegory of different characteristics and features of the photographic world: what Nadar calls, in a discussion of his aeronautic experiences, the "photographopolis."[8] This photographopolis refers not only to Paris as a city that is entirely photographic—according to Nadar, Paris is not only photographed, but essentially photographic in nature—but to a world that, having become a series of images, is increasingly composed of proliferating copies, repetitions, reproductions, and simulacra. What interests me about the memoirs is not only the itinerancy of a camera that moves from Nadar's portrait studio to the streets of Paris, from Paris's catacombs to its aerial photographs of a Paris in transformation, but also the way in which Nadar's memoirs inscribe within its movement an entire constellation of photographic figures, as if photography itself had traveled into his language. What is remarkable is that, in a text that presumably is a record of his life as a photographer, an account of the history of photography from its beginnings to the time of the memoirs itself, Nadar does not reproduce a single photograph, as if to suggest that a photograph is unnecessary in a text that is photographic in form. Indeed, Nadar's text performs, within the forms and itinerancy of its language, what it wants to convey to us about the history of photography and about photography itself. The memoirs appear as a machine of repetition, since several of the texts that compose it had already been published by Nadar earlier (although he sometimes alters them in the memoirs). The memoirs thus form a palimpsestic anthology not only of Nadar's previous writings but also of the texts he cites and recirculates in his work. The text is itself a constellation of then and now that seeks to offer a history of photography in the nineteenth century and beyond. Nadar's text is not a chronicle, however, because it does not offer a sequence of chronological events, a historical record in which the facts are narrated without adornment, or any attempt at literary style. It is, in Benjamin's sense, a question of *Darstellung*—a matter of representation, presentation, performance, and, in a chemical sense that Nadar would have appreciated, of recombination. Written in sections and therefore moving forward in accordance with a series of interruptions, Nadar's memoirs enact a "method" of representation that proceeds, like a performance, in the mode of digression and detour. Each of his vignettes is therefore an opening onto the reading labyrinth that is at once his life and text. Like Benjamin, he knew that "memory is not an instrument for exploring the past, but rather a medium," a kind of "theater" in which remembrance is staged and performed.[9]

Nadar stages the entanglement of his life, his text, and the act of remembrance in the very title of his memoirs, *When I Was a Photographer*. Since we know that he took photographs throughout the entirety of his life, the past tense of the title suggests that the memoirs are written after his death, from beyond the grave. No longer simply alive, but not yet entirely dead—or rather, at the threshold of life and death, dead but still writing—Nadar writes, but as a "dead man." In doing so, he suggests that photography names a dispossession that, dividing him from himself, telling us that living and death are inseparable, figures his death by anticipating it. That Nadar always thought of himself as existing between life and death is confirmed everywhere in his writings. In an early review of the paintings exhibited at the Universal Exhibition of 1855 in Paris, for example, and in order to signal that he has left lithography behind for photography, he signs: "Feu Nadar présentement photographe"[10]—the Late Nadar, presently a photographer. The already dead Nadar lives on, survives, like a kind of ghost, and, instead of producing lithographs, takes photographs. Suggesting that photographs are taken by the living dead, he lets us know that there is never just one Nadar, even as he inscribes a death within each successive self. Still, as Stephen Bann has noted, in a discussion of another text whose title insists on the past, Nadar's 1856 *Quand j'étais étudiant* (When I Was a Student), "Nadar did not by any means relinquish his past. Just as the printmaker, editor, and caricaturist of the 1830s and 1840s was succeeded by Nadar the photographer, so the latter was succeeded in his turn by another Nadar. ... That Nadar looked back at the adolescent Nadar in the spirit of communicating his acute sense of the passing of time."[11] Bearing witness to this passing of time by registering the difference between his different selves—the fact of his multiple identities, the fact that he does not remain the same Nadar from one moment to the next, that one Nadar must always give way to another—Nadar suggests the distance between a history that appears in a linear, successive chain of selves and events and a history that cannot erase the past and therefore carries it forward into the present in a more convoluted, nonlinear manner. As he writes in a later 1881 edition of *Quand j'étais étudiant*, looking back on a past whose significance he cannot retrieve:

> In the old casket closed for nearly half a century, one discovers—a vestige without scent or color—the flowers that once lived, the fragments of yellowed papers whose meaning can no longer be represented, lost forever. ... Thus I discover in this little old book that had its propitious moment the faded memories, the confused essays of my extreme youth and my adolescence, passed in the

old Latin Quarter, before even Bohemia thought of giving itself a name—and I leave the casket open, at the risk that the new air of the present time might succeed in reducing its contents to dust.[12]

There would be much to say about this rather remarkable passage, but I wish to emphasize the identification that Nadar makes between his self, at least his earlier self, and a book, as if this earlier memoir—another "When I Was ..."—were indistinguishable from this self, as if the self were a kind of book and the "little old book" a kind of self. If Nadar here offers a figure for his memoirs (a figure that bears the promise and desire of all memoirs: to embody the history of a self), he also associates this book, this self, with a casket, as if to say that all books are a means of burial, a kind of funerary box.[13] To write one's memoirs may be less to give an account of one's life than to give an account of one's death, even of one's several deaths. The Nadarian self appears like an old, withered and yellowed set of pages, a collection of "faded memories" and "confused essays," none of which can any longer be read and all of which will be reduced, in time, to dust. There can be no memoir, in other words, which does not reduce the self to ashes, which does not register the finitude of its subject. In Nadar's case, this dissolution of the self is legible in the various ways in which the account of his life as a photographer inevitably must include the history of an entire era, even of several eras. Nadar's title, *When I Was a Photographer*, not only refers to the period during which Nadar practiced photography—especially because Nadar expands what can be considered photographic—but also points to the *When*, the era in which he lived. To tell the story of a life, in other words, even part of a life, requires that we also tell the story of the era, the society, the country, and all the relations—personal, historical, economic, and political—in which the life has lived and died, and even survived this death in writing. This is why the wildness of Nadar's text—"the indistinct pell-mell of facts and dates" that so often seems to inform his writing—seeks to match what he calls in the final section of his memoirs, "1830 and Thereabouts," the "pandemonium of people and things" he views as the signature of his era.[14] This era bears witness to, among so many other things, inventions of all sorts, advances in science and in all kinds of technology, new modes of transportation and communication, changes in fashion and controversies over religious beliefs, transformations within the political sphere, increased numbers of riots and new techniques for discipline and punishment, the rise of artificial lighting and the proliferation of newspapers and advertisements, new markets and the Haussmannization of Paris, the spread of theater into every corner of society, and, increasingly, the importance and consequences of photography and its images—of its ability to transform the ways in which we view the world, and even inhabit it. In Nadar's words, "A whole new world is moved in this universal April ... everything is again put into question. Paris, heart and brain, is on fire" (*W*, 204; *Q*, 331–332).

II

Nadar's memoirs open with an account, entitled "Balzac and the Daguerreotype," of the early reactions and responses to the invention of photography. In Nadar's telling, photography appeared in the form of a series of questions that, challenging all of our presuppositions, ask us to reconceptualize the relations between perception and memory, life and death, and presence and absence. In response to its arrival, people are said to be "stupefied," "stunned," "fixed" in place—arrested, that is, as if in a photograph.[15] For Nadar, the introduction of photography transforms everyone into a kind of photograph—perhaps especially when one resists posing in front of a camera. This is why—even though photography, electricity, and aeronautics are for Nadar the premier emblems of modernity, belonging as they do to the innumerable "inventions" produced by what he calls "the greatest scientific century"—nothing is more extraordinary than photography, because it extends the limits of the possible, and responds to the desire to make material "the impalpable specter that vanishes as soon as it is perceived without leaving even a shadow on the crystal of the mirror" (*W*, 3; *Q*, 13). That photography requires the existence of such things as phantoms and ghosts is confirmed in what is perhaps the most famous passage in this section, one in which Nadar refers to Balzac's theory of specters and, in particular, to the spectrality of photographic images. In Convolute Y of his *Arcades Project*, Benjamin explains that Nadar "reproduces the Balzacian theory of the daguerreotype, which in turn derives from the Democritean theory of the *eidola*" (*AP*, 674). Benjamin does not cite his source, but he clearly refers to the following passage from Nadar's opening vignette:

> … according to Balzac, each body in nature is composed of a series of specters, in infinitely superimposed layers, foliated into infinitesimal pellicules, in all directions in which the optic perceives the body.
>
> Since man is unable to create—that is, to constitute from an apparition, from the impalpable, a solid thing, or to make a *thing* out of *nothing*—, every Daguerreian operation would catch, detach, and retain, by fixing onto itself, one of the layers of the photographed body.
>
> It follows that for that body, and with every repeated operation, there was an evident loss of one of its specters, which is to say, of a part of its constitutive essence. (*W*, 4; *Q*, 15–16)

As Balzac would have it, then, all bodies are made up entirely of layers of ghostlike images. Every time someone is photographed, a spectral layer is removed from the body and transferred to the photograph. Repeated exposures therefore lead to the loss of subsequent ghostly layers. Benjamin makes it clear that he is aware of Balzac's theory by citing, a little later in the same convolute, a passage from Balzac's own *Cousin Pons*:

> If anyone had come and told Napoleon that a man or a building is incessantly, and at all hours, represented by

> an image in the atmosphere, that all existing objects have there a kind of specter which can be captured and perceived, he would have consigned him to Charenton as a lunatic. ... Yet that is what Daguerre's discovery proved ... just as physical objects in fact project themselves onto the atmosphere, so that it retains the specter which the daguerreotype can fix and capture, in the same way ideas ... imprint themselves in what we must call the atmosphere of the spiritual world ... and live on in it *spectrally*. (*AP*, 688)

As Balzac suggests, photographic images are based on ghostly images that emanate from physical objects themselves and are then captured by the camera.

Balzac here presents the outline of an eidolic theory of images. As Benjamin's comment on Nadar suggests, this theory had already been elaborated in antiquity in the work of Democritus and, as he notes in his *Berlin Chronicle*, by Epicurus.[16] The most extensive and influential account of Epicurus' writings on the image can be found in Book IV of Lucretius' *De rerum natura*. There, Lucretius describes:

> the paradoxical nature of simulacra, or, as the Greeks *call* them, eidola, those images that appear in the mind and for which there are no counterparts in the outside world: projections and dreams, fantasies, and that category of non-existent beings that flit through the air, willy-nilly, drawn from the outermost surface of things ... these simulacra are the outer shapes of things that constitute a film they throw off in the world.[17]

According to Lucretius, objects are incessantly represented by an image in the atmosphere and therefore appear there as a kind of specter; more precisely, objects are represented by a series of images, by an almost inconceivably rapid sequence of discrete filmic images emanating from the object and serving as a filter for the viewer.[18]

Objects and bodies are therefore condensed composites of multiple layers of images; thus, no image is ever closed or identical to itself. This insight holds for all images but is especially legible in the portraits that helped secure Nadar's reputation as a photographer. These photographs always presume that the image before the viewer is already multiple—and has been from the beginning. Benjamin makes a similar point when he cites Brecht in the *Arcades Project*: "With the older, less light sensitive apparatus, multiple expressions would appear on the plate, which was exposed for rather long periods of time," yielding a "livelier and more universal expression." By comparison, "the newer devices no longer compose the faces—but must faces be composed? Perhaps for these new devices there is a photographic method which would decompose faces" (*AP*, 687). This decomposition of the face—of the many faces that were photographed by Nadar—seems to result from the accumulation of multiple layers of more or less instant images. Insofar as the portraits present a temporal stratification of multiple images, none of which is ever just one, the subject's face is never simply a face but an archive of the network of relations that have helped constitute this particular face and body—the pose it adopts, the clothes it wears, the look it takes, and what it wishes to mime. Nadar himself suggests that the portrait always must bear within it just such a network, however invisible it may remain, and even if its traces are encrypted within the photograph's surface:

> Photography is a marvelous discovery, a science that occupies the highest intelligences, an art that sharpens the most sagacious minds—and the application of which is within the reach of any imbecile. ... The theory of photography can be learned in an hour and the elements of practicing it in a day. What cannot be learned ... is the sense of light, an artistic appreciation for the effects produced by different and combined sources of light, the application of this or that effect according to the physiognomy that, as an artist, you must reproduce. What can be learned even less is the moral understanding of the subject—that instant tact which puts you in communication with the

model, helps you to sum him up, guides you to his habits, his ideas, according to his character, and enables you to give, not an indifferent reproduction, banal or accidental, such as any laboratory assistant could achieve, but the most convincing and sympathetic likeness, an intimate resemblance.[19]

However, this intimate resemblance or portrait requires that the photographer be able to read what is not visible on the surface of the face or body of the person before him, "what was never written" in it, but which nevertheless has left behind its traces.

Like the face and body, the photographic portrait is also a palimpsest to be read, a kind of archive; it always bears several memories at once. To say this, however, is perhaps also to say that every photograph is already, in advance, part of a series or network, even if this web of relations remains unnamable and indeterminate and is generally not emphasized, as it is here. Nadar's understanding of his portraits may even tell us what is true of every photograph: every photograph is already fissured by its own seriality, but a seriality that—like the innumerable ghostly layers that form the skins or films of the body in Lucretius (and later in Balzac)—cannot be understood in terms of succession, because they are constantly separating themselves out of things, even as they condition our perception. This multiplicity and seriality are legible in Nadar's next vignette, because it, too, is a story of ghostly, photographic repetitions.

III

Nadar opens the second section of his memoirs, "Gazebon Avenged," by reproducing a letter he presumably had received twenty years earlier, in 1856, from the owner of the Café du Grand-Théâtre in Pau. In the letter, the owner, named Gazebon, claims that a Mr. Mauclerc—"an actor in transit in our city"—has in his possession a daguerreotyped portrait of himself that was supposed to have been taken of him by Nadar in Paris while Mauclerc remained in Eaux-Bonnes. Gazebon writes to Nadar to request that the photographer take a photograph of him from Paris while he remains in Pau, and do so by the same electric process that had produced the image of Mauclerc. He requests that the portrait be taken in color and, if possible, while he is seated at a table in his billiards room. He promises Nadar that he will display the portrait prominently within his establishment and that, because his café receives every day "the best Society, and even a large number of English gentlemen, especially in the wintertime," this commission will bring Nadar even greater visibility than he already has (*W*, 9; *Q*, 19–20).

Nadar claims to "reproduce" the "original" letter here, but it is, of course, only a reproduction in a memoir. Nevertheless, Nadar quickly remembers that this "original" is a reproduction in yet another sense, since it has its own precedent in a letter Gazebon had sent to him two years ago—again prompted by Mauclerc, who was "already then '*in transit in our city*'"—inquiring about the value of a gilded copper engraving of which, according to Mauclerc, Nadar possessed the only other one of its kind. Nadar states that he never replied to this original letter and this time, too, he decides not to answer Gazebon's more recent request. That this opening scene begins in the oscillation between singularity and repetition, seeing and not seeing, remembering and forgetting, and with a structure of citation that will punctuate the entire story, suggests the repetitions and recirculations that structure the citational character of photography itself—its capacity to double, repeat, reproduce, and multiply what already is doubled, repeated, reproduced, and multiple—and, in doing so, suggests that what is to come will tell us something about the nature of photography.[20]

Immediately after declaring his decision not to reply to this second letter—this double of the first one—Nadar offers us a twilight scene that will serve as the setting for the rest of the section. In this scene we can begin to read another series of doubling, photographic effects. Nadar writes:

> Can you imagine anything more satisfying than those moments of rest before the evening meal, after a long day's work? Driven from bed before dawn by the preoccupations of work, the man hasn't stopped acting and thinking. He has given everything he can, without counting, struggling against a fatigue that becomes more and more oppressive:
>
> I will fall tonight like a slaughtered ox,
>
> and it is only at sundown, when the time of liberation rings, the time for everyone to stop, that, the main door of the house finally closed, he gives himself grace, granting a truce, until tomorrow, to his over-exhausted limbs and brain.
>
> It is this sweet hour par excellence when, … restored to himself at last, he stretches himself with delight in the chair of his choice, recapitulating the fruit of his day's labor. …
>
> Yes, but, even though our main door is closed, the back door always remains half-open, and if our good luck is to be perfect today, he will come to us for some good, intimate, comforting banter, … he, one of those whom we love more than anybody else and who loves us—one of those whom our thought always follows, since their thought is always with us. …
>
> Exactly that afternoon, one of the most beloved and best came to see me, the highest soul with the most alert and clearest spirit, one of the most brilliant foils cited in Parisian conversation, my excellent Hérald de Pages—and what a nice and intimate chat we were having, leaving fatigue and all the rest far behind!—until a visitor is announced to us. (*W*, 11–12; *Q*, 23–24)

This remarkable scene takes place at sundown, at the liminal moment between day and night, light and darkness, and therefore within a photographic temporality and topos. Moreover, in this transitional moment, and in the context of several other threshold figures, especially the several doors

Nadar mentions, the shift in pronouns—from *you* to *he* to *I* to *we*—suggests a self that, like Mauclerc, is always in transit, always passing from one self to another, never simply identical to itself, and since, in Nadar's "photographopolis," everyone and everything is photographic, the characters in this vignette themselves become moving photographs. The entire scene stages, in the most theatrical sense, a self that, always on the move, can never be located precisely, and at this moment in which the self relaxes, stretches itself—perhaps even across other selves—Nadar makes impossible a determination of whether the allegorically named "Hérald de Pages" (the one who announces writing to come) actually arrives "in person" or is a double of Nadar who simply enters through the always open back door of his unconscious.[21] Whether Hérald de Pages is a visitor who comes to see Nadar at this twilight hour or an internal "double," Nadar presents a self whose identity is essentially linked to and dissolved in relation to this other. Divided from itself—because it is inhabited by an other, because, bearing this trace of the other, this self is no longer simply itself—the multiplicity of this self will be confirmed later in the story and in relation to what happens when one enters a photographic space. Moreover, that we have already entered this photographic space is reinforced by the details that will be revealed in the ensuing encounter with the announced visitor.

The visitor is a 20 year-old man. He claims that he has to speak to Nadar and that, although he would have returned until he found him, he felt able to insist on seeing him today because of the connections they already share: the young man's mother used to work for Nadar's mother, and they also share a friend, Léopold Leclanché, who recently died. Insofar as mothers are always another name for photography—mothers and photography are both means of reproduction and mourning is the photographic experience par excellence, Nadar and the young man's relation is mediated, even before they meet, by photography. That the young man was born in the year that

Nadar received the letter from Gazebon requesting that Nadar take his self-portrait from afar is entirely fitting because, as Nadar soon will reveal, the young man has come to ask Nadar to sponsor his new discovery of long-range photography.

After providing Nadar with an account of his experience in the sciences and in several new technological advances, including the velocipede, electronic chronometers, the telephone, and, more recently, photophony, the young man asks Nadar to consider his story:

> — Sir, would you admit, only for a moment, as a hypothesis, that, if, by some impossibility (but it is not for me to remind you, especially you, that, pure mathematics aside, the great Arago would not accept the word: impossibility), if, then, a model, any subject whatsoever, were in this room where we find ourselves right now, for example, and on the other side, your camera man with his lens were in his laboratory, either on this floor, or on any other floor above or below us, that is, absolutely separated, isolated from this model of which he is unaware, which he cannot see, which he has not even seen—and which he has no need to see—would you admit that, if a photograph could be taken here, in front of you, under these strict conditions of segregation, the operation thus executed over such a short distance would have some chance of being reproduced over greater distances? (*W*, 15–16; *Q*, 30–31)

Although Nadar immediately responds to the young man by stiffening—"I dared not move a muscle," he says, becoming in this way himself a kind of photographic effect—Pages springs up and exclaims: "So, you say that, across all distances and beyond your field of vision, you hope to take photographs?," to which the young man replies: "I do not hope to take them, sir; I take them ... I haven't invented anything; I have only encountered. I can take only a small credit there, if at all: that of removing the obstacles" (*W*, 17; *Q*, 32–33). The young man then produces a torn page from a review of his experiment, and Nadar and Pages read the following account:

> One of the most curious experiments took place yesterday, Sunday, at two o'clock in the afternoon, in the town hall of Montmartre. A very young man, almost a child, Mr. M … , had obtained from the office of the Mayor the necessary authorization for his first public experiments of electrical photography across all distances, that is, with the model beyond the practitioner's field of vision. The inventor had asserted that, from Montmartre, he would take photographs of Deuil, near Montmorency.
>
> His Honor the Mayor of Montmartre, and several Council members, were present at the experiment, as well as some residents of Deuil, who were to indicate the points to be reproduced.
>
> Several photographs were obtained one after the other, produced immediately on demand, and everyone recognized the sites reproduced. Houses, trees, people were standing out with perfect clarity.
>
> People warmly congratulated the young inventor, who was trying to escape the great enthusiasm of the crowd with a modesty that increased even more the public interest in this truly remarkable discovery, the consequences of which already appear to be incalculable. (*W*, 17–18; *Q*, 34–35)

The allegory of photography that Nadar wishes to stage here increasingly becomes vertiginously self-reflexive: beyond the claim that the young man can photograph what he cannot see—that photography can make the invisible visible—what is remarkable here is that the young man photographs a town called simply "Deuil," which means "mourning." In taking a photograph of mourning, the photographer not only takes a photograph of an experience at the heart of photography—*mourning* may even be another name for photography—but also takes a photograph of photography itself.

In reaction to this photograph, both Nadar and Pages are speechless and stunned, again frozen as if in a kind of photograph, as if this photographic revelation itself transforms them into photographs. This transformation is reinforced in the following remarkable passage, in which Nadar makes it clear that when one enters a photographic space (and, at this point in the story, there is no other kind of space), one always advances as an other; indeed, as multiple others:

> Yes, of course, I gave in, I would have given in ten times already if ... —if I had not been forcibly arrested by a singular hallucination ...
>
> *
>
> As in phantasmagorical phenomena and with the obsession that attends certain cases of double vision, it seemed to me that the features of my noble Hérald and the honest face of the young worker were merging, blending into a kind of Mephistophelean mask from which appeared a disquieting figure that I had never seen before but I recognized immediately: Mauclerc, deceitful Mauclerc, "in transit in our city," mockingly handing me his electric image, from the country of Henry IV ...
>
> And I seemed, myself, to be Gazebon, yes, Gazebon himself, Gazebon "the Gullible" ... —and I would see myself in my Café du Grand-Théâtre in Pau, awaiting, from Nadar in Paris, my portrait "by the electric process" and, in the meantime, to kill time, serving a beer to "the best Society, even to Englishmen, seated, if possible, in my billiards room." (*W*, 19–20; *Q*, 37–38)

That every self here becomes someone else, and even more than one other, suggests the continual distortions and displacements from which the photographic subject emerges, but always as an other. In experiencing the other's alterity, for example, Nadar experiences the alteration that, "in him," infinitely displaces and delimits his singularity. This movement of disfiguration, linked to the chiasmic plurality of the passage's interwoven figures, makes it impossible to determine who speaks the rest of the story. Where everyone can become someone else—for example, in the aleatory, ghostly space of photography—no one is ever simply himself. Because figures are always haunted by other figures, are always bearing the traces of the other, they are always themselves and not themselves at the same time. What gets signaled here is not only the structure of photography in general, a structure that names the loss of identity that attends the entry into photographic space, but also a mode of writing that performs at the level of its sentences and words what it wants us to understand. This becomes clearer when, after the young man leaves, Nadar is left to appreciate his performance: he suggests the young man was simply following a script that would permit him to trick Nadar, and his sometimes mouthpiece, Hérald. As he puts it to Hérald:

> Notice to what degree our young artist was correct in his entire presentation: his entrance, modest, reserved, his attire standard: all this perfect; the use of sentimental opening lines, the evocation of the two old mothers (which never fails ...), the ingratiating exordium drawn from the character of the orator; the voluble list of facts and dates, difficult to verify on the spot, swirling to dazzle us like the balls of a juggler, the compliments, a bit exaggerated, but this always happens: and in order to achieve this perfect whole, think of all the preparations, of all the training! And he's still so young! (*W*, 23–24; *Q*, 44–45)

A theater, Nadar reminds us, is always also a place of memory and anticipation, where what has been is rehearsed and repeated as what is to come. The story ends with a reminder of the citational character of the young man and, by implication, of all of us. We live, Nadar seems to suggest, within quotation marks, in relation to both mourning and photography.

IV

That this citational structure can be linked to the madness of a mimesis gone wild is elaborated in Nadar's fourth vignette, "Homicidal Photography." Even within a strange collection of self-reflexive stories, this fourth story is a particularly intense allegory of photography's capacity to address and enact violence, and of its capacity to be mobilized toward different ends within different contexts. It is also a compelling account of the way in which everything can be viewed as photographic, even the influence that one person can have on another. In it, Nadar tells the story of a pharmacist who, with the help of his wife and his younger brother, murders his wife's lover. While the story seems somewhat distant from Nadar himself—it is one of the few vignettes that does not present him as its primary character and is not presented directly in his voice, at least not clearly so—it nevertheless encrypts several references to his own personal life and, in particular, to his capacity to influence his younger brother, often negatively. It therefore touches on the sometimes violent force of mimesis, and perhaps even on the murderous character of the photographer himself.

Even if the story did not reference Nadar's own photographic desires—along with his relation to his brother, Adrien—it would be difficult to say that it is entirely fictional and, indeed, neither the characters nor the story are invented by Nadar alone. As Jérôme Thélot has noted, Nadar's readers would have recognized in the story a well-known murder that they would have read about in several newspapers and books, since the particular details and horror of the "Fenayrou Affair" had been widely circulated to the public through the press and various scandal sheets.[22] The murder of the pharmacist, Louis Aubert, planned and executed by the Fenayrou couple, with the help of Marin Fenayrou's younger brother, occurred on May 18, 1882. The murderous trio threw Aubert's body into the Seine, and it was discovered a few weeks later, on June 7. The crime is sensationalized in the press from that day until the end of the trial, which lasted from August 9 to 12. Only Marin Fenayrou—also a pharmacist, and therefore a double of his victim—is condemned to death; his wife is sentenced to forced labor for life, and the younger brother to forced labor for seven years. Nadar knew all of this when he first wrote his text in 1892[23]—especially since many images of the events had circulated, including images of everyone involved in the matter and, indeed, of the scene of the crime itself. Nevertheless, because he does not disclose the names and details of the case until the end of his retelling of the story, the characters appear to be fictional. If he delays any reference to the actual events, it is partly because, instead of wanting to restrict his story to the historical affair, he wishes the affair to be read more generally as a kind of self-portrait not so much of the pharmacist and the criminal—even though in the story these two can be the same person—but of the photographer, and perhaps even of this particular photographer. Indeed, it is because the pharmacist is a figure for the photographer that Nadar can tell us that "the pharmacist is not there" (*W*, 40; *Q*, 68).

This identification between the pharmacist and the photographer—and their shared capacity for violence—unfolds gradually. The story opens drily and anecdotally, with a description of a run-down pharmacy in the Madeleine quarter of Paris, and the early pages establish the story's atmosphere, which is, by turns, melancholic, dreary, desperate, despairing, even suffocating. We learn that the pharmacist's family had wanted him to be a doctor but that, not succeeding in medical school, he had become a chemist; that he seduces a young girl into marrying him and uses her dowry to set up his pharmacy; that, never able to make ends meet, things are very bleak. He hires an assistant whose situation seems to mirror this desolation and who, for a short time, becomes the lover of the unhappy wife. On discovering her infidelity, the pharmacist creates an elaborate plan to murder the assistant, with the help of his wife and younger brother. Much of the story traces the various ways in which the pharmacist imposes his will on his wife and brother, and also the different forces that act on him.[24] In each instance, a suggestion becomes a kind of command, a statement influences another's actions and thoughts, and this other is molded in relation to the other's desires.

Despite the elaborateness of the plan—and perhaps because of it—everything explodes when the cadaver is found in the Seine. A photograph is taken of the dead, terribly decomposed body, and its circulation in the press begins to move the crowds who see it against the murderers. The story is therefore also a story about the effect a photograph can have, but this effect has already been at work throughout the story, in all the different ways in which one character imitates, copies, or even becomes, like a photograph, the doubled trace of another one. This is true even of Nadar's own encrypted relation to the story. Having abandoned his studies in medicine, Nadar is like the pharmacist who, having wanted to be a doctor (or perhaps not wanting to, but instead following the wishes of his parents), is now only a would-be doctor. Moreover, in the same way that the pharmacist manipulates chemicals and drugs in his laboratory and can either cure or poison his clients, the photographer also manipulates substances and chemicals and can produce either a good, lively image or a bad, deadly one. Beyond the fact that Nadar always referred to his photographic studio as a laboratory, he also viewed photography itself as a kind of pharmacy, and often emphasizes all the chemicals he uses in his practice.[25]

If Nadar is attracted to the story, then, it is because it encrypts several references to his photographic practice, but also to his familial history. Insofar as Nadar focuses on the way in which the pharmacist—ever attended by his younger brother, who, always imitating him, surrenders his identity and agency to him—exerts a controlling influence over his brother, he recognizes his brother Adrien's own fate, and registers the extent to which his force and influence may have affected his brother. Indeed, Nadar first begins writing his account only a few months after Adrien is committed to a mental institution in 1890, and may have done so not only because he saw in the criminal pharmacist an allegory of the photographer but also because he saw in this story the drama of a younger brother driven to madness because of his inability to resist the elder brother's force. That Nadar considered the more psychological dimensions of the story is confirmed by his evocation of Hippolyte Bernheim's theory of hypnosis and suggestion in the postscript that he adds to his tale (*W*, 53–55; *Q*, 92–93). We can see here that the suggestive power that Félix has over Adrien is analogous to the relation that exists between the husband and his wife, the murderer and his co-conspirators, and the photograph of the cadaver and the crowd that is mobilized in relation to it.[26] The metaphor of this almost compulsory form of mimesis—described as having a crushing force—eventually determines the description of the cadaver in the photographic image:

> One month, six weeks, after the evening at Croissy, a sailor catches with his hook, under the bridge, an unformed mass, a hideous apparition in the silt. ...
>
> It is the cadaver of a drowned man in total putrefaction, so abominably fashioned that the human form soon becomes illegible. The limbs had been taken and violently bent against the body: lead chains crush them into pallid turgescence and, thus, this gaunt mass seems like the pale belly of a giant toad. The skin of the hands and feet, all wrinkled, is raw white while the face has taken on a brownish tinge. The two eyeballs, the eyelids turned inside out, like two eggs and as if ready to burst, bulge out of the pallid head: between the lips swollen into folds, the wide-open mouth leaves the swollen tongue hanging, torn into pieces by fish. ... The fleshy parts were already saponified; what remains of hair or beard no longer sticks. Punctured many times, the skin of the abdomen, green in places and blue or violet in others, vomits by each of these holes the unraveled intestines, and these hoses float like banners, like the tentacles of an octopus. ... Never had decomposition by death resulted in anything more horrible than this heap without a name, this infamous carrion, disemboweled, so deliquescent as to make even a grave-digger faint. (*W*, 50–51; *Q*, 86–87)

The body mutilated and deformed by torture, decomposed by the undulating waters of the Seine, and destroyed by the ruinous force of violence, is, according to Thélot, "the physical trace of what the pharmacist suffered, crushed by his fixed idea, what the younger brother suffered, crushed by his older brother, the wife crushed by her husband and her lover, and what the fascinated and furious crowd will suffer in its desire to crush the guilty ones with its obsessional vindictiveness, after having been crushed by its drive to the image. *This force of annihilation is therefore the other name of suggestion*—as the cadaver is the other name of photography."[27] In this dead body—emerging from the waters of death into the light, exposed to the looks cast on it, immediately followed by the horror of this terrible apparition—in all of this, Thélot notes, we recognize another "hideous apparition":

> the one in the watery solution of the photographer's basin, the image that trembles under the avid gaze, the imprint on wet paper where the human appearance, arrested by the lens, cadaverized by the shot, and misrecognized by the blind and cold apparatus of the photographic operation, arises deformed, dreary, and crushed. The cadaver caught in the Seine evokes the dead body that appears in the photographic exposure. This cadaver bears the imprints of physical abuse, as the photograph the imprints of what it represents.[28]

The cadaver is a photograph, and, because of it, we can identify the man whose body has been found, and we can "track down" his murderers. While people try to figure out what happened, the police photograph the horror. The devastated body of the pharmacist's victim can now be identified with the flat image of itself (with what Roland Barthes would call "flat Death")[29] and, indeed, the fascination with the cadaver results from the photograph itself. But this identification between the cadaver and the photograph was already anticipated, even if in a displaced manner, in the very moment in which the pharmacist first imagines his revenge, since, at that moment, he himself becomes a kind of photograph, a photographic negative that undergoes a process of enlargement and already has the capacity to kill. As the narrator reports:

> Darker than ever, the husband is possessed by a fixed idea; even though he dries up, even though he consumes himself in research, he does not yet know how to find, he will never know how to find, what can extinguish his hatred, this hatred that immediately elevates and reveals him, enlarges him—a negative, a nothing until then—in the eyes of his alarmed wife. All right, finally! Suddenly, here is the man, here is the valiant, terrible one—the one who commands and who is obeyed: the one who will kill … (*W*, 46; *Q*, 80)

Like the crime that leaves its traces, photography records an imprint on malleable matter. The wife under her husband's spell is "inert," Nadar tells us, "like wax to be molded" (*W*, 42; *Q*, 72) and, in this way, she figures the relations of submission that characterize all the relations in the story: that between the younger brother and the older one, that between the pharmacist and his "fixed idea," and that between the image and everyone who sees it. The image exercises its power and influences the entirety of Paris: "since yesterday, people have been swarming the newsroom of *Le Figaro*, and all of Paris will pass by there" (*W*, 51; *Q*, 88). Nadar expresses an anxiety over the power of the image and, in particular, its capacity to move people wherever it wants to: "but such is the disorder of Justice itself, since this is what it is called, in front of the accursed image of perpetrated murder, that this photographic print ends up sovereignly substituting itself for all the rest: it drives everything" (*W*, 52; *Q*, 90). "It is the photograph that has just announced the SENTENCE," he notes, "the sentence without appeal—*DEATH!* …" (*W*, 51; *Q*, 88).

Here again Nadar simply reports what his readers already would have known. A photograph of the cadaver was taken and the negatives were displayed in the editorial halls with lights behind them. The crowds that view the images are moved to vengeance just as the husband was when he discovered his wife's affair, and their desire for what they presume to be justice begins with this photograph. What Nadar witnesses here, and what he elaborates elsewhere in his memoirs, is, in Thélot's words, "the birth of a modern journalism that invents the mutual reinforcement of words and images in its production of contagious opinion."[30] What is perhaps most remarkable in Nadar's telling of the story, however, is its insistence that this process of contagious imitation or mimesis is itself an entirely photographic one. This identification between photography and the way in which a person (who, according to the logic of this vignette, is himself or herself already photographic) acts upon another is in fact elaborated in the "Preface to the Second Edition" that the French sociologist and criminologist Gabriel Tarde wrote to the 1895 edition of his *Laws of Imitation*. There, in a long passage in which he discusses imitation directly in photographic terms, he writes:

> Now I am well aware that I am not conforming to ordinary usage when I say that when a man unconsciously and involuntarily reflects the opinion of others, or allows an action of others to be suggested to him, he imitates this idea or act. And yet, if he knowingly and deliberately borrows some trick of thought or action from his neighbor, people agree that in this case the use of the word in question is legitimate. Nothing, however, is less scientific than the establishment of this absolute separation, of this abrupt break, between the voluntary and the involuntary, between the conscious and the unconscious. Do we not pass by insensible degrees from deliberate volition to almost mechanical habit? And does the same act absolutely change its nature during this transition? I do not mean to say that I deny the importance of the psychological change that is produced in this way. But on its social side the phenomenon has remained the same. No one has a right to criticize the extension of the meaning of the word in question as unjustifiable unless in extending it

I have deformed or obscured its sense. But I have always given it a very precise and characteristic meaning, that of the action at a distance of one mind upon another, and of action which consists of a quasi-photographic reproduction of a cerebral image upon the sensitive plate of another brain. If the photographic plate became conscious at a given moment of what was happening to it, would the nature of the phenomenon be essentially changed? By imitation I mean every impression of an interpsychical photography, so to speak, willed or not willed, passive or active. If we observe that wherever there is a social relation between two living beings, there we have imitation in this sense of the word (either of one by the other or of others by both, when, for example, a man converses with another in a common language, making new verbal proofs from very old negatives), we shall have to admit that a sociologist was justified in taking this notion as a lookout post.[31]

This passage could serve as the epigraph to Nadar's vignette, since it articulates the logic that underlies the entire story. In the story, there is not a single moment in which one character is not following the script of another; even Nadar, we discover, is following, even as he revises, the earlier script of the "Fenayrou Affair."[32] In each instance, the tendency to be influenced by others, to permit oneself to be imprinted upon by another, transforms the subject into a photographic surface, and this process of transformation—which in the story touches and drives everything—works to crush and even erase a person's agency. It is in this way, Nadar suggests, that photography displays its homicidal tendencies. These tendencies also account for why the memoirs are littered with corpses—from the body of Leclanché that serves a mediating function between Nadar and the young inventor of long-range photography to the corpse of the pharmacist lover to the corpse whose body lies in the funeral home scene that opens the vignette entitled "The Professional Secret," and to the millions of corpses that populate the Parisian Catacombs.

V

When Baudelaire refers in "Spleen II" to "A pyramid, an immense vault, / which contains more bodies than the common pit. / ... a cemetery abhorred by the moon,"[33] he is referring to what, in a passage cited by Benjamin in his *Arcades Project*, François Porché calls "the ancient ossuaries, now leveled or entirely gone, swallowed up in the sea of time with all their dead, like ships that have sunk with all their crew aboard" (*AP*, 99). These ossuaries point to another city in the midst of Paris, a city whose inhabitants far outnumber the living beings of the metropolis above: the underground catacombs.[34] The creation of the Municipal Ossuary beneath the city corresponds almost exactly to the timing of the Revolution: ordered in 1784 by the Conseil d'État, and opened the following year, the catacombs were meant to relieve the stress on the Cemetery of the Innocents and, even more successfully than the Revolution, created a kind of equality that could not be found above ground. As Nadar writes in his account of his photographic descent into the Parisian underground: "In the egalitarian confusion of death, a Merovingian king remains in the eternal silence next to those massacred in September 92. The Valois, Bourbons, Orléans, Stuarts, end up rotting indiscriminately, lost between the wretched of the Court of Miracles and the two thousand 'of the religion' [that is, Huguenots] that were killed on the night of St. Bartholomew" (*W*, 78; *Q*, 129). Moreover, he adds, celebrated figures from Jean-Paul Marat to Maximilien Robespierre, from Louis de Saint-Just to Georges-Jacques Danton and the Comte de Mirabeau, all succumbed to the anonymity of the catacombs. By the late nineteenth century, the catacombs contained the remains of nearly eleven million Parisians. In his memoirs, Nadar refers to this underground city as a "necropolis," a city of the dead (*W*, 83; *Q*, 137). Like photography, Paris—as a city that exists both above and below ground—names the intersection of life and death.

Nadar took his camera underground into the catacombs and the sewers in 1861. Much of his account of this work details the difficulties and challenges he encountered while experimenting with electric light. Among other things, Nadar's underground work literalizes the relation between photography and death that he had already signaled in the earlier vignettes, and that he understands to belong to photography's signature. Whether the bones are put haphazardly on top of one another or are neatly organized, the catacombs are signs of our mortality:

> But the nothingness of the human condition has no limits and the standards of eternity demand even more: these skeletons, all pell-mell, are themselves disaggregated, scattered in such a way as never to be able to be found in order to be reunited on Judgment Day. By the hand of special workers, employed annually for this service, the ribs, vertebrae, sternums, carpi, tarsi, metacarpi, and metatarsi, phalanges, etc., the whole menu of the bones, are pushed back, compacted into more or less cubic masses under the crypts—in *jams*, as they say here—, and held in front by heads chosen from the best preserved of them: what we call the *façades*. The art of the excavation workers combines these strings of skulls with femurs arranged in a cross in certain symmetrical and varied arrangements, and our funerary decorators devote themselves to them—"in order to make the view interesting, *almost pleasant*," says the good Dulaure. (*W*, 78–79; *Q*, 129–130)

Operating with an aesthetics of display, within the effort to aestheticize death, the workers seek to produce a treat for the eyes, a visual pleasure. Moreover, as Christopher Prendergast has noted, Nadar's lighting sometimes gives "a bizarrely polished look" to some of the skulls, which transports us "back into the world of the *grand magasin*, as if the skulls were so many shining spectral commodities placed on display."[35]

This is not the only reminder of the aboveground city in Nadar's underground, however. The skeletal remains also recall the masked faces in the opera or theater. These theatrical resonances are reinforced by Nadar's use of mannequins to represent workers in his photographs.[36] As Nadar explains in a passage that Benjamin cites in his *Arcades Project*:

> With each new camera setup, we had to test our exposure time empirically; certain of the plates were found to require up to eighteen minutes.—Remember, we were still, at that time, using collodion emulsion on glass negatives. ... I had judged it advisable to animate some of these scenes by the use of a human figure—less from considerations of picturesqueness than in order to give a sense of scale, a precaution too often neglected by explorers in this medium and with sometimes disconcerting consequences. For these eighteen minutes of exposure time, I found it difficult to obtain from a human being the absolute, inorganic immobility I required. I tried to get round this difficulty by means of mannequins, which I dressed in workman's clothes and positioned in the scene with as little awkwardness as possible; this business did nothing to complicate our task. (*AP*, 673–674)[37]

While the mannequins were meant to add to the photograph's realism, they instead accent the image's theatricality. Presumably working to order the remains of the dead, they, along with the images in which they appear, evoke the tradition of *vanitas*, something Nadar himself suggests in his memoirs (*W*, 80; *Q*, 132). In this world in which the boundaries between life and death, or persons and things, have begun to blur, the mannequins who push wagons, shovels, and bones in numerous pictures suggest the death-in-life on which Nadar so often insists, the shadowy transitoriness and finitude of all living beings, a finitude whose traces cannot be erased, either in life or in death. This is why Nadar emphasizes the palimpsest-like relation between the underground network of tunnels and the aboveground network of streets. Nadar's Paris is always double, is always more than one, which is why, like the mannequins which serve as doubles for the workers, it is another name for repetition and citation, and perhaps for photography itself.

VI

In his 1864 book, *À terre et en l'air: Mémoires du Géant*—parts of which are incorporated into his later memoirs—Nadar explains that his interest in aerial photography grew out of his interest in mapping the city from a bird's-eye view. When Nadar looked to the skies, however, as when he looked to the sewers and catacombs, he encountered more than anything else his finitude, even as he continued to wish he could exceed it. As he puts it, describing the sensation of being in the air above Paris, "[t]here only complete detachment, real solitude. ... [In] the limitless immensity of these hospitable and benevolent spaces where no human force, no power of evil can reach you, you feel yourself living for the first time ... and the proud feeling of your liberty invades you ... in this supreme isolation, in this superhuman spasm ... the body forgets itself; it exists no longer."[38] This passage is rewritten and elaborated even further in Nadar's memoirs. There, clearly referencing the earlier passage, and emphasizing the play between the soul and the body and the more general experience of liberty, he writes:

> Free, calm, levitating into the silent immensity of welcoming and beneficent space, where no human power, no force of evil, can reach him, man seems to feel himself really living for the first time, enjoying, in a plenitude until then unknown to him, the wholeness of his health in his soul and body. Finally he breathes, free from all the ties with this humanity which ends up disappearing in front of his eyes, so small even in its greatest achievements—the works of giants, the labors of ants—, and in the struggles and the murderous strife of its stupid antagonism. Like the lapse of times past, the altitude that takes him away reduces all things to their relative proportions, to Truth. In this superhuman serenity, the spasm of ineffable transport liberates the soul from matter, which forgets itself, as if it no longer existed, vaporizes itself into the purest

> essence. Everything is far away, cares, remorse, disgust. How easily indifference, contempt, forgetfulness drop away from on high—and forgiveness descends ... (*W*, 57–58; *Q*, 96)

But amid the clouds, and despite the experience of freedom and calm that seems to attend flight, when Nadar looked down at his beloved city, instead of simply feeling that he was "living for the first time," he registered and experienced a landscape of ruins. The photographs show what he saw: Paris as it existed in the late 1850s; that is, a Paris in transformation because of Haussmann's efforts to renovate and rebuild the city. Taking off from the Champs de Mars, Nadar's balloon flight enabled him to glimpse the developments in the northwest of Paris that were meant to accommodate the wealthy bourgeoisie. The picture titled *First Result of Aerostatic Photography* shows the new roads that were altering the city's identity, as well as buildings and landmarks such as the Parc Monceau, Montmartre in the distance, and the Arc de Triomphe, all of which were now resituated—and therefore redefined—in the context of Paris's transformation. Another image shows us the arch at the center of the Place de l'Étoile, which was one of Haussmann's signature accomplishments (and, because stars belong to the history of photography, this emblem confirms Paris's photographic character). As Shelley Rice notes:

> in the clean sweep of their diagonals, in their geometrical organization, in their focus on crossroads and places of exchange, the photographs of Paris itself are indeed the doubles of the photographs of the underground. ... All of Nadar's documentary images of Paris, whether taken above or below the ground, are about dynamism, circulation, change, and, as a result, about a new, thoroughly modern kind of death.[39]

But what is this death? This is the question that all photographs ask us to engage, and it can be posed at each step of Nadar's photographic journey and on each page of his memoirs. Indeed, his encounter with death is legible in the persistence, for more than four decades, with which he remained open to the photographic registration of ruins and death (including those ruins which are the mortal bodies that so often sat before his camera, which is why his studio can also be understood as a mortuary chamber, something he himself suggests in his memoirs). But death is also legible in the disappearance of the places and people that he photographed during this time. The world he photographed—including a Paris that belongs to the past, to yesterday—this Paris no longer exists and it was already, even as he was photographing it, in the process of altering and disappearing. As Baudelaire would write in "The Swan," registering the transformations that Parisians living in the age of Haussmann witnessed every day, "*Old* Paris is gone (no human heart changes half so fast as a city's face)." "Paris changes," he adds, "But in sadness like mine / nothing stirs—new buildings, old / neighborhoods turn to allegory, / and memories weigh more than stone."[40] Suggesting that Haussmann was destroying more than simply objects and space, Baudelaire also indicates that he was erasing and demolishing the repositories of memory-images, the neighborhoods and stones that bore the traces of the city's history and memories. Paris was now littered with ephemeral ruins, which, in turn, became a kind of lens through which the city could be read and rediscovered. Through its ruins—those of the city, but also those of the people who lived there—Paris redefined itself. The city was transformed by at least three forces of destruction: the Haussmannian destruction, the Prussian bombardment during the siege of Paris, and the Commune of 1871. But the Haussmannian moment was the first step in the direction of demolition and ruin. Haussmann saw himself as a "demolition artist" and he was known as "the Attila of the straight line," "the Attila of expropriation."[41] Viewing demolition as part of the great work of progress instead of as the violence it also was, Haussmann sought to break with the past and, in so doing, he destined the now unmoored memories to wander aimlessly through the new metropolis. This is one of the reasons photography—in its capacity to capture moments and places that are in the process of vanishing—became such an important medium during this period. In Benjamin's words, "when one knows that something will soon be removed from one's gaze, that thing becomes an image" (*ML*, 115). This is also why Nadar's aerial photographs (and not only these) recall the traces and specificity of a particular culture and history, even as they inevitably mark the disappearance, loss, and ruin of this same culture and history. His images signal an act of mourning that remains in love with a city that could be said to have died several times, even if it is still living, even if, in its living, it remains haunted by its past and its deaths. Precisely this survival, precisely this living on, reminds us that things pass, that they change and alter, and this is why, throughout his literary and photographic career, Nadar always remained most interested in, and most faithful to, this process of change and transformation. Indeed, the very law that motivates and marks his writings and his photographs is this law of change and transformation.

In several instances, this law is legible in the technological and scientific advances that arrived with photography and aerostatic flight. This is particularly evident in the section of the memoirs that Nadar devotes to the siege of Paris, "Obsidional Photography." There, Nadar tells us that, during the Siege of Paris by the Prussian army in 1870, he offered his services as a balloonist and photographer to help transport mail across Paris. At first making regular observational ascents and conveying his findings to the military authorities, Nadar decided it would be more helpful to interrupt the communications blockade ordered by the Germans. He launched his first siege balloon from Place Saint-Pierre in Montmartre and he carried military dispatches, government paperwork, registered mail from officials, and over a hundred pounds of personal correspondence of ordinary Parisians who, until this moment, had remained isolated from the rest of the world. The flight was successful, but it had not solved the entire problem, since although mail could go out, it could not yet come in. Nadar's solution, inspired by an engineer who comes to visit him in order to discuss his idea for overcoming the problem, is an extraordinary anticipation of the circulation of microfilm across long distances (echoing the long-distance experiments discussed in "Gazebon Avenged"), and even of the sending of compressed zip files.[42] He writes:

> An engineer, employed, if I remember correctly, by a large sugar factory, and since he had never been engaged with photography, it was with all possible reserve, and with his good will as excuse in case he is wrong, that he brings to me, on the off chance that I would be interested, the theory that had crossed his mind.
>
> —Since the question, he says, is how to transport by pigeon the most considerable quantity of messages, I presume that in every major postal center—Lyon, Bordeaux, Tours, Orléans, etc., or even, if necessary, concentrating all services in a single point—everyone brings to the office of outgoing mail his correspondence, written on one side only, with the recipient's address at the top, written as clearly as possible.
>
> A special photographic studio is installed there under an experienced practitioner.
>
> All the letters brought are placed alongside each other on a mobile surface, in a number to be determined, a hundred, two hundred, five hundred, a thousand. A two-way mirror keeps them in place by pressing them down.
>
> This set, once completed, is then adjusted vertically to be immediately photographed at the minimal reduction possible—to the hundredth, the thousandth, what do I know?
>
> Only that, instead of photographing on glass or paper, as with ordinary shots, the operation must be performed simply on collodion, whose substance seems to me the prototypical entity, thanks to its lack of grain, transparency, flexibility, and, above all, thinness.

> This micrographic image of an almost zero weight is mounted on one of the quills or claws of the bird, under the usual conditions of dispatch by bird.
>
> Once at its destination, the counter-operation: enlargement of the micrographic image of every missive, amplified to its current format, in order to be cut immediately, folded into an envelope, and addressed to each recipient. (*W*, 135–136; *Q*, 221–222)

Nadar is taken by the idea and he approaches a photographer who specializes in micrography, René Dagron, to see if he is willing to help execute the plan. Dagron agrees and, introduced by Nadar to the head of the Post Office, who approves everything, he immediately sets up his camera, photographs hundreds of letters with a single exposure, and then reduces the photograph to a miniaturized negative that can be carried by pigeons. Within weeks, pigeons are transporting thousands of letters on small rolls of collodion film above the Prussians, then returning home to roost on Paris rooftops. All of this happens, of course, as the contours and landscape of Paris are being transformed by acts of violence on several fronts, as the Prussian bombardment puts the destruction of the capital on view.

In a certain sense, Nadar the photographer, because of his fidelity to the finitude and evanescence of things, already signals and bears the mourning of Paris—this city that, as he always suggested, belongs to death. This is why even the mourning of Paris, the mourning of a Paris that has disappeared and shows the body of its ruins—but also the mourning of the Paris which he knows, even as he photographs it, will disappear tomorrow—is itself destined to pass away, but always in another act of mourning. Benjamin reinforces Nadar's sense of Paris's finitude when, in Convolute C of his *Arcades Project*—a section devoted to "Ancient Paris, Catacombs, Demolitions, [and the] Decline of Paris"—he cites Gustave Geffroy's comments on Charles Meryon's engravings of Paris (comments that could be used to describe Nadar's own photographs of Paris): "[h]is work as an engraver represents one of the profoundest poems ever written about a city, and what is truly original in all these striking pictures is that they seem to be the image, despite being drawn directly from life, of things that are finished, that are dead or about to die" (*AP*, 96). But, as Nadar also knew, death is not simply a matter of things disappearing even in relation to the photographic act that would seek to preserve them, because another form of mourning is possible, one in which photographs capture scenes which, although visible today, will disappear tomorrow. Nadar knows that everything passes. The figures and people in his photographs, the sites, the objects, all these are destined to death.

In his 1882 *Under Fire* (Sous l'incendie), Nadar confirms his sense of the finitude of all things in what is perhaps one of the most remarkable moments in his oeuvre, a dialogue that he stages between himself and death. Simply entitled "Duo" and dedicated to the French poet and writer Théodore de Banville, the dialogue is divided into two parts, with the first part taking place in a library and the second "in the woods." He had already prepared the path to this dialogue earlier in the book's first section, "Posthumous Paris," in which he writes of the devastation and destruction that has besieged his beloved city. There, he writes, "in the midst of this abandon, this silence, before these ruins of yesterday and these ruins of tomorrow, the thought of the Death of Things comes to me."[43] He refers again to the ubiquity of Death in the dialogue when, addressing Death, he states that "in the immense solitude of the plains, in the populous streets of the city, you are always present to me and I accompany you" (*SI*, 260). Nevertheless, even though he feels surrounded by Death, he asks Death to let him finish the pages he has begun writing, even under Death's shadow. "Why have you begun?," Death replies. "Why finish? Leave behind these vain desires. You only have one truth that will never deceive you: to be with me. — Come! / Come! Everything here distracts you from me ... around you are books of famous authors whose names I will erase tomorrow. ... Against all this rebellion, I will throw my grand shroud of snow. And with one deep layer of cotton I will cover and annihilate everything, forms, colors, noises, and sounds! ... Who dares to breathe before me?" (254, 256–257). Toward the end of the dialogue, and despite his acknowledgment of the inescapability of Death, Nadar tells her: "Everything that moves me, everything that pushes me irresistibly toward you by some fatal, algebraic progression, cannot suffice to defend me against the excessive suffering, the intolerable heartbreak, of saying goodbye to those I love," and she replies, implacably, "you render harsh what for you is the sweetest. Those who you say are yours are mine, not yours: it is through me, and only through me, that you can ever be united with them" (261–262). What this dialogue demonstrates, among so many other things, is the sense of mortality that punctuated Nadar's very real love of life, that actually encouraged him to take great risks, to permit himself to experience the wonder of friendships, inventions, art and theater, and all the scientific and technological advances to which he was a witness. His strong sense of death and mortality is what gives him the right to live, to fly, and to experience all the joy that is legible in his memoirs.

But this is also why, within the world of Nadar's photographs, within his "photographopolis," there can be no photograph that is not associated with death, and why the sections of his memoirs on which I have touched here are everywhere marked by a sense of death. Whatever the represented thing may be, whatever its theme, whatever its content—and even when death is not shown even indirectly—the thing represented is still touched by death, by the fact of its passing. Even the sun—from which all photographs take their point of departure—will one day pass, will one day no longer cast its light on the earth. Because photography belongs to the dying sun it also, for Nadar, belongs to Paris, the dying city of light. Paris is the city par excellence of photography; it *is* a photograph, and within Nadar's world Paris and photography constitute themselves as the allegory of each other. Nadar thinks of this

Paris-Photograph every day. But what happens within his imagination in relation to Paris? What haunts him? What encourages him to focus, like a kind of camera, on the relations among photography, death, and the day and night that touched each of his subjects?

Nadar's photographs are the indices of his particular vision, the traces of a declaration of love, and, if we listen to the silence of his photographs, we perhaps can hear him say, across this silence, and to the Paris and people he loved, and loved to photograph, even as they were vanishing:

> I can only find myself in relation to you, even though I know that, because of this relation, I can never be simply myself. Obsessed with you, and by you, I lose myself in the madness of a single desire: to alter time. I want nothing else than to arrest time, to stop it, to seal it within the surface of a photograph. I want nothing else than to archive and preserve, within a series of photographs, within the series of written photographs that my memoirs are, not only the speed of light but also the night and oblivion without which we could never see, and, yes, the death and mourning without which neither I nor you can be said to live. I want to touch and preserve this passing, this itinerancy which belongs to both life and death, mine and yours, and which offers me a series of shifting reflections, as if in water, in which I can see myself, but as the one who is no longer just myself, as the one who is no longer here.

Translators' Note

Quand j'étais photographe was first published in its full, final form, and with a preface by Léon Daudet, in Paris in 1900 by the Ernest Flammarion publishing house. There is a debate over the publication date of the book, with some art historians claiming that it was 1899,[1] and with the Gallica online library from the Bibliothèque Nationale de France simply noting that it was published between 1895 and 1905. The 1899 edition, however, did not include the final vignette, "1830 et environs," that was subsequently included in the text's second edition, published in 1900. It is as if the publication date could be listed, playing off the title of the second edition's final vignette, as "1900 and Thereabouts."

Since we have based our translation on the edition published by Seuil in 1994 under its L'école des lettres imprint, the only current and complete edition of the book available today, and since this edition includes the added, final vignette, we have referenced the publication date of the second edition as the date of the book's initial publication.

In regard to the memoirs themselves, the first thing to mention, of course, is the tension that exists in the French title itself, since it implies a witness who is speaking from the vantage point of someone who was once a photographer but is perhaps no longer one now. Because parts of the memoirs had been published earlier, while he was a photographer—Nadar incorporates these early versions into the memoirs—and because he never really leaves photography behind, it is as if he were writing his memoirs from beyond the grave, which would account for the title's insistence on a continuous state of past existence. We might even say that Nadar's memoirs come to us in the form of an act of mourning—for a self that perhaps no longer exists, or has been transformed into one of the many versions of Nadar that he lived and overcame during his lifetime, one after the other. We have even permitted ourselves to think that the memoirs would have remained in this act of mourning until they were translated and given another life.

At the same time, Nadar's memoirs resist translation, and not only because they represent the enigma that he was, the dispersed and always moving subject who, like Mauclerc in "Gazebon Avenged," was always "*in transit in our city.*" What makes the text even more intensely difficult to translate is that, in a very real sense, it performs and enacts, within its very movement, what Nadar wants to convey about the always shifting, changing nature of Parisian life in the nineteenth century, and about the rapid transformations brought about in this century by advances in technology and science, and especially by photography. As Maria Morris Hambourg has suggested, "trying to follow the thread" of Nadar's stories "is rather like trying to catch a butterfly without a net."[2] Indeed, part of the difficulty of translating Nadar is that he is primarily a conversational artist. He writes as he speaks, or speaks as he writes, and at every moment he seeks to give form to the fugitive character of his existence; whether he is in the catacombs or in the skies, in the streets of Paris or in his aerial balloons, he attends to the transience of all things, but in a way that surprises and dazzles at every turn. In the words of his friend Charles Bataille, Nadar is "one of the most irresistible characters of the time. He is opinionated, passionate, spontaneous in his hates and in his loves, willful, changeable as a thermometer in his impressions. He dazzles you every minute with the glitter of his speech, which is full of turbulent and unexpected images, which gives you shivers like the knives of Chinese jugglers."[3] Like the society to which he belongs, his language is in constant flux, moving from one topic or figure to another, and never resting on a single one long enough for us to get our bearings.

Putting aside the often very technical vocabulary—drawn from medicine, chemistry, emerging nineteenth-century technologies and sciences, aerial navigation, and especially photography—Nadar's language is impassioned and full of enthusiasm, even if at times wordy, drowning in adjectives, and mostly subjective. It almost always seems to precede him, however, to take him, to lead him in unpredictable directions without his knowing it, which is why he so often stays with what seems, but only seems, to be an insignificant detail. If he often rambles, wanders away from what would seem to be the point, it is because he wishes to find a language that can match what is always about to change or vanish. This attention to movement has its analogy, then, in all the different ways his stories seem to be propelled by the logic of their own dissolution, by the way in which Nadar can go around and around and in all different directions before arriving somewhere. It also has an analogical relation to the multiple styles with which the memoirs are written—from their many dialogues to the sometimes endlessly pedantic but nevertheless instructive and minute descriptions of his balloons or even of Étienne-Jules Marey's laboratory, from the often humorous and sarcastic verbal portraits of Parisians to the sometimes utterly gorgeous and poetic descriptions of relationships, the French countryside, experiments of all kinds, and even our finitude. This is why Nadar's thought and language require a patience and willingness that cannot always be guaranteed in his readers, and perhaps why his book has remained waiting for its translators, translators who, during the years in which it has taken them to translate his text, have come to experience a kind of friendship with him. If he extends the patience and willingness required to read his memoirs carefully to his friends, it is because the memoirs come to us in the form of an exultation of friendship, since so much of what we know about Nadar has to do with his relationships with some of the most famous artists and writers of his time. The memoirs are, among so many other things, a kind of homage to his friendships and to his love for Paris, and this even though he also retains a strong critical stance toward the city and many of its inhabitants.

If Nadar's memoirs almost seem to work against their being translated, it is because it is only when a work remains untranslatable that it can be said to be translatable: that there is, in other words, a task for the translator. But the essential untranslatability of the work means that the translator can never know if he or she translates or even that he or she is a translator: we can never recognize ourselves in the act of translation. In the words of Kiki Dimoula, "translation is an act of self-abandonment, indeed of self-oblivion," since it is only in losing himself or herself that the translator can "enter unprejudiced into otherness."[4] The task of the translator is therefore not *to translate*—if this means merely to transfer a meaning from one language to another, or to communicate the meaning of a text to someone who does not know another, foreign language—but instead to remain faithful to the work's alterity, to its untranslatability; to enact, within the very movement of his or her language, his or her infidelity to the original. Indeed, it is only in relation to this infidelity that the translator can be said to "translate" at all, since it is what makes a new life for the original possible, what tells us that the original can change and become something else. This taking of what is already there, and then transforming it and mobilizing it in a new and different context, is part of the signature of Nadar's writing practice but also of the way in which his inventive and creative activities unfold. Indeed, Nadar views the act of writing as a force of transformation and perhaps even of revolution.

As Walter Benjamin would put it in the remarkable essay that he wrote to introduce his translation of Baudelaire's "Tableaux parisiens"—an essay famously entitled "The Task of the Translator" ["Die Aufgabe des Übersetzers"]—translation must resist its desire "to communicate something," its wish to render the sense of the original.[5] The justification for a translation, he tells us, "does not derive from the sense of what is to be conveyed"—since the translator's "task of fidelity" requires an "emancipation from this sense" (TT, 261)—but from an act of translation that remains faithful to the mobility, strangeness, and incomprehensibility of both the original and language in general. The original is in fact important to the translation only insofar as it relieves the translator and his or her translation of the obligation to preserve a relation to it, to repeat it in another language. The original gives its translator the license to be unfaithful, the freedom to invent a relation to a language that is yet to come, and even to invent this language itself.

The encounter between translation and original takes each language beyond its own limits: it frees them from themselves, even as it enables them to remain in themselves, in language. In his or her freedom, the translator must be able to break through the "decayed barriers" (TT, 261) of his or her own language. As Benjamin notes, citing Rudolf Pannwitz, "the basic error of the translator is that he preserves the state in which his own language happens to be instead of allowing his language to be powerfully affected by the foreign tongue. … He must expand and deepen his language by means of the foreign language" (262). For there to be translation, then, even the translation of what remains untranslatable, language must be changed and transformed. It must diverge from itself, and what this divergence ensures—a divergence that belongs to what makes language language—is language's strangeness and inexhaustibility. In this dispersal of meaning, translation does not transform an original foreign language into one we may call our own, but instead renders radically foreign the language we believe to be ours. Indeed, "all translation," Benjamin suggests, "is only a somewhat provisional way of coming to terms with the foreignness of languages" (257)—including our own. This is why translation must always enact a gesture that is plural and multiple, divided and overdetermined, and why it can always be interpreted as a movement of love or aggression toward the body of every language it touches.

Translation therefore tells us, if it can tell us anything at all, what is true of all texts. In addition, by setting the original in motion, by confirming and bearing witness to the fact that language and meaning can change, translation de-fetishizes, de-canonizes, de-sanctifies, de-nationalizes, and de-constructs language (and it is here that we perhaps can register, even if only in a provisional and preliminary manner, what we might call the politics of translation). It exposes the mobility, instability, and foreignness of language, and thereby prevents it—and the sentence or book in which it takes place—from becoming a fetish. It comes to us as a force of liberation. Indeed, Benjamin notes, it is the task of the translator "to liberate the language imprisoned in a work" by transposing it, by re-creating it beyond the limits of his "own" language (TT, 261). This is why, instead of making itself similar to the meaning of the original, the translation must "lovingly and in detail incorporate the original's way of meaning [Art des Meinens], thus making both the original and the translation recognizable as fragments of a greater language, just as fragments are part of a vessel" (260). Linking the work of translation to the artistry with which language comes to mean something—rather than to what the language means—Benjamin not only evokes the "greater language" which serves as the medium of translation (and is perhaps translatability itself) but also points to the love without which translation could never take place. To translate a work is to engage in a labor of love, in a movement or gesture of love. This gesture does not seek to reproduce or represent. It seeks, like all acts of love, to respect the work's infinite alterity and strangeness, to render its meaning, fleetingly and in all its fragmented and broken fragility, only at the point of contact (the infinitely small point of meaning), as a kind of kiss or caress.

For Benjamin, however, the more untranslatable a work is, the more faithful it is to the mobility and strangeness of its language, "the more it remains translatable, even if its meaning is touched upon only fleetingly" (TT, 262). This means, for us, that the originals most worthy of being translated are those that most fiercely resist the work of translation, most unwillingly surrender their sovereignty to an other. This is why, Dimoula notes, "the only painless duty of the translator is bringing the dictionaries of two languages, strangers to one another, face to face and forcing them to speak to each other But [his or her] heaviest and most exhausting task, henceforth tantamount to an ex nihilo creation, is convincing a word to leave its country and entrust its meaning—great or small—to an unknown guardianship."[6]

We have hoped to encourage Nadar's text to entrust itself to our guardianship. We have tried to be faithful to the strange wonders of this text, to all of its sinuous, wandering, and ever-expanding richness. We have wanted to retain the experience of simultaneously getting lost and finding oneself in his language, and, in so doing, to enable a new generation of readers to experience the wildness, the beautiful eloquence of a book that teaches us what it means to survive in language, in another's language, and perhaps even in this modest and grateful gift of renewal and transformation that we call "translation."

When I Was a Photographer

Balzac and the Daguerreotype

When the word spread that two inventors had just succeeded in fixing every image presented in front of them onto silver plates, there was a universal stupefaction that we cannot imagine, so accustomed are we, after so many years now, to photography, and so inured to its popularization.[1]

There were some who stubbornly refused to believe that it was possible. A usual phenomenon, since by nature we are hostile to everything that disconcerts our received ideas and disturbs our habits. Suspicion, hateful irony, the "eagerness to kill," as our friend Sand used to say,[2] arise immediately. Wasn't it just yesterday, the furious protest of that member of the Institute invited to the first demonstration of the phonograph? With what indignation did the distinguished "*professor*" refuse to waste one more second with this "ventriloquist hoax," and what a scene he made as he stormed out, swearing that the impertinent charlatan would have to deal with him ...

— "How!," Gustave Doré—a clear and free mind if there ever was one!—asked me one day while in a bad mood, "How is it possible that you don't understand the enjoyment one has in discovering the chink in the armor of a masterpiece?"

As the "Sublime always produces the effect of a riot,"[3] so the unknown strikes us with vertigo, and shocks us like insolence.

The appearance of the Daguerreotype—which more legitimately should be called the Niépcetype[4]—therefore could not fail to provoke considerable emotion. Exploding unexpectedly, totally unexpectedly, surpassing all possible expectations, diverting everything that we thought we knew and even what could be hypothesized, the new discovery indeed appeared as, and still is, the most extraordinary in the constellation of inventions that already have made our still unfinished century—in the absence of other virtues—the greatest of the scientific centuries.

Such is in fact the glorious haste of photography's birth that the proliferation of germinating ideas seems to render incubation superfluous: the hypothesis comes out of the human brain in full armor, fully formed, and the first induction immediately becomes the finished work. The idea runs to the fact. Scarcely has steam reduced distance, when electricity abolishes it. While Bourseul[5]—a Frenchman, the first humble employee of the Post Office—points to the telephone and while the poet Charles Cros[6] dreams of the phonograph, Lissajoux,[7] with his sound waves, makes us *see* the sound that Ader transmits beyond our range, and that Edison recorded for us for all time; Pasteur, simply by examining more closely the helminths intuited by Raspail, imposes a new diagnostic that throws away our old codex; Charcot opens the mysterious door of the hyperphysical world, intuited by Mesmer, and all our secular ideas of criminality collapse; Marey, who had just stolen the secret of rational aeronautics held down by weights from birds, reveals to man in the immensities of the ether the new domain that will be his from tomorrow on—and, a simple fact of pure physiology, anesthesia elevates itself, with an almost divine aspiration, to the mercy that lifts physical pain, which is henceforth abolished from humanity ... And it is this, indeed, all this, that the good Mr. Brunetière calls: "the failure of Science"[8] ...

Here we are well beyond the remarkable accomplishments of Fourcroy, at that supreme hour when the genius of a nation in danger *would order discoveries*, beyond even those of Laplace, Montgolfier, Lavoisier, Chappe, Conté, and of all the others, so well beyond that, in the face of this set of events, of almost simultaneous explosions of Science in our nineteenth century, its symbolism also must be transformed:

"the Hercules of antiquity was a man with the full force of his age, with powerful and large muscles; the modern Hercules is a child leaning on a lever."[9]

But all these new wonders, have they not been erased by the most astonishing and disturbing one of all: the one which finally seems to give man the power to create, he, too, in his turn, by materializing the impalpable specter that vanishes as soon as it is perceived, without leaving even a shadow on the crystal of the mirror, or a ripple in the water in a basin? Was it not possible for man to believe then that he actually was creating, since he seized, apprehended, fixed the intangible, preserving the fleeting vision, the flash, engraved by him today in the hardest bronze?

In short, Niépce and his fine accomplice were wise to have waited to be born. The Church always has shown itself to be more than cold toward innovators—when it was not too warm toward them—, and the discovery of 1842 seemed mostly suspect.[10] This mystery smelled devilishly like a spell and reeked of heresy: the celestial rotisserie had been heated up for less.

Everything that unhinges the mind was gathered together there: hydroscopy, bewitchment, conjuration, apparitions. Night, so dear to every thaumaturge, reigned supreme in the gloomy recesses of the darkroom, making it the ideal home for the Prince of Darkness. It would not have taken much to transform our filters into philters.

It is not surprising, then, if, at first, even admiration seemed uncertain; it remained unsettled, as if bewildered. Time was needed for the Universal Animal to make up his mind and approach the Monster.

In front of the Daguerreotype, things went "from the lowest to the highest," as the popular saying goes, and the ignorant and the illiterate were not the only ones to have this defiant, almost superstitious, hesitation. More than one of the most beautiful minds suffered the contagion of this first recoil.[11]

To mention only one from among the very highest, Balzac felt uneasy before the new marvel: he could not defend himself against a vague apprehension about the Daguerreian operation.

He had found his own explanation, for whatever it was worth at the moment, returning somewhat to fantastic hypotheses à la Cardan.[12] I think I remember well having seen his particular theory explained by him in detail in a corner somewhere in the immensity of his work. I do not have the time to research it, but my recollection is very clear and precise because of the prolix account that he gave me in one of our meetings and which he repeated to me another time, since he seemed to be obsessed with the idea, in the little violet apartment that he occupied at the corner of rue Richelieu and boulevard Richelieu: this building, famous as a gambling house during the Restoration, still was called at that time the Hotel Frascati.

Therefore, according to Balzac, each body in nature is composed of a series of specters, in infinitely superimposed layers, foliated into infinitesimal pellicules, in all directions in which the optic perceives this body.

Since man is unable to create—that is, to constitute from an apparition, from the impalpable, a solid thing, or to make a *thing* out of *nothing*—, every Daguerreian operation would catch, detach, and retain, by fixing onto itself, one of the layers of the photographed body.

It follows that for that body, and with every repeated operation, there was an evident loss of one of its specters, which is to say, of a part of its constitutive essence.

Was there an absolute, definitive loss, or would this partial loss repair itself consecutively in the mystery of a more or less instantaneous rebirth of the spectral material? I suppose that Balzac, once he began, was not the kind of man to stop along the way, and that he would walk until the end of his hypothesis. But this second point was never brought up between us.

Balzac's terror before the Daguerreotype, was it sincere or simulated? If it was sincere, Balzac had only to gain from his loss, since his abdominal abundances, and others, permitted him to squander his "specters" without counting. In any case, it did not prevent him from posing at least once for that unique Daguerreotype that I owned after Gavarni and Silvy, and is now in the possession of Mr. Spoelberg de Lovenjoul.[13]

To claim that it was simulated would be rather tricky, without forgetting, however, that the desire to shock had been for a long time the most fashionable sin of our elite minds. These originals, so real, of such genuine frankness, seem to enjoy so thoroughly the pleasure of presenting themselves paradoxically in front of us that we had to invent a name for this disease of the brain, "*the pose*," the pose that, with their moribund look, the hunched, consumptive Romantics have transmitted perfectly in the same way, first under the naïve and brutal allure of the naturalist realists, then up to the present rigidity, the fixed and thrice-locked posture of our current idiographic and self-centered decadents—the punctilious themselves more annoying than all the others together, eternal token of the imperishability of Cathos and Madelon.[14]

Be that as it may, Balzac did not have to go far to find two disciples for his new parish. Among his closest friends, Gozlan, in his prudence, immediately got out of the way;[15] but good old Gautier and the no less excellent Gérard de Nerval immediately followed suit to the "Specters." Any thesis beyond verisimilitude could only agree with the "impeccable" Theo,[16] the precious and charming poet, floating in the vagueness of his oriental somnolence: the image of man is prohibited, after all, in the countries of the rising sun. As for the sweet Gérard, forever mounted on the Chimera, he was already predisposed: for the initiate of Isis, an intimate friend of the Queen of Sheba and of the Duchesse de Longueville, every dream would arrive in the form of a friend ... —but talking of specters, both the one and the other, and without any qualms, were among the very first to pass before our lens.

I could not say for how long this cabalist trio resisted the entirely scientific explanation of the Daguerreian mystery, which soon passed to the domain of the banal.

It can be assumed that our Sanhedrin had the same end as everything else and that, after a first very lively agitation, we very quickly finished up not speaking about it. As they had come, so the "Specters" had to leave.

Never again did they come up in any other meeting or visit of the two friends to my studio.

Gazebon Avenged

Dear Sir,

Mr. Mauclerc, a dramatic artist, in transit in our city, has shown to me and the patrons of my establishment, a daguerreotiped (sic) portrait of himself taken, he said, by you in Paris, while he was in Eaux-Bonnes (by means of the electric process).

Many people who ignore the progress of electricity have refused to lend credence to Mr. Mauclerc's claims, which I myself did not doubt for a moment, since I have been somewhat occupied with the Daguerreotipe for a time.

I therefore am begging you, sir, to make my portrait using the same process and to send it to me as quickly as possible.

Since I receive everyday the best Society, and even a large number of Englishmen, especially in the wintertime, I urge you to take the greatest possible care with this commission, which will no doubt be to your benefit, since many people have the intention of writing to you in order to have their portrait done.

I would like it in color and, if possible, taken while I am seated at one of the tables in my grand billiards room.

I have the honor of saluting you.

GAZEBON,
Proprietor of the Café du Grand-Théâtre,
Grande-Place.
Pau, 27 August 1856.

On the back and body of the letter, as was the practice before the use of envelopes, with the stamps of Pau and Paris, plus the canceled Imperial seal, was the following postal address:

Monsieur NADAR,
Daguerreotipe artist,
Rue Saint-Lazare, 113
Paris.

*

I had read and reread this curious letter—which I reproduce here word for word, with its spelling and punctuation—, admiring equally the gullibility of Gazebon and the knavery of perfidious Mauclerc.

Having "*been somewhat occupied with the Daguerreotipe for a time*" had left me thinking ...

And, in a vague memory that slowly was becoming precise, I managed to find again these two names of the naïve café proprietor from Pau and of the mischievous comedian.

Some two years before I had received from the same Gazebon, under the instigation and auspices of the very same Mauclerc—already then "*in transit in our city*"—a first "sensational" epistle.

It concerned an atrocious clock in gilded copper, a masterpiece of Restoration bad taste: entitled *Malek Adel on His Charger*. This ubiquitous Malek Adel—one could see him everywhere—had been reduced to seeing himself being refused asylum by even the meanest secondhand dealers.

This Mauclerc "*in transit*, etc.," nosing about the café, and coming across this last souvenir of the books of Mrs. Cottin,[1] the insidious Mauclerc exclaimed, swearing to the innocent Gazebon, that he had there in his possession a treasure of the first order in upscale curiosities, listed by all the connoisseurs, and of which the one and only other copy in the world was in my hands. In such a way, he had thus easily incited his chosen victim to write to me and to come to an understanding with me—in order to keep the prices high.

I had abstained from responding and, since this first effort by Mauclerc had no effect, at least as far as I was concerned, he charged again, pushing his Gazebon on me a second time.

So much for Gazebon, who "[receives] everyday the best Society, and even a large number of Englishmen"; but why me, why this obstinacy, this obsession to choose me specifically and to pursue me as their chosen vessel, to impose on me the complicity of such misdeeds? Mauclerc, "*dramatic artist, in transit in our city*," what do you want from me?

Without allowing myself to be touched by his so-marked preference for my collaboration, a preference that I want to believe is flattering on the part of this Mauclerc, I didn't find myself in the mood even this second time to give him an answer.

I left Mauclerc to turn around and witness his scheme explode all by himself, and the heroic Gazebon to await his portrait "taken in color and, *if possible*, while he is seated in his billiards room"—in the plural.

But this letter begged to be kept as a specimen, and, as a collector pins a rare butterfly, I gave it a place in a special box.

It is not unpleasant and even justified, in the last days of a long and rather full career, to have received and to reread letters like this one.

Except that, who would have told me that fifteen or twenty years later the good old Gazebon would have found his avenger and that ...

But let's not get ahead of ourselves.

*

Can you imagine anything more satisfying than those moments of rest before the evening meal, after a long day's work? Driven from bed before dawn by the preoccupations of work, the man hasn't stopped acting and thinking. He has given everything he can, without counting, struggling against a fatigue that becomes more and more oppressive:

I will fall tonight like a slaughtered ox,[2]

and it is only at sundown, when the time of liberation rings, the time for everyone to stop, that, the main door of the house finally closed, he gives himself grace, granting a truce, until tomorrow, to his over-exhausted limbs and brain.

It is this sweet hour par excellence, when, rewarded for his work—our great human advantage—by his work itself, and restored to himself at last, he stretches himself with delight in the chair of his choice, recapitulating the fruit of his day's labor …

Yes, but, even though our main door is closed, the back door always remains half-open, and if our good luck is to be perfect today, he will come to us for some good, intimate, comforting banter, where detestable discussion would never take it upon itself to interfere, he, one of those whom we love more than anybody else and who loves us—one of those whom our thought always follows, since their thought is always with us: perfect agreements, cemented communions until beyond the last hour, made possible by long years of affection and esteem …

Exactly that afternoon, one of the most beloved and best came to see me, the highest soul with the most alert and clearest spirit, one of the most brilliant foils cited in Parisian conversation, my excellent Hérald de Pages—and what a nice and intimate chat we were having, leaving fatigue and all the rest far behind!— until a visitor is announced to us:

— I'm not here! Leave me in peace!

— But this one has already come three times without finding you, and he just told us that, if you could not receive him now, he would come back; he absolutely needs to talk to you.

— Who is he?

— I don't know: a very young man who looks like a worker, bareheaded and with a white shirt.

— Let him come up … intervenes the good Hérald, who has already sensed (I know him!) something interesting …

— All right!!! … Let him come up.

*

The young man appears wearing a white shirt and bareheaded.

He begins by apologizing for being in work clothes: having been occupied all day, he had not been able, afraid that he would never find me again, to return to the home of his mother, with whom he lived on the heights of Clignancourt, to change.

He was about twenty years old, at most, a direct and clear look, his bearing reserved, modest yet self-assured. He spoke with remarkable ease, and had none of the drawn-out accent of the Parisian lowlifes. Altogether a very pleasant young man: a typical example of the good French worker: intelligent, quick, resourceful.

After his apologies and thanks, he explained that, despite his absolute need to see me, he perhaps still would have hesitated to bother me if there were not already some familiar territory between us: his mother, whose name he says and repeats to me, had been in my mother's service in Lyon and had very happy memories of her; in addition, he himself had worked for almost two years for Léopold Leclanché, the son of an old friend of mine, the translator of Cellini's *Mémoires*.

— ... the one, sir, you had nicknamed *Farouchot* (he was laughing heartily as he was telling us the story!) and whom we had the misfortune of losing before his son: a great loss this one, too, sir, for me and for everyone, since Mr. Léopold still had many inventions in front of him, perhaps even more precious than his electric battery, and he was kind enough to show an interest in me, a great interest. I have lost a lot with his death.

— You are an electrician then?

— Yes, sir. I've always liked my trade, and anything related to it: physics, chemistry, calculus. I attend community courses every evening or I read books and special reviews: this is my great, my only pleasure. I know nothing or almost nothing, but I keep up with what others know. I also like going to all the shops where I can learn something: that is why, after having worked for eighteen months at the Maison Breguet, I left: there is only manufacturing there, and it is the laboratory that attracts me. I was employed at Mr. Trouvé's, in the rue de Valois, while he was working on his dual-motor electric velocipede. I worked—I wanted to know it all, see it all—at Mr. Froment's on his clocks, at Mr. Marcel Deprez's on generators and on energy transmission—a great thing of which we have not yet heard the last word, sir!—then with Mr. Ader on his telephone[3] ...

— Ah! You know Mr. Ader, too?

— Oh! Yes, sir; a very fine gentleman, who knows a lot and who will have a lot to tell us some day! And despite this, modest, too modest!

— Indeed.

— You know him, too? ... Isn't it true, sir, that I'm not mistaken? Finally, I was even lucky enough to be accepted by Mr. Caselli to help with his research on autographic telegraphy.[4] It is there especially ...

— But just how old are you?

— Well, sir, I'm almost twenty.

— You do not even look that old. But, let's see: you are an electrician, you are studious, certainly intelligent, you know my friend "Farouchot" and my friend Ader; you've been around: fine! But surely that isn't all you've come to tell me.

Here, a moment of silence. The young man is hesitant, timid, embarrassed. Finally, after a visible effort:

— Mr. Nadar, I won't permit myself to tell you the reasons why it is to you that I have come, why it is to you, to you alone, that I had to come, and why I would have come again if I had not been able to reach you: I find nothing worse than flattery and I would not want to appear a flatterer to you ...

I must have frowned at that point, and he must have noticed:

— First and foremost, sir, I beg you not to take me for an arrogant person, which I have no reason to be; but what I have come to reveal to you is so ... extraordinary, so beyond, even for you, what is recognized as accepted, classified, catalogued, that I first must make an appeal to you: to kindly agree not to judge me right away as crazy or impudent, to listen to me, to hear me without crying out ...

— Go ahead!

— And I must also ask you, gentlemen, not to do me the honor of taking me for an inventor. I am only a young man, very ignorant, and it is not at all a discovery that I claim to bring to you. It is only a simple find, a chance, a coincidence in the laboratory. Moreover, you would be surprised at the simplicity, at the banality of the thing: I am speaking of my find by itself, from a scientific point of view, not in regard to its consequences. I was led there naturally by the latest published experiments on photophony. I said to myself: if the results obtained by Mr. Graham Bell and Mr. Summer Tainter have established that all bodies can emit *sound* under the action of *light*, why would we refuse to accept from light itself what light can offer us?

— And? ...

*

Here, another silence: then, with resolution, looking at me even more directly:

— Sir, would you admit, only for a moment, as a hypothesis, that, if, by some impossibility (but it is not for me to remind you, especially you, that, pure mathematics aside, the great Arago would not accept the word: impossibility),[5] if, then, a model, any subject whatsoever, were in this room where we find ourselves right now, for example, and on the other side, your camera man with his lens were in his laboratory, either on this floor, or on any other floor above or below us, that is, absolutely separated, isolated from this model of which he is unaware, which he cannot see, which he has not even seen—and which he has no need to see—would you admit that, if a photograph could be taken here, in front of you, under these strict conditions of segregation, the operation thus executed over such a short distance would have some chance of being reproduced over greater distances? ...

*

De Pages jumped up as if the young electrician had touched him with his live wire ...

As for me, a little stunned, as you can imagine, I was examining my interlocutor: his clear gaze, that of a good young man, remained directly fixed on mine.

— And so, sir, I have come to you to ask you a favor—a favor that is nothing to you, and everything to me: to only and simply be kind enough to allow me to have a photograph taken in your studio, in front of you, by one of your technicians—, under the indicated conditions of isolation or conditions that you will indicate yourself, with any model you wish to choose, a photograph, no more than one photograph, which will suffice to demonstrate whether what I suggest is possible or not. Obviously, I myself have neither the equipment nor the photographic materials, and, in any case, this side of things is not my interest.

This is all I had to ask you, sir, and you see that the inconvenience that I have come to request of you is not very great. As for my part in this, it will not inconvenience you much more: I do not take up much space and I will not be in your way with the eleven hundred grams that my little Griscom motor on my knees weighs[6]—and which is all I need.

And I will be very grateful to you, since it will be a great honor to me to have been heard in a house like yours. I'm not talking about the results from the point of view of financial profits, which concern me less than the rest. With my eyes closed, I here put myself in your hands—which I know.

I hadn't even flinched.

My friend De Pages, excited, was seeking my eyes as eagerly as I was avoiding his, making numerous signals to me that I didn't wish to see. Very clearly, he thought I was somewhat cold. Unable to hold back any longer, he intervened:

— So, you say that, across all distances and beyond your field of vision, you hope to take photographs?

— I do not hope to take them, sir; I take them. But I wouldn't know how to say it again to you and you will see it anyway: I'm not an inventor, I haven't invented anything; I have only encountered. I can take only a small credit there, if at all: that of removing the obstacles. Do you remember, Mr. Nadar, what you wrote about the first cogwheel of Stephenson's locomotive: "The first obstacle in most of the new manifestations of the human spirit is that we proceed almost constantly from the complex to the simple"?

— And he cites his classics! ... De Pages tells me, laughing.

— I've simplified, that's all. Only ... only, gentlemen, I owe you a confession ... My duty is to tell you ...

— ? ...

— ... to warn you that I have already attempted a first experiment, an experiment that, after your kind reception today, I must regret, since it was public. I should even have the newspaper that reviewed it on me ...

He put his hand into his pocket, then, with a growing agitation, he searched successively his other pockets:

— O! My God! I must have left it in the workshop!!! ...

Then, all happy:

— No! Here it is! ...

He unfolded and handed the page to me—some *Courrier* or other, or an *Écho de la banlieue*.

At the head of the "News Items" column we read—De Pages, transfixed, with his shoulder against mine:

> One of the most curious experiments took place yesterday, Sunday, at two o'clock in the afternoon, in the town hall of Montmartre. A very young man, almost a child, Mr M ... , had obtained from the office of the Mayor the necessary authorization for his first public experiments of electrical photography across all distances, that is, with the model

beyond the practitioner's field of vision. The inventor had asserted that, from Montmartre, he would take photographs of Deuil, near Montmorency.

His Honor the Mayor of Montmartre, and several Council members, were present at the experiment, as well as some residents of Deuil, who were to indicate the points to be reproduced.

Several photographs were obtained one after the other, produced immediately on demand, and everyone recognized the sites reproduced. Houses, trees, people were standing out with perfect clarity.

People warmly congratulated the young inventor, who was trying to escape the great enthusiasm of the crowd with a modesty that increased even more the public interest in this truly remarkable discovery, the consequences of which already appear to be incalculable.

*

We reread again this extraordinary account ...

We were dumbfounded, and we would have been so with less.

In fact, the very day before, we were coming out of the Exhibition of Electricity, fully dazzled, even blinded by its miracles, troubled by this mysterious power we now have domesticated and which rushes to our call even before our call—even better, summoning itself for our slightest needs or whims, always there, invisible and present, like some diabolical servant ...

We had just seen it, the one we cannot see, accomplish all duties, perform all offices, realize all the desires of our imagination, as soon as they are formulated or only conceived, waiting, subdued and ready, for our commands to come. This agent, both omnipotent and impeccable, this servant unrivaled in all its liveries and all its names: telegraph, polyscope, phonophone, phonograph, phonautograph, telelogue, telephone, topophone, spectrophone, microphone, sphygmograph, pyrophone, etc., etc., we have seen it lifting and transporting our burdens for us, propelling our ships, our carriages, carrying our voice from region to region and keeping, *ne varietur*, the sound up to its least perceptible modulations, writing, drawing far beyond the reach of our hand, at all distances, chiseling, sandblasting, gilding, silver plating—feeling our pulse and setting our clock, calling the firemen before we even see the fire and the diggers before the rising of the water level, fighting in our place either by keeping watch like a sentinel, or by regulating the speed of our missiles or by blowing up the enemy's forts, indicating to the surgeon the bullet lodged in our body, stopping our launched horses or our locomotives dead in their tracks, and also arresting thieves, plowing our soil, winnowing our wheat, improving and aging our wine, and shooting game for us, monitoring our cashiers while guarding our cashboxes, and preventing even our good representatives from cheating when they vote until we obtain the blessed machine which at last will manufacture representatives who will not defraud us in anything; a first-class worker, in all arts and professions, and a jack-of-all-trades, one at a time or all at once, if you wish, market porter, postman, lamp man, engraver, farmer, physician, artillery man, bookkeeper, archivist, carpenter, substitute soldier, tenor and police officer ...

In fact, why not photographer, this universal Jack-of-all-trades, and even long-distance photographer?

And good old Hérald, born to be credulous always, with all his spirit so fine, so sharp (like our good Latour-Saint-Ybars, gone before us ...),[7] Hérald was reproaching me, he was returning my silent resistance with his gaze illuminated before all the infinite prospects of this new path which was opening before us ...

Eh! Yes, of course, I gave in, I would have given in ten times already if ... —if I had not been forcibly arrested by a singular hallucination ...

*

As in phantasmagorical phenomena and with the obsession that attends certain cases of double vision, it seemed to me that the features of my noble Hérald and the honest face of the young worker were merging, blending into a kind of Mephistophelean mask from which appeared a disquieting figure that I had never seen before but recognized immediately: Mauclerc, deceitful Mauclerc, "in transit in our city," mockingly handing me his electric image, from the country of Henry IV …

And I seemed, myself, to be Gazebon, yes, Gazebon himself, Gazebon "the Gullible" … —and I would see myself in my Café du Grand-Théâtre in Pau, awaiting, from Nadar in Paris, my portrait "by the electric process" and, in the meantime, to kill time, serving a beer to "the best Society, even to Englishmen, seated, if possible, in my billiards room."

And "taken in color"! …

*

And while the good young man was waiting silently for an answer, his eyes always fixed on mine, fiery De Pages continued to sparkle …

— Well, Nadar, you say nothing?

— What do you want me to say?

— But what do you have to lose? And why do you care about one more or one less photograph? In the end, what is he asking from you?

Here, the young man, with a resigned sadness in his half-smile, said:

— Oh! No, it's not that! I understand very well what stops Mr. Nadar … Yet, when he will have seen, seen with his own eyes, that this phantom is nothing, less than nothing …

— Suppose that I do not stop: how will you arrange your conducting wires here?

—You will recoil even more this time, sir. And yet, I cannot, in conscience, tell you what is not so … Sir, I have no need of wires.

— What do you mean!!!

— No, sir, I'm not an original, for it's not since yesterday but since 1838, I think, that Steinheil already had replaced his wire with the ground itself as a conductor, and Bourbouze had observed tellurian currents with a galvanometer.[8] But, in any case, the way had long been indicated by the first experiments of the Royal Society of London, when Watson, Cavendish, and a third whose name escapes me (ah! Martin Folkes!) used the Thames as a conductor, not along its current, but across it, and when they even increased the path by adding to the width of the river a stretch of land: an experiment that was repeated later with voltaic current.[9] But isn't air itself recognized today as a conductor? Why then would we doubt today what has been known since 1747, for more than a century, and why would we be such enemies to ourselves as to resist using this knowledge? Finally, the photo-phone, this mirror that vibrates across all distances under the action of the word, this miracle, wasn't it obtained without a wire? It is true that the selenium that produced it for us has been waiting since 1817, when Berzelius discovered it, for us to want to take the trouble to accept it.[10] But it's always as you have said: "the human spirit proceeds from the complex to the simple ..." Since the wires were useless to me, sir, I dispensed with wires.

From dumbfounded, I went to being absolutely stunned ...

But the match had been won, and our young man had already felt it, since in order to be absolutely sure that he had won the city by planting his flag, he added, more familiarly and with the smile of a good boy:

— And now will you permit me, Mr. Nadar, to express my surprise at having encountered such resistance in a man known for so many diverse initiatives, in a man who—the first!—thirty years before anyone else dreamt of it, predicted, explained, and even baptized the *Phonograph*? For it was indeed in 1856, in an article in the *Musée français-anglais*, that you ...

— Ok, ok ... Enough!!

— ... you who took the first underground photograph by

artificial lights and also the first photograph from the basket of an aerostat; you who in 1863 were so instrumental in the chimera of balloons pretending to be dirigibles and you who have proclaimed since then the exclusive principle, accepted by everyone today, of heavier-than-air machines for aerial navigation ... you who ...

— Have mercy!! ... Come whenever you like.

— Ah! Thank you, sir!!!

— And when will you come? De Pages asks, having reached boiling point.

— Sir, if it's not inconvenient, I will come on the sixteenth of this month, at the time that Mr. Nadar would like to designate.

But Hérald:

— The sixteenth! ... but today is only the fourth!!! Why lose these twelve days? Why not earlier? ... tomorrow? even today?

— I am sorry, sir; I cannot before the sixteenth.

— Why?

But the young man is already moving toward the door, bowing to take his leave.

De Pages grabs him by the sleeve of his shirt.

— But why such a delay?

— Excuse me, sir, if I cannot give you an answer: I have personal reasons, of no interest whatsoever. I'll come on the sixteenth.

— But what possible reasons could you have to delay by twelve days a demonstration of such great importance to you?

— I can only repeat to you, sir: it is a personal matter and there is no need for anyone to intervene.

But De Pages is not one to be beaten and will not let go. He pushes, he presses with such vigor that the young man, crushed beyond his last defenses, begins to give in ... De Pages inflames his arguments persuasively:

— Come on, from you to us, really between us, what's the obstacle? ...

— My God, sir, you insist so much that it would be bad form of me to refuse such benevolence further. Since you wish to know, I will tell you that it's only the fourth and I must wait until the fifteenth to be paid at the workshop …

— …For? …

— … For one or two small purchases of products needed for my experiment: last Sunday at Montmartre, I used up the last of my very few supplies. It is an insignificant cost, barely forty francs: but you understand—I'm sure you understand—that I feel very strongly about providing them myself …

"Here we are!" I thought.

It is I, this time, who searches for De Pages's gaze … But nothing escapes the one who watches: the young worker turns again toward Hérald and, choking, with a tear trembling at the corner of his eyelashes:

– There!!! … You see, sir! … I was sure! Mr. Nadar thinks ill of me! … Yet he himself is my witness that I did not want to say anything about what concerned me alone; but you insisted so much that I gave in and now I am taken for a schemer, a miserable beggar …

It's necessary to calm him, to console him, to reassure him … I help Hérald in this and finally the young man leaves with his two louis, but how much we had to beg him! …

He will return tomorrow morning, at ten o'clock, *exactly* at ten o'clock.

There he went.

*

As I'm saying nothing:

— Well??? … Hérald asks me.

— So much for your two louis! …

— What? Do you believe that this was nothing but a game, that this boy is a liar, that he will not come back tomorrow?

— … and it wasn't very expensive after all! Notice to what degree our young artist was correct in his entire presentation: his entrance, modest, reserved, his attire standard: all this perfect; the use of sentimental opening lines, the evocation of the two old mothers (which never fails: see Dennery! See

Coppée! ...),[11] the ingratiating exordium drawn from the character of the orator; the voluble list of facts and dates, difficult to verify on the spot, swirling to dazzle us like the balls of a juggler, the compliments, a bit exaggerated, but this always happens: and in order to achieve this perfect whole, think of all the preparations, of all the training! And he's still so young! Believe me, there is in him a future minister for our horse-trading, and even conservative, Republic.

— But the names of friends he mentioned?

— Random information, obtained very easily from the first person who happens to be next to me for ten minutes or from anyone who knows me.

— And the newspaper article?

— How is it, my dear Hérald, that it is you, who has known so much about newspapers, you, who were the real, the initial founder of the *Petit Journal*, with its four million readers today, it is you who is taken in by a news item slipped into one of the two first and last issues of some short-lived tabloid by the complacency, or—who knows?—the complicity of a journalist comrade? You believe in newspapers, you who have created several of them! Despite your intelligence, you have remained a trusting man! ... But no, all this means nothing or very little, and what we should admire, first of all, is much less the intelligence spent on all this pseudo-scientific knowledge than the way he used it, so skillfully laying it out and manipulating it on the tapestry of prestidigitation! We encounter here a first-rate performer and I am very happy to have made the acquaintance of this strong man. He will go far! ... Yes—and I am difficult!—this is a good job, since you've seen me consent to let myself be bitten. Here, then, is Gazebon avenged! On me! And by me!

Are you happy, Mauclerc! You and your hideous smile ...

— But, my friend, how do you account for so many preparations, for all this effort, to achieve what? the puny result of two illicit louis?

— Excuse me, excuse me! You're right here about that number two. We were worth more than that and he could have taken us for at least five: which is proof that even the best horse stumbles. But can you imagine that it was for me, for me alone, for this one and only presentation, that he set up this theatrical performance that must have required the work of so many studies and rehearsals! That could hardly be compensated. No: what this pleasant boy has served us here, he will deliver, depending on the location, to all the photographers of the world, in Paris, in the suburbs, in the provinces, abroad, seasoning the sauce of his entrée and of his sweet-talk according to the situation, the taste, and the stomach of each, since there will be no one too humble for him to cook for. And since none of the chosen, none of the privileged ones whom he favors, one after the other, with this very special honor of his confidence and with the unexpected promise of limitless profits to be shared, since no one will dare to announce to his neighbor that he has been tricked, each one keeping the secret of his complicity, the mine is inexhaustible: now that is really what practical people call "a racket." And at the same time, it has all the philosophy of adventure.

After a silence:

— The question remains, De Pages said again. To sum up, you who so complacently (which I find reprehensible) let the favorite saying of our very charming but detestable friend G ... "Everything is possible, even God!" be repeated in front of you, you refuse absolutely to ever admit the possibility of photographing a model beyond our field of vision?

— I would find it as rash to deny the possibility as to affirm it. I remain floating, exactly like my old friend Babinet, escaping the dispute that Biot was pushing on him.[12] The atheist denied this God, of which you have just spoken, with such a furibund insistence that Babinet, in order to close the discussion, said: "Then you are absolutely certain that God does not exist? Well, my friend, you are *even more superstitious* than me. I really know nothing at all about it." And my opinion being only of very relative worth here, I will conclude by holding onto, in full innocence, this other saying of the same Biot, so profound, so essential, the eternal word:

There is nothing easier than what was done yesterday; nothing more difficult than what will be done tomorrow.

P.S. — When we wrote these words, we scarcely imagined that the technical question raised so imaginatively here would soon be taken up in actual fact by our eminent correspondent and friend Doctor Ed. Liesegang, of Vienna.

See, regarding this subject, the very interesting article translated in the *British Journal of Photography*, which finally discredits Mauclerc to the greatest glory of Gazebon, who is hereby rehabilitated ... Hang yourself, Nadar!

P.P.S. — ... And from this very morning, with the successful wireless telegraphy of Marconi, what can we not dream of! ...

Marseille, June 1899.

The Blind Princess

— Has Mrs. Ratazzi arrived? I asked, glancing over the list of appointments for the day.

— No, sir.

— I see there: *Princess of Solms*?

— Yes, sir, but this is not Mrs. Ratazzi: this is the Princess of Solms, sister of the King of Hanover. Her son and daughter came themselves to make the appointment: their mother is blind. The two young people are charming; they were sorry not to find you. They said that their family knows you and that they themselves almost came to know you in the past, too.

In the past, indeed ...

In these personal recollections, it would be impossible to exclude the detestable "me." It would even be uncomfortable to reduce it.

Still, I begin by asking to be excused for having to take the long road and to recall an old history ignored by the present generation and which, moreover, since 1863, has had enough time to be forgotten by everyone, despite the sensation it created then.

*

In my first ascents in quest of aerostatic photography—so difficult then and so easy now, since the path has been cleared, that everyone can play as they wish—I, like everyone in the air and even on earth, did not fail to give myself over to the eternal human dream: aerial navigation.

Several abrupt descents during which, by a little fresh wind, my wicker basket crashed into trees and walls, very quickly gave me something to think about.

"If I can't simply stop my balloon under this insignificant breeze, where the slightest increase in speed tangles my anchors, tears my cables, and drags me through everything, then my claim to steer it against the currents would be more than impertinent."

From this so simple first observation, a whole logical chain of other observations, no less decisive, had determined my conclusion:

"The aerostat (and this name that it received at its baptism seemed to define its unique destiny), the aerostat could never be a ship. Born a buoy, it will die a buoy. To direct balloons is a chimera."

*

On the other hand, I was nevertheless thinking that man has the right to fly in the air at his will, since animals fly there.

I came to think then that birds and flying insects direct themselves in the air only under the fundamental, absolute condition that they are precisely unlike balloons: in fact, they do not rise, like the balloon, because of a simple difference in specific gravity and, contrary to the balloon, where air presses on the balloon, they press on the air. Without which they would not fly.

Those excellent professors, from the moment I paid attention to them, quickly taught me that flight, strictly speaking, aerial self-propulsion, can only be dynamic, mechanical, in agreement with other components, static, etc.

Finally clearing away the false starts on which, despite the lamentable and ridiculous series of endless discoveries,[1] the man repeatedly returned to the sublime but misleading discovery of Montgolfier; it was necessary, therefore, as homeopathy had done vis-à-vis allopaths, to reverse the proposition in order to extract the problem and finally to pose it in its true, absolute, exclusive terms:

TO BE DENSER—HEAVIER THAN AIR—IN ORDER TO MASTER THE AIR—that is to say, as everywhere and in all things: —*To be the strongest in order not to be defeated.*

*

It was something; it was nothing.

Nothing but a formula: who would develop it?

Certainly not I, who has none of the virtues of the engineer, who has never been able to digest logarithms, by nature resistant to expressions like A + B, and who has always been reproached above all for barely knowing how to count.

But who will explain the great unknown to us, which one of us will set in motion this colossal revolution that will overturn from top to bottom (think about that for a moment) all the conditions of our present existence, and before which all the discoveries of which humanity is so proud will be erased?

On the other hand, wouldn't this superhuman glory be too heavy for one person alone?

In the face of such a complex thesis, in which all our knowledge participates, wouldn't it be necessary to call upon all researchers, all believers?

So, with a dear friend, whom I have since lost, the Excellent La Landelle, and Ponton d'Amecourt, struck by an analogous madness (*sapientem stultitiam*), I founded a *Society for the Encouragement of Aerial Navigation by Exclusively* HEAVIER-THAN-AIR *Machines*—and with the same stroke, no longer counting, I created our specialized journal *The Aeronaut*.

They came from everywhere, inventors, mechanics, algebraists, physicists, chemists, and others—from the Corps of Engineers and of the Navy, from the Department of Mining, from the prestigious, specialized Grandes Écoles, etc. Almost immediately there were six hundred of us, and each Friday evening these faithful souls gathered to discuss and present theories and plans.

But there again, to discuss was not enough: experiments were needed, experiments ad infinitum, in this science of synthesis, which had to be created from scratch. Money was needed, a lot of money.

Where to find it? ...

I had never had any source of income other than my work,

and from the government at that time, I didn't want to accept absolutely anything, despite a good will that I should acknowledge today, a good will remarkably insistent in the face of my recoil.

In summary, I found myself alone encouraging my Society for Encouragement. It was not enough.

*

I then had the idea of asking for the treasure that we needed, precisely at that aerostation that I wanted to exclude: I constructed at great expense an aerostat of previously unheard-of dimensions, containing 6,000 cubic meters of gas, and able to lift, in addition to the weight of its enormous materials, up to forty-five artillery soldiers (which it actually did) on the platform of its two-story wicker basket.

The ascents of this monstrous balloon throughout the entire universe were to fill the coffers of our Association, and each capital, each great city, would pay its part of the ransom for the future of aerial navigation.

And in fact, first Paris twice, then Brussels, Lyon, Amsterdam, gathered in great numbers around the enclosure of the *Géant*.

I had not been mistaken, then, except on the essential point where Florian's monkey deviates;[2] I had forgotten to light my lantern, that is to say, I had not known how to organize my financial accounts, where hundreds of thousands of francs poured in, only to disappear ...

And all my great effort resulted in nothing, except a grim struggle of ten years, of anxieties and efforts to honorably pay everything—which finally was done!

But this is of interest only to me.

*

It must seem that I am distancing myself more and more from the Princess of Hanover at the very moment when I am rushing toward her under full sail.

But what can I do in the face of so many memories, especially when I find myself standing again before the GRAND CAUSE—where it is impossible for me to stop! ...

*

The second time we went up in the *Géant*, then, we left the Champ de Mars at seven o'clock in the evening, and we dropped out of the sky, through a bad maneuver of our crew members, at eight o'clock the next morning in Hanover, where we were dragged for seven leagues in the space of thirty minutes—nearly the normal speed of express trains.

Imagine that you thus cover seven leagues in half an hour, in tow behind the express train, in a basket at the end of a cord—and you can see what a dance this was ...

Nevertheless, there were no casualties: one person broke his arm, I fractured a leg and had a few sprains—and the very dear companion who had too bravely wanted, in the words of the civil code, "to follow her husband everywhere," was cruelly bruised. The other passengers got away with contusions or insignificant injuries.

We were taken in rather great pain to the city of Hanover, which was not too far, and we were installed a little too sumptuously on the first floor of the Grand-Hotel, reserved for our little group—by the order of the King.[3]

I wouldn't know how to describe the concern and kindness that flowed both from the Palace and from the French Embassy. Day and night, flowers and fruits were sent to my poor wounded wife by the Queen—whom I was to encounter in Paris several years later, bathed in tears, mad from all her grief, by the deathbed of her husband, both of them reduced by their Prussian brother to live in a furnished room on the rue de Presbourg ...

Twice a day, without fail, an aide-de-camp of the King came to inquire after us.

This aide-de-camp was a real giant, whose build appeared even more formidable under his white uniform.

I had the time, during the hours that he spent at my bedside, to observe that this magnificent war machine harbored a remarkably fine intelligence, developed by the most complete scientific education. Needless to say, the manifest evidence of our "heavier-than-air" aerostat had quickly gained there another adept for our Society of Encouragement.

That officer was the Count of Wedel.

I hadn't seen him since Hanover.

But one day, looking through the newspapers, I came across his name in the international news section.

I read with regret that Count Wedel had just left the personal service of the King, and even the region of Hanover, immediately after a very unfortunate duel; he had shot a Duke—whose name was lost for me in the *burg*, *stein*, or *berg* endings, typical of the old German families ...

*

But finally, after all this past, we have arrived here in the present:

The Princess of Solms has just been announced. Enter her daughter and her son who guide and support her; her eyes closed, smiling with anticipation, she proceeds with that sliding and prudent step particular to the blind.

This absent look is the same as that on the face of the King, her brother, struck by a similar blindness, without my ever being able to know if this duality was congenital. But the King, himself, would not admit it, and everyone remembers the innocent deception of the large binoculars that he frequently pretended to use at the Opera.

Like his sister, and as if in perfect identification with her, the King also had his guardian angel, Princess Frédérique, his daughter, who never left his side, until death: accomplished perfections, these two Antigones, and, the one like the other, obstinately refusing marriage for the pious, jealous egoism of filial devotion …

*

The blind Princess had been seated: the operations of the laboratory got under way.

From one pose to the other, I would sit between the two young people, who had immediately won me over with their familiar and cordial ease, both even more pleasant than when they were announced to me. Their eyes did not leave their mother, whom they seemed to protect …

They recalled to me all the details of their memories of our stay in Hanover: their endless visits to the basket and the aerostat, shattered into pieces, their curiosity about all the incidents of our catastrophe, their playing harmoniously with my son, a child, then, younger than them, whom we had immediately brought from Paris upon the news of the accident and whom the Queen sent for from the Palace every morning. They did not stop asking me questions, inquiring about what I had been able to attempt since then, about what I was planning to do.

And as I was answering their questions, in this fragmented conversation, interrupted by the necessities of my work, for my part I would ask them for information on certain points that had remained inexplicable to me in bed during my convalescence. From the back of the studio, and well separated from us, the mother would take some part in the conversation in the intervals between poses.

One last time, returning to sit with them, just as they were about to leave:

— And by the way, would you be kind enough to give me news of a very charming man of whom I have kept the fondest memory, and of whom I haven't heard since his terrible duel: Count Wedel? …

*

Lightning striking all three of us on the spot could not have produced such a commotion ...

The two young people, as if charged by an electric current, leaped up, both of them stretching out toward a single point: their mother—white as a sheet, holding her breath ... —while the young girl raised her hand toward my mouth in order to close it, and the young man—rapidly, stridently, as if suffocating—whispered:

— *Silence!!!* ...

— I remained mute, understanding nothing ...

But already the two young people were turning back toward one another, looking each other directly in the eye—and what deep thoughts in the soul of that look!—entirely agitated, even undone, but with an immense sigh of relief ...

Their mother had heard nothing, and was still smiling ...

And then, against my ear—very softly, all too softly—the young man whispers to me:

— The man whom the Count of Wedel killed two years ago was our older brother.

We have been able to hide this catastrophe from our mother, thanks to her blindness. But with the coincidence of the Count's disappearance, we always have feared, we still fear always, the possibility of some encounter ...

Until now, for our mother, our brother has been, for two years, on a grand tour, around the world.

Every fortnight, we read his letters to Mother, always eagerly awaited: the letters that *HE* addresses to her—and which we write, my sister and I ...

She thus awaits his return, counting the days ...

One word more—*and you could have taken her from us ...*

*

Derisory fragility of our human destinies: all these pious and long ruses disposed, combined, attended by the most tender love, all these holy subterfuges, all this breathless fervor, could have been thwarted, subtly and tragically annihilated in a second—all this sweet hope tenderly taken in by the mother, all this calming consolation from the others, all this falls down, collapsing suddenly in order to be irremediably swallowed up in the most terrifying of despairs, the one that cannot be consoled, before which we are speechless ... —because of a single word spoken by accident, during a fortuitous visit to a photographer's studio, in a foreign country ...

I still choke up, every time I remember it.

Homicidal Photography

A small pharmacist's shop, in the rich quarter of Madeleine, improvised at an acute angle as a result of the failure of the architect's or the *pseudo*-architect's bevel joint, and much more cramped than one generally would choose for this business.[1]

From the very first glance, the store is scantily, insufficiently stocked. "Supplies" are not renewed there: one feels that they have forgotten the way because they have lost the faith. The "*specialist*" is born too canny, having been taken in once, to let himself be taken in again.[2] The little that has survived in the display cases is discolored, faded, anemic, so spaced apart that it seems to be cold. The clientele, almost stillborn, is diminishing. Not even a cat, as we say: barely, here and there, a lowly maid comes, having disembarked just the day before and who, not yet au courant about the neighborhood, in her innocence, has put her hand on the latch of the door of unhappiness. The misery! Nevertheless, this discouraged hole is well-kept; what little is found there is strictly in place and as ordered as possible, having had, alas! time to be dusted twice.

At the counter, a woman. What is it that they come to do, these women, at the counters of pharmacists? Could you please get out of here? This is not your place! ... The woman is young, not ugly but not exactly pretty, what connoisseurs call "interesting": brown, pale, looking thin, with a bitumen-like face,[3] prematurely weary of everything and nothing, exhaling from head to toe the implacable, immortal, and mortal boredom.

Desperately, like yesterday, like tomorrow, she leans over the previous day's hollow serial novel, similar to the novel from the day before yesterday, the same as the novel after tomorrow.

It is there that, every day, from night to morning, lacking other food, she grazes. And her life passes like this, oriented around this emptiness ... Two children, two little girls, born one after the other in quick succession, have changed nothing of this, being dispatched immediately into the care of a nurse.

And the pharmacist? The pharmacist is not there. The pharmacist is never there. The pharmacist is at the races, of which a tolerant government has accorded us this daily benefit —or, if he is not there, he is riding one of these carriages with postilions and five horses on which figures, naïvely greedy or sinister, are stacked up, young pigeons and old pigeons promoted as hawks—or rather, the pharmacist is with the bailiff to ask for "time"—or yet at the brasserie, the hangout of the shady moneylender...

*

Of this shop where nothing is sold and where there is nothing to sell, of this counter that does not have money either to receive or to give, of this pharmacist bookmaker and of this lamentably idle woman who could sit somewhere else to read these bad novels—the explanation?

It is simple.

The man and woman come to us like so many others from any other province: these, from the heart of Aveyron. The man, the son of peasants, has struggled to finish his studies at the seminary. The ambitious love of the mother and father had suffered, sought, invented heroic privations, to push breathlessly, to push further, to push again the son who is their pride and from whom they await their glory: he will be a doctor! As for the younger boy, this second one could not have been anything more than a good artisan. This one, in reality still more obtuse and whom extensive study cannot even help to refine, they have made a plumber—between zinc and "glazing" —and this is enough, since the first-born, as they say, has taken everything for himself.

But our glorious one did not succeed in his final exams; rejected on his third attempt, he was obliged to withdraw. He will not add to the suspect group of adventurous doctors without patients and without money, gathering in the seediest places—we have seen many of them!—doctors who advertise on the fourth page and on municipal buildings, practitioners of all trades, including political horse-trading, or, like the young Lebiez, cutting old women into small pieces.[1] Our man fell back on the pharmacy and he just scraped through his exams; a little further and that would have exceeded the height of his genius.

For two years, then, he was "the apprentice," moving from one office to another, at first in Rodez, then elsewhere in the province. But Rodez is not Paris, the Paris of dreams, and "being the apprentice" or "cramming for exams" does not accomplish anything. It is necessary to be established, licensed, to buy or to create a business. With what? Ambition eats scruples, always and especially for the lower classes. The only known method in this case is to take over any dowry whatsoever that allows one to move on to subsequent actions, to seize the dowry first, no matter where or how, in the same way in which a little fear and a quick exit is enough for the petty thief to grab any cap in the window of a hatter.

Our penniless oaf could not count on his good looks to seduce the Cydalises with an inheritance. The narrow and dark mind, the mediocre soul, can be read on that low forehead where the thick mop of hair falls almost onto the bushy eyebrows: the forehead of an acephalous, at best a mandrill, furnishing just enough room for one meager idea at a time. The twisted little eyes, almost bloody, flee under the unkempt thatch, and from that bestial profile, the instinctive analogy would immediately be with the melancholy taciturnity of the badger. In addition, this gracious man remains obstinately mute, always. Eh! What could he say to us?

How, in what encounter, by what fortuitous coincidences, has this unattractive and voiceless animal found beside him, readily at hand and having just the day before come out of the convent, the young girl with the money he needed? By what parental conniving, by what strategy of looks and schemes, by what spells, did the gang manage to grab the loot, modest as it was, and this girl so prepared in advance to accept any of the life about which she knew nothing, not having even the shadow of desire, attraction, or repulsion—submissive, inert, like wax to be molded? And she is a "lady," raised so differently from us peasants; this is evident at first glance, even though she barely says a word, or nothing at all.

It is true that there is a flaw (the skeleton in the closet ...), and the secret is public knowledge, like all family secrets in the provinces: —the older sister who had died *mad* ...

But it does not befit us to be difficult.

*

So the marriage took place between this silent passivity and this concentrated deviousness. The young couple immediately departs for Paris, taking with them the younger brother, inseparable from his elder brother whose superiority fascinates him to the point of ecstasy: the zinc worker will find "day jobs" there, exactly as elsewhere. They leave behind the bloodless, aged parents, continuing to tighten their belt.

And in Paris the battle is immediately engaged.

Not the battle, the rout. Paris does not even have to bite to incapacitate such innocents: these species are volatilized upon entering its ambient atmosphere, for them unbreathable.

A few months were enough to punish their temerity. The tiny dowry was spent entirely on the planning and initial stocking of the shop, smothered before being opened by the crushing competition of its neighbors. The good landlord who had, from the first day, eyed a second leaseholder for this still new establishment, which cost him nothing, spurs his bailiff to deliver the final blow. The entrepreneurs have not yet been paid in full. But they can go bankrupt; this does not concern him. In truth, it would not be worth it for these honest landlords to make the law themselves if it did not place them above such miserable details.

The pharmacist has been thrown off his horse at the first clash. Bewildered by the speed of the collapse, he loosened his grip and sought recourse elsewhere, sniffing left and right, primarily, like all the famished, to fill his empty stomach. Desperate in the face of the possible, he runs after the implausible in the fields of the Chimera. He has come to intensify, with his sterile unit, the aleatory and illicit world that, as the impudent have dared to say, "improves the equestrian race in France," begging for a small coin with the bet as his carrot.

*

An incident in this monotony.

In seedy cafés and dens in backrooms where this unhealthy race finds itself, our wandering pharmacist met another poor devil, perhaps even more miserable than himself, a young student pharmacist looking for work, lodging, a bit of bread, in search of anything. Then, something unexpected, what seemed to be three times closed forever in the Aveyronese, was opened up all by itself: a soft, warm pity suddenly melted this frozen soul, softened this stone. This man who never had an outpouring vis-à-vis his own parents, who remains obscure, impenetrable even to his young wife, opened the door of his heart to this stranger, offering to share his distress with him—we will do what we can!—confiding his disappointments, anxieties, hopes, confessing everything to him, believing him and in him, loving him, making him his guest: *GUEST!* A word so great that it is enough for him alone to embrace at the same time him who receives and him who gives ...

Then this dead shop seemed to live for an instant: we saw again this little door at the back knocked on, behind the counter, on which is written a little ambitiously: LABORATORY—a mostly intermittent and even deserted laboratory, despite the formal injunction of the law—, the law which we are here as elsewhere disposed to revere. My goodness, what does it give us in return!

But this was for the newcomer only a temporary solution: a time to touch the earth to regain his footing and to go even further, higher. Where the north wind blows, the indifferent nomad does not stay put any more than the rat remains in the sinking ship.

The test, moreover, becoming harder by the hour, comes to its end. The final blows are precipitated by an acceleration of speed, as in every instance in which bodies fall. The battle of stamped papers is in its final cartridges. More than one night later, it is getting late when the zinc worker brings from the suburb his "day's wages" to keep the pot boiling. This is the psychological moment when our Aveyronese trio will remain fixed on itself.

Indeed, the bird of passage, the young clerk, has just left—quietly, naturally, almost without saying goodbye or giving a warning—leaving behind him an even more lonely solitude, an even more abandoned abandonment …

*

In sum, so far nothing more banal than this failure of an insipid epic of little people. It is the eternal, universal story, vulgar ad nauseam, of the daily battle of all these subjacent multitudes that struggle as they flow toward the final hole in the ground, similarly habituated in their conformities. Nothing of significance in the action, or barely worth noticing in the actors.

Nevertheless, in the everydayness of this minor household, we will suddenly see these predisposed destinies reveal themselves to the world in a burst of thunder, then develop and realize themselves, through the horrors, in the fateful monumentality and progression of a Shakespearean drama …

A spark is enough to burn the forest.

Here, it took only a last fragment of an old ticket torn to pieces—forgotten by the broom in a dark corner for weeks and picked up by the most fortuitous effect of the maliciousness of things—to reveal everything and to make it explode.

You remember the other wreck taken in: the assistant pharmacist of whom we hardly had time to catch a glimpse? Oh well, as fast as his ill-fated passage through this house was, the betrayal that entered with him had the time to open the door to adultery.

In fact, between, on the one hand, the husband always absent and, on the other, the wife always desperately idle at home, the third term of the proposition could not but intervene. It did not fail to take place: at the right moment, by one of those games familiar to every stage, the coefficient, the second, found himself playing the primary role ...

Destroyed by the irrefutable revelation, the unfortunate woman confesses everything. She has betrayed everything, everything—even this meager cashbox which she was in charge of protecting and whose nearly empty contents she was stealing for this fugitive. He went away, the ignoble one, only when there was nothing left—nothing! ...

*

In these adventures, there is only one rule of law. It is the bridge of asses.

The husband makes his preliminary investigation, takes his time to examine, to weigh what would be best for him to do with the two lives he from now on finds himself having at his disposal: *jus utendi et abutendi.*[5] Will he kill the wife or the lover, or the lover and the wife? This, this alone concerns him: it is at his discretion. He is asked only, and in order to remain until the end within the bounds of propriety—*omne punctum*![6]—to present himself, his deed done, before the judge:

— Your Honor, what would you have done in my place?

Whereupon there would be no need at all for deliberation: and hands up, the jury will proclaim the acquittal unanimously—without ever, not even once, even one of these brave men of the jury having thought, for one second, to ask the murderer this simple, essential question:

— You, Avenger, you who kill adulterers, weren't you ever an adulterer yourself, and indeed the first? ...

But, for the moment, it is not a question of such delicacies. ...

*

I omit the rage, the grinding of teeth, the bites, the tortures in this disaster forever without bottom or limits: it is necessary to run toward revenge!

Nothing else exists anymore, not even the collapse to come the following day.

One question only: the traitor in the house, the thief of honor and of everything, will there ever be enough blood to quench such thirsts?

The wretch is there, nearby. With the money of some other woman—from where else would he have taken it?—he came to settle, he, too, in a shop close by which seems to threaten to prosper; indefatigable hunter, like Nimrod in front of the Eternal,[7] already the infamous one goes around all the matrimonial agencies in order to track down another woman to whom he can sell himself.

Darker than ever, the husband is possessed by a fixed idea; even though he dries up, even though he consumes himself in research, he does not yet know how to find, he will never know how to find, what can extinguish his hatred, this hatred that immediately elevates and reveals him, enlarges him—a negative, a nothing until then—in the eyes of his alarmed wife. All right, finally! Suddenly, here is the man, here is the valiant, terrible one—the one who commands and who is obeyed: the one who will kill—, the Male! ...

In regard to the accomplice, he has made a silent truce: he will decide later! ...

For the moment, he does not want anything between him and his single-minded thought ...

She, before him, is crushed, annihilated, ready to obey him in everything, to further the punishment of the other, the perjurer, the double perjurer ...

Glued to his older sibling's eyes, the brother waits for only one sign—his arm raised to strike ...

*

Let us not forget, in order to understand well and to understand everything, that this avenging trio, from a reality more dramatic in its perfect agreement than that of *Don Juan*, comes directly from the sinister zone whose provinces are tinted totally black on the criminalist maps and on information maps for the public. It is the country where people kill the little old man by dragging him under the nasal sound of the organ, the land of the widow Bancal and of Bastide-le-Gigantesque, where the rocks endlessly return the echo of "the lament of 'Fualdès.'"[8] In this region inherently, naïvely scelerate, the sun, which intoxicates like a strong wine, releases vapors that smell of blood. The viper's bite is more deadly there; the plants with vivid colors, wolfsbanes or foxgloves, exude more acrid, more subtle poisons. The rattle of the cicada becomes obstinate in order to cover the step of the murderer, and, from the Pyrenees to the Abruzzi, the knife naturally seems to push the fingers, as if to extend and perfect the hand that kills ...

In a good judicial system, where everything counts, this in its turn will not be forgotten.

*

Finally, everything is laid out, prepared, ready. This man who, the day before, did not know how to find enough to pay for a piece of bread or a stamp, immediately has found everything he needs to rent an isolated house near Paris, in Croissy, at the edge of the bridge, and also how to defray all travel costs and other expenses, in such a way that the irrevocable execution could not be stopped for a second or hindered by some miserable question of detail.

Under his dictation, it is the woman—the woman herself—who will write to set up a last appointment with the felon lover ... Stupefied, stupid like the instrument under the orders of the husband, which has suddenly become formidable in front of the crime to be accomplished, and without even thinking to remember that she also has to avenge her lost life, the shame and remorse of her double betrayal betrayed in turn, she obeys, and, even beyond the horrible, she will obey: as if predestined by the ancient fatality, it is she—the sister of the other sister, do not forget! The sister of the mad one—it is she who will lead there, right under the knife, the man she has loved ...

But, that evening, she will wait for him at the Gare Saint-Lazare in vain—and it is also in vain that the other two will wait for him there, in the isolated house at the end of the bridge ... He did not come: everything has to begin again.

Let's begin again! This time he will come: a letter is used as the bait: "... An unexpected, amazing godsend has come our way, which there is no time to explain to him, it is written. But, at least for now, there are a thousand francs for him, waiting for him ..."

This time he runs (of course!) to the station, in the evening, at a quarter past eight, just in time for the eight-thirty train, exactly as he had been instructed ... The woman is there, heavily veiled:

— It is me!

— But why go so far? Why ...

— I'll explain on the way. Let's flee! If we were seen! ...

Here they leave—and they arrive. In the full car, it was impossible to exchange a word: finally they can talk a bit, while walking, almost running: "... it was necessary that he would come to know this little house, quite secure, well-hidden, discovered and just rented on purpose for him, for both of them, thanks to a little fortune fallen from the sky ... But there will be time to talk to each other about this—later ... —Let's hurry! ..."

And she drags him, pulls him—him, somewhat indecisive, with a vague uneasiness, carried away toward the unknown through the darkness of the gloomy night ...

Finally, here is the deserted little street.

— It's here!

A key—the second key ... —opens the door ...

— Come on, enter!!!

He is pushed into the darkness—and again pushed from the entrance into a second room ... The two doors are closed behind him ...

At that moment, all of a sudden, a flashing gleam bursts out from two hands: the executioners are before him, with naked blades ...

He falls, riddled by blows ...

*

Now the rest goes without saying: plans studied and studied again, everything well explained, stipulated, without possible contradiction, mistake, or surprise, the trio splits up, each taking his or her own way—and the avenging and avenged husband is led by the first passerby to the police station or to the town hall:

— Sir, here are the keys to a house where I just killed my wife's lover; you will find in the young man's pocket a ticket that will prove to you that I did not mistake him for another; I make myself a prisoner.

Politely, you are offered a chair. So that the preliminary investigation is finished quickly and does not disturb you for too long, we will work twice as hard. As for the acquittal, the case is classic.

*

Not at all!

These brains, annealed under the sun of the Midi, need melodrama, staging: they need to complicate, to do too much, to strike at the wall of Poe's cellar from where the denouncing meowing will come out. How many stories and how many tasks! The corpse, limbs folded, twisted, in order to keep it, they had to tie it with lead pipes, brought from Paris by the plumber; then painfully hoisted it onto a handcart, rented in advance; then they rolled it to the bridge, and from there—pluff! ... to the water!—After all this, they finally return to Paris—en famille ...

After everything, even like this, even admitting that the discovery of the murder will take place without a prior, unsolicited statement by the murderer, that is, in the worst-case scenario—Well! after all, what?

The fact remains, it will always remain the known, proven, irrefutable fact of adultery committed, adultery avenged. At the most, if there is anything to regret it is that they have deviated on a point of the consecrated rites, and of the usual practices.

And since there will only have been one transgression of the adopted observance, a simple defect in form, the condemnation will be more than benevolent—if condemnation there is.

— Wait! ...

*

One month, six weeks, after the evening at Croissy, a sailor catches with his hook, under the bridge, an unformed mass, a hideous apparition in the silt ...

It is the cadaver of a drowned man in total putrefaction, so abominably fashioned that the human form soon becomes illegible. The limbs had been taken and violently bent against the body: lead chains crush them into pallid turgescence and, thus, this gaunt mass seems like the pale belly of a giant toad. The skin of the hands and feet, all wrinkled, is raw white while the face has taken on a brownish tinge. The two eyeballs, the eyelids turned inside out, like two eggs and as if ready to burst, bulge out of the pallid head: between the lips swollen into folds, the wide-open mouth leaves the swollen tongue hanging, torn to pieces by fish … The fleshy parts were already saponified; what remains of hair or beard no longer sticks. Punctured many times, the skin of the abdomen, green in places and blue or violet in others, vomits by each of these holes the unraveled intestines, and these hoses float like banners, like the tentacles of an octopus … Never had decompo sition by death resulted in anything more horrible than this heap without a name, this infamous carrion, disemboweled, so deliquescent as to make even a gravedigger faint …

The men of law visit the scene, begin the process. They search, they search, they have already found.

But, before everything, the service of the Prefecture has photographed the horror, and a devil of a journalist, always on the lookout, gets hold of the first print: since yesterday, people have been swarming the newsroom of *Le Figaro*, and all of Paris will pass by there.

*

There is a unanimous outcry in front of the accursed image:

— Oh! The villains! Oh! The monsters!—To have reduced to such a state "*this poor young man!*"—He was not even thirty years old, Madam!—To death! … To death!! … To death!!! …

And for a moment, I thought I heard, shrill over all the other curses and clamor, this very sharp falsetto—from a very beautiful person, with a very respectable air, believe me!—which, in another time even more atrocious than this one, and as a countertenor to all the shouts, pierced my eardrum, in the middle of the boulevard, while a band of Communard prisoners were passing.

— *Tear their nails out!* …

Silence on the bench of the accused! Silence on that of the defense council! The defense is heard, the debate closed.

It is the photograph that has just pronounced THE SENTENCE[9]—the sentence without appeal: "*DEATH!* …"

The whole mob set to barking, howling on this trail of blood where no power could stop it now. And it is mainly the woman whom they are against, and it is mainly the women who are against her, the women in jealous hatred, in eternal hatred of woman—always ready to finish off, with the relentless ferocity of the hen house, the wounded companion—always ruthless to the adulteress and furious as if this one had dishonored them all.

And why, then, this one—whom that other one, "*the poor young man*," made a deceiver, an adulteress, a thief, the miserable one lost forever, in order to abandon her when she didn't have even a penny to give him anymore—, why wouldn't she have the right to vindicate herself, she, too? Who was betrayed more than her, indeed? But no: not one voice, not one claim, not one criticism should attempt to rise above this tornado of carnage! Jesus of Nazareth would be stoned next to the adulteress here.

—*DEATH!!!* ...

*

In this drama, as monstrous as it is and *sensational* in its staging, and moreover vulgar in its conception and execution—above all necessarily stupid, like all crime—, what remains stupefying for us is the intellectual poverty of the judge—of the judges—and also of the defense, from the point of view of judgment, deduction, and the most simple psychological intuition.

Nevertheless, and despite the more serious reservations expressed, what a curious study for the "professionals," what resources for the defense, the observation of coincidences, antecedents, all the early signs! But such is the disorder of Justice itself, since this is what it is called, in front of the accursed image of the perpetuated murder, that this photographic print ends up sovereignly substituting itself for all the rest: it drives everything. Not even a mention of that older sister, stupid or crazy; not even a glance at the very important statement about their private life, their earnings, their everyday resources and their provenance in the infamous one, the ex-*m*actotum of the Fenayrou pharmacy,[10] the newcomer, the initial author of so many ills!

—*DEATH!!!* ...

*

And in what concerns me as I refuse my part in the social complicity of the unjust sentence, under the frenzied clamor of the universal hue and cry, the savage maledictions, even worse the cruel irony, I see—pardoned, acquitted, almost crowned and even better forgotten—, I see, in front of everyone, and forever calm in the vast and beneficent forgiveness of death, I see the first culprit, the primary cause, the first factor of this primary disturbance, of these lies, these ruses, these thefts, these anguishes, these rages, the traitor of the hearth, of friendship, of tenderness, the villain who pushes the wife, the mother, everyone: "*the poor young man*"—without whom these three ordinary beings, no more or less unhealthy than many others, would have continued to push ahead, one by one, all the more or less difficult days of this mundane life, which is everybody's life: but, because of him alone, they are lost forever! I remain simultaneously seized by horror and infinite pity before the convicted who will pay for the one who, deserving of condemnation, is absolved, forever thrown, they and their little children—*who have done nothing*—into the horrible and the irreparable ...

But *PHOTOGRAPHY* wanted it this way this time ...

P.S. — At the moment in which I was writing these lines, by chance I encountered in Baignots de Dax a young doctor of the Navy's first class—Dr. Offret—who was for four years affiliated with the penitentiary of Nouvelle-Calédonie (New Caledonia) where Fenayrou had been transported, his wife having remained in France in prison.

— Fenayrou, Dr. Offret told me, had limited intelligence, but especially an unhappy character ... gloomy, restless, always dissatisfied with everything and everyone. He had at first been placed at the pharmacy in Bourail, which was the natural center of the penitentiary colonization, an idea that was soon abandoned. There, because of his claims and complaints, he became so unbearable to everyone that he was sent, alone, to be the ferryman to the almost deserted station of Houilou. This is where he died around 1887 of *stomach cancer*.

We know the affinities of this illness with hypochondria and melancholy ...

Dr. Offret gave me information no less curious about another famous assassin, the medical student Lebiez, with whom he had studied in high school in Nantes. Lebiez, from the time he was in college, was *an epileptic*.

In the sinister and singularly propitious milieu where Dr. Offret had to spend these four years, he wasted no opportunity in continuing as a doctor his studies in psychology, looking for, in the autopsy reports, the confirmation of the various indications of facial asymmetry, of the development of the zygomatic bones, the protuberance of the maxilla, and an entirely new diagnostic of pilosity. When the analysis of the brain cannot comprehend the liquefied pulp of the young guillotined Menesclou,[11] it arrests scientific evolution in general at the moment when the most serious disturbances were being produced ...

All of these observations are entirely consistent with the theory of professors Bernheim and Lombroso[12]—so sharply attacked by our old school of criminal medicine—that any villain who is not considered a madman is inevitably considered an idiot.

On the other hand, the softness that we attribute to our juries, especially in the face of the application of the supreme penalty, this softness, always and everywhere increasing, would it not be, together with other signs of the times, the symptomatic guarantee of a future disruption of our idea of criminality? Does the human conscience have to wait long for the old formulaic question: "*The accused, is he guilty?*" to be finally replaced by: "*The accused, is he dangerous? ...*"

The First Attempt at Aerostatic Photography

"Nothing will ever be equal to the moment of hilarity (*sic*) that overtook all my being. As soon as I felt that I was fleeing the earth, I did not experience pleasure, but happiness. Having escaped from the terrible torments of persecution and calumny, I felt that I was responding to everything by rising above it all. This moral sentiment was soon succeeded by an even more vivid sensation: above us a sky without clouds; in the distance the most delicious sight ... —Oh, my friend, I said to Mr. Robert, what happiness! ... I wish I could hold here the last of our detractors and tell him: 'Look at this, wretched man!!! ...'"

In these affectionate terms, the physicist Charles[1]—the first, with his companion Robert, to be lifted in the air by hydrogen gas—expresses himself after his initial ascent.

And forever, for all those who went up after Charles as well as for those who will go up in the basket of an aerostat, the sublime impression, emotional or physical, will invariably remain the same.

Free, calm, levitating into the silent immensity of welcoming and beneficent space, where no human power, no force of evil, can reach him, man seems to feel himself really living for the first time, enjoying, in a plenitude until then unknown to him, the wholeness of his health in his soul and body. Finally he breathes, free from all the ties with this humanity which ends up disappearing in front of his eyes, so small even in its greatest achievements—the works of giants, the labors of ants—, and in the struggles and the murderous strife of its stupid antagonism. Like the lapse of times past, the altitude that takes him away reduces all things to their relative proportions, to Truth. In this superhuman serenity, the spasm of ineffable transport liberates the soul from matter, which forgets itself, as if it no longer existed, vaporizes itself into the purest essence. Everything is far away: cares, remorse, disgust. How easily indifference, contempt, forgetfulness drop away from on high—and forgiveness descends ...

Another ecstasy, however, calls us back to the admirable spectacle offered to our charmed gazes.

Underneath us, as if to honor us by accompanying our step, the earth unfolds into an immense carpet without borders, without beginning or end, in varying colors of which green is dominant, in all its nuances and in all its combinations. Fields in irregular grids look like those "*quilts*" in multicolored but harmonious pieces put together by the patient needle of the housekeeper. It seems that an inexhaustible box of toys has been abundantly spread on this earth, the earth that Swift revealed to us in Lilliput, as if all the factories of Karlsruhe had emptied their stock there. Toys these little houses with red and slate-gray roofs, toys this church, this prison, this citadel, the three dwellings to which all our present civilization comes down. Even more of a toy this hint of a train which sends to us from down below its shrill little shrieking whistle, as if to draw our attention, and which, so cute, moves slowly along—despite its fifteen leagues an hour—on its invisible rail, decorated with its small wisp of smoke ... And what is this other rather white flake which I make out down there floating in space: the smoke of a cigar? No, a cloud.

This is indeed the planisphere, since there is no perception of differences in altitude. Everything is "*in focus.*" The river flows at the top level of the mountain; there is no perceptible disparity between the fields of alfalfa equally leveled and the established forests of ancient oaks.

And what purity of lines, what extraordinary clarity of sight in the smallness of this microcosm where everything appears to us with the exquisite impression of a marvelous, ravishing cleanliness! I found neither slag nor stain. Nothing but distance to escape all ugliness …

*

The invitation to the lens was in this case more than formal, imperative, and, so intense that our absorption was pushed to the vagueness of a dream, in truth it would have been necessary never to have even half-opened the door of a laboratory so that we wouldn't have been immediately taken by the thought of photographing these marvels.

And since chance apparently wanted me to be the first photographer to be lifted in a balloon, it happened that a precedent fell on me that very well could have belonged to anyone else.

*

First of all, I had glimpsed here two of the most interesting applications.

From a strategic point of view, we are aware of what good fortune it is for a general in a war campaign to encounter the bell tower of a village from where a Master Sergeant can make his observations.

I was carrying my bell tower with me and my lens was able, successively and indefinitely, to shoot positives on glass which I would send directly from my basket to the headquarters, by means of a very simple form of delivery: a small box which would slide down to the ground through the length of a rope that would bring instructions back up to me, if necessary.

These images, immediately enlarged by projections under the eyes of the commander in chief, would present to him the entirety of his chessboard, as they would register progressively the minutest details of action and ensure for him incomparable superiority in conducting his part in the game.

Then—*cedant arma!*[2]—I would proceed to another no less important task.

*

Long ago, in Brittany, when there was a division of property between two families, the parents of each side would take their children there. They would place indicative markers, and immediately rush to the children and cover them with punches:

— In this way, the memorable beating that you have just received always will remind you on this day of the place, always to be respected, where the markers have been put.

This somewhat primitive mnemonic procedure has long been abandoned; but with what have we replaced it?

"This gigantic work of registering the land," I said to myself, "with its army of engineers, surveyors, chainmen, draftsmen, accountants, had required more than a billion and more than half a century of work—to be done poorly.

"This year, today, I can finish it by myself in thirty days—and perfectly.

"A good captive aerostat, a good camera, these are my only weapons.

"No more preliminary triangulation, painfully built up on a stack of trigonometric formulas; no more dubious instruments, plane tables, compasses, alidades, graphometers; no more chains of convicts to drag through the valleys, hills, plowed fields, vineyards, swamps: we do not have to bother people at home anymore.

"No more of these uncertain works, prepared without uniformity, pursued and completed by approximation, without cohesion, without control or guarantee, by unsupervised personnel who sometimes can be made to forget their hours of work by the billiards hall in the next town.

"Miracle! I who all my life have professed a hatred of geometry that is equal only to my horror of algebra, I produce with the rapidity of thought plans more faithful than those of Cassini,[3] more perfect than the maps of the Ministry of War!

"And what simplicity of means! My balloon held captive at the same height from each of the points determined in advance, I automatically record in one blow the surface of a million square meters, that is to say, one hundred hectares. And since in a single day I can travel through some ten stations, I can record in one day the land register of a thousand hectares!"

*

What a triumph!

In the future—thanks to me!—no more disputes, no more litigation—not even in Normandy.

And from the personal point of view of *business*, which I perhaps will be permitted not to forget entirely, I already foresee the pleasant perspective of a legitimate profit, which, well earned, will not be the despicable kind.

I made inquiries.

England has no land registry. At most, a civil state of public property.

Nothing in Russia, nothing in Italy, nothing in Spain, nothing anywhere.

Even by us, in France, even though all our provinces, except Corsica, are registered, the work was done in such a way that a number of localities in the Seine, in Eure, etc., just decided to have everything done over again. For three or four provinces, this redoing will cost no less than six hundred thousand francs from the budget, not including the additional one-off charge imposed by the municipalities. On this little point only, almost a million a year!

And all the rest! ... It's enough to make one dizzy. The imagination runs wild ...

But, despite its enticing aspect, this "business" side is not the one that preoccupies me the most, and I must confess completely here: in my heart of hearts, I surprise myself by being somewhat exalted at the thought that the year 1855 will perhaps not be too unworthy of its elder, the year 1783, and that I will have, that I will be the first to have, the honor of developing two new and most precious applications of the French discovery of our Montgolfier ...

Absolute certainty, after all, for who could prevent my lens from returning to me what, like my eye, it sees? And if it happens to lose itself in the eccentricity of some distortion, nothing seems easier than to rectify its spherical aberrations mathematically with any mnb^2 whatsoever.

But the inconvenience of the mobility of my basket still remains, as captive as it is, with all its movements, back and forth, forth and back, left or right, top to bottom and bottom to top, without forgetting the gyrations. But all my precautions are taken and, although we have yet neither the gelatin-bromide nor the always-victorious ingenuities of the glorious High Priest of the Snapshot, our friend Marey, I do not doubt that the distance of objects will make my task easy.

And without delving any further, passing immediately as always from the dream to action, I run to register my patent.

(I will have gotten so many of these patents!—And for what! ...)

*

But in the Photographopolis the word had already spread, and, even before being launched, photography-from-the-balloon shakes our little world. Friends come running.

What is today—some thirty-five years later—an everyday, elementary task, at the level of the lowest assistant in the laboratory, seemed then to everyone impracticable, improbable. It is always necessary to repeat Biot's saying:

"Nothing is easier than what was done yesterday, nothing more impossible than what will be done tomorrow."

Practitioners shake their heads, but they are not the least of the suspicious, who include all the top guns. It is Bertsch who leaves his astronomy laboratory to say to me that I am attempting the unrealizable. The elder Bisson confirms; the good Le Gray says to me:

— You'll spend money that you don't have, and break the neck you do have, for nothing!

And my excellent master Camille d'Arnaud begs me to remain quiet.

But who or what can stop me once I have given in to one of my sudden bursts of enthusiasm? …

I have already chartered a balloon, plus a member of the Godard tribe to maneuver it[4]—and the date is fixed.

*

Feverishly I prepared the organization of the laboratory that I have to install in my basket, since we are not yet in the blessed time when our descendants will carry a laboratory in their pocket, and we must cook up there. Thus, all our equipment is there, in its place. And we should not forget anything, since it is not convenient to go up and down too often.

The basket, as spacious as the six hundred cubic meters of the aerostat allow, that has to lift with its cables only my technician and me, has been fitted to perfection. Everything is methodically within reach, stowed away or hung up in its place. We are there as if we were at home, and Bertsch would immediately exchange his narrow little sentry box on rue Fontaine-Saint-Georges, this real umbrella cover from where he ogles his planets, for our aerial laboratory.

The tent is hung in the circle of the aerostat, impermeable to the slightest diurnal ray with its two-sided orange and black jacket, and with its all-too-little skylight of yellow aphotogenic glass which gives me just the light needed. It's hot down there, for the operator and for the operation. But our collodion and our other products do not know it, immersed as they are in their ice baths.

My lens, vertically fixed, is a Dallmeyer, this says it all, and the click of the horizontal guillotine that I have devised (another patent!) in order to open and close it in one breath, works impeccably.

Finally, I have guarded against the movements of the basket, in the best way possible: our upward force is such that our cables, departing not from the basket but from the equator of the aerostat, are so tight as to nearly make the balloon's jacket burst. I will operate only in calm weather and, if the elasticity of my ropes and cables is felt at my altitude, fixed at three hundred meters, I will reduce it to two hundred, to a hundred: I must succeed.

*

Finally, everything is here, everything is ready!

I board …

— First ascent: result—zero! …

— Second ascent: —nothing!! …

— Third ascent: —nothingness!!! …

I had initially been astonished—then anxious: here I am terrified …

What is happening? …

*

And I go up, I go up and up again and again, always—without any success.

With each new failure, however hard I search, however hard I look and look again: nothing has been forgotten or neglected, nothing is wrong. Ten times, twenty times, my baths have been filtered, refiltered, replaced, all my products changed.

How is it that invariably, inexorably, I obtain only a series of plates veiled by black soot, without a sign, without even the suspicion of an image? How is it that, as if under a cast spell, I cannot get out of these opaque, fuliginous plates, from this night that pursues me?

"The others," could they have been right?

Impossible. I will never admit that the lens does not *render* at all what it *sees*. Of course, it must be an accident, just an accident in the laboratory, unexplained until now, an accident which prolongs itself cruelly, indeed, and perseveres beyond the plausible—but about which I will be right!

I will not budge: whatever the cost, I will continue my ascents until I get to the bottom of this.

*

But "whatever the cost" is easily said. Every successive ascent, financed by me alone, costs a lot and exhausts my more than meager resources; everything that I earn, everything I have is spent there, and the thousand-franc notes run out quickly …

In addition, here comes the winter, scarcely propitious to my attempts. Will I then have to stay with my shame of being defeated and to bite my fists until next spring, waiting to begin again?

One time, one more time, let's try! And with all my force of application, with all the concentration of my will, this last time, I try …

Again, nothing, nothing, nothing!!!

A spell!!!

*

In every one of these ascents, when, wearily unable to extricate myself from the black series, I would end up putting off the new attempt until the next time, I would not forget, as one might think, a beautiful "*Release everything!*," offering to myself, at least as a consolation and compensation, the pleasure of a free ascent. Like the pastry chef who, for lack of customers, eats his own sweets.

This last time, insisting, I had prolonged my useless struggle longer than the previous ascent, and the night was falling together with us as we were descending, very near Paris, in an unknown little valley, almost deserted and charming then, called Petit Bicêtre.

There was no wind. We had just sat gently next to a big apple tree. One of the Godard crew members was preparing to empty and fold his balloon:

— Stop! …

I was struck just then by an idea—why shouldn't I try one more time the next morning, independently of the results, since I am here, all ready? The expenses are incurred, the gas is paid, and, my valve well closed, there is no danger that gas will escape while the balloon is dilated tonight, since already the cold is biting. I will therefore leave the balloon where it is, well moored to this honest apple tree and, in any case, under good surveillance. I will load my basket with millstones and send my assistant, who will bring me other newer products, to Paris.

A night passes quickly, even at Petit Bicêtre—and who knows if tomorrow morning, finally? ...

*

I am up at dawn. The weather is overcast, a gray and icy drizzle falls. Decidedly I am not lucky.

But there is something else, too: I can't see my balloon anymore!!! ... Yes, here it is! But in what state?

This balloon to which we said goodnight a few hours ago, so tall and proud on its peduncle like a majestic mushroom, I find it again folded in on itself, collapsed, shapeless. The cold of the night has condensed its gas, and in addition to the net, the ropes have been weighed down by this so inopportune drizzling rain. The bad luck continues. Will I be able to go up at least?

The basket is emptied of the millstone. While we maintain it without difficulty, I clear off the so carefully installed laboratory, the tent, everything, even my famous horizontal guillotine (in patent!), which I will substitute with my hand: I will carry with me only my camera obscura and my plate glass prepared with a frame.

I take my place in the basket: it barely makes a half-turn around itself without leaving the ground, as if discouraged and unable to make such a big effort.

In this almost nothing, there is nevertheless a small indication of ascent and it is evident that even a very small lightening will be enough to get me up, since this weighing in quintals is ultimately as delicate and sensitive as that of the centigrams on the pharmacist's scales.

There can be no hesitation: I will lighten the load by unfastening my basket: I will hold onto the circle. Then, despite the cold, I take off my coat, which I let fall to the ground, then my vest, and then my boots, then … But can I say this, and how to say it? Having taken off everything in regard to the exterior (there are no ladies? …), I even relieve myself of *everything* that can weigh me down—and I rise at last to approximately eighty meters … I have immediately opened and closed my lens and I shout impatiently:

— Descend!

I am pulled to the ground. With a leap, I rush into the inn where, palpitating, I develop my image …

What happiness! There is something! …

*

I persist and I try again: little by little the image appears, quite indecisive, quite pale—but clear, certain. …

I emerge triumphant from my improvised laboratory.

It is only a simple positive on glass, very feeble in this so hazy atmosphere, all stained after so many adventures, but what does it matter! It is impossible to deny it: here beneath me are the only three houses of the small town: the farmhouse, the inn, and the police station, as befits every traditional Petit Bicêtre. One can distinguish perfectly on the road a tapestry maker whose cart stopped before the balloon, and on the tiles of the roofs the two white doves that had just landed there.

I was right then!

*

But how, why, could I only this desperate time obtain what had been refused to me so implacably until then?

Suddenly, an illumination, and I at last have the explanation that my lay reader, more sagacious than me, has already guessed.

This time, not having gas to spare, I ascended with the valve *closed*—this valve that the elementary prudence of all aeronauts always leaves wide open, at every departure, in order to give vent to the excess gas which expands as the balloon rises, and therefore to prevent an explosion.

Now, during each of my ascents, this valve, gushing, would spew out sulfured hydrogen in torrents onto my developing baths: silver iodide with hydrogen sulfur, a wicked couple irrevocably condemned to never produce children. By not having imposed here an immediate divorce, and from the very first encounter, I undoubtedly had deserved to pay even more dearly for my lack of observation and deduction.

But if I have had shortcomings, I forgive myself for them, as I am so happy finally to have "broken the spell."

Since the explanation of my mistakes has been revealed, I am, in all tranquility, quite sure to obtain up there all the perfect shots that I will need, to prove to the great scientists that I was right against them—and my son will be able to say that his father was the first to have the honor of actualizing aerostatic photography. He will do other things, too, more and better: "the first preoccupation of a father," my excellent cousin Charles wrote to me, "must be to leave behind a son better than him."

*

And to all those who come I display my negative, however imperfect it may be, explaining the hows and whys it was transported ... But what a new stroke of lightning on the very evening of that beautiful morning!

A friend visits me at dinnertime. Naturally, he has barely come in and I have already shown him the famous negative, and all excited, with my usual lyricism when I have mounted a new hobbyhorse, I tell him both my theory and my continual failures, and their explanation, and my experience of that morning and my expectations (patented!) ...

And then the friend—like ice:

— But, my poor good man, it is known, your business, well known! You're by no means the first. I read all this, not even eight days ago, printed fully ... The book is very curious. It's by a Mister ... Mister ... wait a second!—A gentleman who has something to do with compressed air ... Mr. ... Andraud! That is it: Mr. Andraud! And *there were* even photographs at this year's exhibition obtained from the basket of a balloon ...

*

The blow is hard!!! ...

A bell rings, and two people already leave in two directions, running in search of the book I have such a thirst to see ...

They finally bring it to me: it has an entirely honest air, with its modest appearance, this villain of a book!

WORLD'S FAIR OF 1855
A FINAL SUPPLEMENTARY PRESENTATION
AT THE
PALACE OF INDUSTRY
Industrial Sciences, Fine Arts, Philosophy
BY
MR. ANDRAUD

The science of power consists in using well the power of science.
—Napoleon

PARIS
GUILLAUMIN AND CO. BOOKSELLERS
Publishers of the Journal of Economists, of the collection
of Principal Economists of the Dictionary
of Public Economy, etc.
14 RUE RICHELIEU, 14
and the author, Rue Mogador, 4
1855

I flip through the pages, feverishly—and I get to page 97 ... There it is!!!

TOPOGRAPHY

No. II. Land Surveying by daguerreotype.

The book falls from my hands …

How had I not read this? … What a beautiful patrimony lost! … Not to mention all the thousand-franc notes thrown there …

Painfully disappointed, I pick up the book again and I skim …

Suddenly:

— But, you brute! I shouted, you can't even read!

"The brute" (it's my friend) couldn't even read, in fact, or rather, like many others, he had read only with his eyes.

The book by the learned engineer was a book of pure science fiction: this *Supplementary Presentation* at the World's Fair: it was Mr. Andraud himself who had put it together, magnificently, it must be said, without sparing millions, as if he were the State, Pereire, or Rothschild,[5] and the prodigious and transcendental dreamer had piled up there all the fantastical but no less precious treasures, all the accumulated *desiderata* in his fecund and three-sided imagination as learned man, as poet, and as philanthropist.

We would find there successively exhibited, explained and described, everything that is still missing from our needs as civilized people—and part of which is achieved today:

— the escalator,
— the balanced-load wheelbarrow,
— a definitive system for paving,
— awnings to cover sidewalks,
— instantaneous vegetation,
— a universal filter,
— plant meats,
— garment reform,
— a new combustible,
— an air clock,
— the universal prime mover,
— the planimetry of a house,
— the theater of science,
— the unlimited propagation of sound (Edison, watch out! …),
— *land surveying by the daguerreotype*, etc.,

and a whole host of other ingenuities disseminated handsomely, without precautions or patents of any kind. What would it matter to this millionaire of ideas if he were robbed!

The episode had alarmed me so intensely that I wanted to see the terrible man who had caused it, which gave me the opportunity to make the acquaintance of a spirit absolutely superior and at the same time of the most modest and likable man. It is unfortunately on a tomb that I lay this wreath in respectful and affectionate remembrance.

I never had the leisure or the curiosity to determine whether Mr. Andraud's book had appeared before or after I got my patent.

It did not matter much: I know now that its author was too affluent in his own right to need to take anything from me and, as for me, I was quite sure that I had not taken anything from him.

There are at certain times endemic synchronisms in human thought, in the moments when our imagination finds itself ordered to respond to our needs. It is in this respect that it was necessary to formulate the saying: *this idea was in the air*.

*

Starting in the first days of the following spring—1856—I obtained, from the first attempt this time, together with a dozen other points of view, a snapshot of the avenue du Bois de Boulogne, with the top part of the Arc de Triomphe, the perspective from Ternes, Batignolles, Montmartre, etc.

This snapshot affirmed *first*,[6] despite its imperfection, the practical possibility of aerostatic photography: this was above all what I had aimed at.

As for its cadastral application, my very eminent friend, Colonel Laussedat, explained to me that it was impossible.

My innate, absolute intractability in the face of everything that is exact science prevented me from following the explanation in its entirety; but before the assertion of such authority, I could only bow—and that's what I did.

Later, I had the satisfaction of seeing a number of magnificent aerostatic attempts effortlessly obtained by Paul Nadar, by the brothers Tissandier, Ducom, etc.,[7] and by many others still—and even by the very obstinate mahouts of the École aérostatique of Meudon, who insist on raising flying fish that do not fly …

Subterranean Paris

IN THE CATACOMBS AND SEWERS

THE FIRST ATTEMPTS AT PHOTOGRAPHY UNDER ARTIFICIAL LIGHT

Four times a year, Madam, exactly at midday, it can happen that you attend a rather strange meeting, often arranged several months in advance, between four or five hundred people who do not know one another.

You see them one by one or in groups of two, three, and four, converge at the appointed hour at the formerly called "exterior boulevards" and the rue d'Enfer—today Denfert-Rochereau—toward a kind of small temple with Doric columns, where the customs checkpoint at the ancient entrance gate was situated. All these people, of one sex or the other, carry a small package in their hands as a sign of recognition. Many brandish, not without some contained pride, a lantern, that one or two have even pinned to their lapel, in the manner of a decorative insignia.

Some take on a grave and even collected appearance; others radiate with a joy that is a little too excessive not to appear forced. They all have the special physiognomy, mysterious and somewhat conceited, of characters to whom a secret, and not unimportant, mission would have been entrusted. Moreover, the occasion to be solemn does not befall us every day.

By the door of the small Temple, they disappear, one after the other, under the earth.

These elect will visit the Catacombs. The various public administrations, from whom they have solicited, in the most respectful terms, this "favor" that rightfully belongs to everyone and is not refused to anyone, take advantage of the occasion of the four annual statutory visits in order to get rid of these unassuming solicitors en masse.

You do not know the Catacombs, Madam; permit me to lead you there. Please take my arm and—let us follow the people!

*

In the courtyard where we are, with its somewhat neglected air, the company, already numerous, surrounds the well and especially the kind of small stone postern from which we will descend shortly. We have around us the various specimens of the genus curious—the insatiable curious and the indifferent curious, by which I mean the disdainful, the serious, the mocking, the eloquent, and the taciturn. Here is—a rare species—the Parisian familiar with Paris, who knows like the back of his hand its Artillery Museum, and for whom the Gobelins factory has no secrets, next to a real autochthonous Parisian who gives a glance to his Paris only when he happens to have a visitor from the provinces. Here is also, in addition, the special public that subscribes to the *Illustrated Père Lachaise*, the same that in the past would buy Volney's *Ruins* and Young's *Night Thoughts* in the heroic times when we used to read everything, even Young and Volney.[1] And here is, finally, the inevitable band of English tourists.

All these people are necessarily a little mixed and they familiarize themselves quickly with their neighbors; nothing is better than the proximity of danger to bridge distances and encourage fraternity. Everyone prepares, lighting his or her lantern. The laughter that, quite forced, bursts out here and there, along with some bewildered looks, testifies, to the glory of Noël and Chapsal's literature course, that everyone has not yet forgotten the unfortunate mortal lost in the Catacombs and, to make his plight worse, put into verse by the abbot Delille.[2] Another brave one in the center of the group has prudently brought with him, as if he was going to pass the winter here, two pounds of candles, a four-pound loaf of bread, and a supply of chocolate; on second thought, if only he believed that he still had time, he would have run in a heartbeat to double his ammunition. But I wouldn't swear that the joker, who more than anyone else makes fun of our cautious pilgrim, would not conceal, if we were to search his pockets carefully, some balls of thread, in memory of Theseus, the man in the Labyrinth. The classic is eternal.

Yet you do not doubt, Madam, you who are brave—brave like a man, that in these statutory visits there cannot be even the shadow of a danger. In line, one after the other, our tourists, counted at the entrance in order to be re-counted at the exit, must only march in perfect security along the restricted route given to them at the ossuary, under the surveillance of guards on sentry duty at every false exit. Without these precautions, the outcome of the expedition through this immense entanglement of Roman quarries from which our Lutèce emerged between the third and the eighth century, and which branch out into thousands of meanders on both sides of the Seine, from Vaugirard to Charenton, from Passy to Ménilmontant, would no doubt have been very different.

*

But the postern is opened. Each person goes slowly down the narrow staircase with its sharp turn. Would it please you to find out that this entrance, the most frequented, is counted as one of the sixty leading into the Parisian Catacombs, and also that its staircase has ninety steps? I would like to believe that these statistics do not interest you any more than they interest me.

Besides, to begin with, I do not know who could assume the responsibility of enumerating exactly the six or seven millions of skeletons that for more than ten centuries have been bequeathed to us here, an unexploited mine of calcium phosphate and potassium nitrate.

Finally here we are at the bottom of the interminable and slippery staircase. Following the first ones in our single file, and followed by others, we walk through a narrow gallery with damp walls whose crushed vault makes the tallest people bend over. The monotonous procession extends and, in order to make it even more unpleasant in this viscous atmosphere, the smoky smell of this succession of candles—and, in any case, isn't there some candlestick lagging behind?—is condensed and congealed in this long airless corridor.

But space becomes wider around us. A door appears to us: on it the inscription:

MEMORIAE MAJORUM

and on both sides:

HAS ULTRA METAS REQUIESCUNT,
BEATEM SPEM EXPECTANTES[3]

It's here. We are entering the ossuary.

Between the huge, roughly squared pillars of stone, built in order to preserve this southern part of Paris from the frequent landslides (one could liken them to the immense site of a meticulous timber merchant), all the bones collected, mostly since 1785, from abandoned cemeteries, ancient churches, and the excavations which, under the Second Empire, have turned a large part of the Parisian soil upside down, are arranged in perfect order. From the time of the Caesars and the Norman invasions until the last bourgeois and peasants were extracted from Vaugirard cemetery in 1861, all those who lived and died in Paris sleep here, lowly multitudes and acclaimed great men, canonized saints and criminals executed in Place de Grève. In the egalitarian confusion of death, a Merovingian king remains in eternal silence next to those massacred in September 92. The Valois, Bourbons, Orléans, Stuarts, end up rotting indiscriminately, lost between the wretched of the Court of Miracles and the two thousand "of the religion" that were killed on the night of St. Bartholomew.

But the nothingness of the human condition has no limits and the standards of eternity demand even more: these skeletons, all pell-mell, are themselves disaggregated, scattered in such a way as never to be able to be found in order to be reunited on Judgment Day. By the hand of special workers, employed annually for this service, the ribs, vertebrae, sternums, carpi, tarsi, metacarpi, and metatarsi, phalanges, etc., the whole menu of the bones, are pushed back, compacted into more or less cubic masses under the crypts—in *jams*, as they say here—, and held in front by heads chosen from the best-preserved of them: what we call the *façades*. The art of the excavation workers combines these strings of skulls with femurs arranged in a cross in certain symmetrical and varied arrangements, and our funerary decorators devote themselves to them—"in order to make the view interesting, *almost pleasant*," says the good Dulaure, evidently seduced, but a statement which Mr. Paul Fassy, in his very interesting work on the Catacombs, has some reason to treat as "partial."[4]

Thus, the skulls that compose this "façade" in front of which we pass come from the rue de la Ville-Levesque, where some of those executed in 1793 were thrown together. Among them, undoubtedly, is Philippe Égalité, Duke of Orléans. Which one? ...

And this little verse from the first chapter of St. Luke, fatal like a sentence, is it pure chance that chose it to be engraved here?

DEPOSUIT POTENTES DE SEDE
ET EXALTAVIT HUMILES.[5]

It is established that they are all there in their mixed up fragments: St. Geneviève and Mirabeau, Marat with Nicolas Flamel "and his wife," St. Vincent de Paul and Cardinal Dubois, Marguerite de Bourgogne with the provost Marcel, Perrault, the architect storyteller, Marshal d'Ancre, Voiture, Cassini, Benserade, St. Médéric, Gaultier-Garguille, Malherbe, Gassendi, Philippe de Champaigne, Lulli, Rabelais, Commines, etc., Frédégonde perhaps lies intermixed with Miss de la Vallière and Miss de Scudéry by the shambles of Turlupin between Pichegru and Father Santeuil.

This is the parade of the great names of France as well as of the small ones. There is not even one of our old families that does not have someone to claim there, Condés and Contis, Soyecourt and Vendôme, La Rochefoucauld, Créqui, Rohan, Montmorency, Villars, Blacas, Brancas, Noailles, Du Lau, La Trémoille, Nicolai, Luxembourg, Molé, etc., lifeless here and there, every trace implacably lost in the uncountable clutter of the most humble, the anonymous, the Durands, Legrand, Petit, Lemaître, Berger, Lenoir or Leblanc.

This fragment that your foot just bumped into, this debris without a name, is perhaps one of your grandfathers, a grandmother perhaps, Madam. And this one has loved, this one has been loved ...

What human vanity, what pride could stand before this final, inevitable promiscuity of our ashes, when, only yesterday, the jaw of a Cardinal Richelieu circulated among the antique stores followed on the track by reporters—when, as with papers in hand, one of the most serious, erudite scholars affirmed to me, the expiatory Chapel, this venerated place of pilgrimage for the last faithful ones, would not contain a vestige of the relics of Louis XVI, but precisely the detested bones of a Robespierre? What nobility, what titles, what cartularies, what seals? Search it, your glorious register, in these heaps and heaps without end, poor fool!

It was decided, especially in recent years, to distinguish the bones of diverse origins. Lapidary inscriptions indicate that this cluster comes from Picpus, another from the convent of the Cordeliers or from the Market of the Innocents. These inscriptions alternate with Latin verses from the Bible and with French fragments, the majority of which are annoyingly unearthed from a tenacious selection of our *minor* poets, Lemierre, Ducis, the already named Delille, and other Campistrions.

A small stream of water, clear and always at the same level in its stone basin, serves as an asylum to five or six small fish imported by the fancy whim of a site worker, who presents them to us with a certain pride. I imagine that, in this almost perpetual darkness, these fish are in the process of becoming blind, like the atrophied vision of species found in underground lakes and cave-dwelling insects. Above the source:

SICUT UNDA DIES NOSTRI FLUXERUNT.[6]

This is certainly one of those deep thoughts to which neither Bourdaloue nor even Mr. Prudhomme could find the means to say no.[7]

Further on, but outside the ossuary, is a very large and deep well, into which we were irresistibly tempted to descend. But be careful: the water is so clear that one can perceive it only when one touches it and I warn you that the footbath is freezing; I have personal experience.

On the side, two examples of architectural sculpture, carved in tuff:

QUARTIER DE CAZERNE (sic)
PORT SAINT-PHILIPPE 1777,

say the artist's inscriptions. These works of patience, which in no way bear comparison with the colonnade of the Louvre, are owed to the leisure of an old soldier named Décure who had apparently chosen to retire there, and who, according to the local tradition, perished there under a landslide, victim of his own imprudence.

Here, too, in order not to forget anything, a heavy table similarly carved in solid stone, on which, according to the same tradition, Charles X had a quick meal.

The legends on gravestones testify that the victims of the

BATTLE AT THE CHÁTEAU DES THUILERIES (sic)
ON THE 10TH OF AUGUST 1792

were reunited in this other place, and then here those of the

BATTLES OF THE PLACE DE GRÈVE, OF THE HÔTEL
DE VILLE, OF THE HÔTEL DE BRIENNE, AND OF

THE RUE MESLAY, ON THE 28TH AND 29TH
OF AUGUST 1788

and there those of the

BATTLE AT THE RÉVEILLON FACTORY,
ON THE 28TH OF AUGUST 1789.

This other inscription is even more striking in its lapidary succinctness:

D. M.
II and III
September
MDCCXCII

A gravestone, the only one that we found here gathered among so many thousands of others of greater interest, still stands to teach us in prose and in verse that it covered the body of Françoise Gellain, wife of Legros, who assisted in the escape of Latude.

Here is the sarcophagus called TOMBEAU DE GILBERT, from which Gilbert is missing. But he cannot be far away.

And the provisional altar where at least once a year, I suppose, a regulatory Mass must be said for so many dead, Catholics, Huguenots, Jews or even Mohammedans, always in wait for the special chapel which the here present pamphleteering Timon de Cormenin, once deadly to the profiteers of the old civil list, never ceased to demand.

Here the path is blocked. This enormous pile of bones, a landslide whose summit pierces the vault, comes from the well of the rue de la Tombe-Issoire (or just simply *Tombissoire*?). In this well, all the human remains unearthed in the eliminated cemeteries and in the debris excavated for the creation of new roads, since death itself cannot safeguard us against expropriation, are unloaded little by little.[8] The workers of the ossuary heap them up in each of these two dump carts which, once full, they push in front of them toward the still empty arches which wait for their "filling."

Next to the pile, a small bier, entirely new. A map recently nailed, written by hand, tells us that the remains that it contains have been designated and reserved to be buried elsewhere. The decomposition in the tomb has not left much to keep, since it is really a child's coffin.

But what! among so many beings, once so dear, only one evoked! Is our family piety extinguished, too, then? And before the conclusive and universal abandonment, wasn't there a way for the officials of this necropolis, where everything vanishes, even the remembrance of the fathers in the memory of the sons, to replace one of the disticties of their Chênedollés of choice by the piercing cry that escapes like a sob from the psalmist's bosom:[9]

Oh, you who were my friends, have pity on me!

*

And yet more bones and inscriptions, always sorted out from the repertoire of academic *minores* and *minimi* ... Haven't you had enough, Madam? The picturesque is quickly exhausted here, the points of view are not varied, and even if we always spun ourselves around we would not see anything different. This mysterious word—catacombs—by itself excites a curiosity that, going back a long way, has taken its time to develop. Not everyone has the leisure, the opportunity, or the thought to descend here—and there were sufficient reasons to come. But you have already discovered, like me, that a few steps in these subterranean passages are enough to satisfy your curiosity. It is one of those places that everyone wants to see and no one wants to see again.

Let us then climb this staircase which appears to our impatience even more interminable than the descent—and here is the sweet air of the outside, here is the light, the sun, life, which chase away from us, like a bad dream—even worse, a boring dream—the memory of a funereal excursion.

*

We now go back down to work.

We will ask our lens to do without daylight in order to "render" to us what "it sees" with us: we will attempt *the first* underground experiment of photography with artificial light, which has already successfully replaced sunlight in our portrait studio.

But, in this place, this requires some explanation.

*

Most of these operations that we commonly perform today with perfect ease seemed, before the first attempt, an impossibility, even an affront to common sense.

As in my attempt at aerostatic photography, so loudly opposed and denied by the experts, I encountered more than one naysayer when I set out to compensate for the deficiencies of daylight with artificial illumination, which would seem necessary, after all, in the majority of cases where sunlight is lacking or insufficient. Having conceived the idea, I began the preparations.

At first, electricity was used for prolonged operations and magnesium in specific conditions. But at that time (1858) electricity was still quite a long way from the practical applications toward which it would soon stride with gigantic steps. We did not have the precious portable accumulators, or the intermediary generators of Gaulard,[10] or all the other equipment we have now, and we were forced to accept all the cumbersome inconveniences of the Bunsen battery. We had no choice.

I therefore had an experienced electrician install, on a solid part of my terrace on the boulevard des Capucines, fifty medium elements that, as I had hoped, turned out to be sufficient in providing me with the required light. I pass over the embarrassment and difficulties of installation and handling, all venial compared to the obstacles that I was to encounter later—when I took them outside.

My first application rightly belonged to the portrait before I launched myself into expeditions taken outside.

*

I naturally began the experience in *anima vili*, on myself and on the personnel of my laboratory.

As mediocre and even detestable as these first negatives were, the news of the attempt had spread in our photographic microcosm, in which everyone kept an eye on his neighbor, and I was soon invited to give a talk for the Circle and journal *la Presse scientifique*, which at that time had its headquarters at rue Richelieu, next to the fountain of Pradier—the pleasant but incoherent sculptor of whom Préault said: "he leaves every morning for Athens and he returns every evening to Place Bréda."[11]

Having immediately transported all my bulky equipment to rue Richelieu, I obtained various negatives—among others, the group of the President and his two assessors at their office—, negatives whose positives I made right away with my electric light source.

These first negatives came out coarse, with clashing effects, the blacks opaque, cut without details in every face. The pupils either extinguished by excessive luminosity or brutally sticking out, like two nails.

In order to perfect them, we needed a second source of softened light, penetrating the shaded parts. I tried bursts of magnesium; but we did not yet have the so propitious lamps invented later, and the use of magnesium, let alone of smoke, presented a number of problems.

I tried to attenuate my light by placing frosted glass between the lens and the model, which did not help me much; then, more practically, I arranged reflectors on white twill, and finally a double set of large mirrors reflecting intermittently the luminous light source of the shaded parts. I thus managed to restore my exposure time to my daily average;

finally I was able to obtain negatives with equal speed and of totally equivalent value to that of the negatives executed daily in my studio.

I would not pause over these experiments and over the gradual progress of research indicated by the most elementary practical sense if we had not seen, some years ago, two photographers, one of whom is well known, dispute excessively in court the priority of processes applied and divulged many years before they took up arms.

*

The presence, at dusk, of that then little-used light would stop the crowd on the boulevard and, drawn like moths to light, many curious people, friendly or indifferent, could not resist climbing the stairs to find out what was happening there.

These visitors of all classes, some of whom were known or even famous, were well received, gratuitously providing us with a stock of models, all disposed to the new experience.

It is in this way that in these evenings I photographed, among others, Niépce de Saint-Victor, G. de La Landelle, Gustave Doré, Albéric Second, Henri Delaage, Branicki, the financiers É. Pereire, Mirès, Halphen, etc., and finally my neighbor and friend from across the street, Professor Trousseau.

*

The possibility of photography in artificial light was therefore from then on secured; it was now only a matter of proceeding to the desired application.

The subterranean world was opening up an infinite field of operations no less interesting than the telluric surface. We were going to penetrate, to reveal the mysteries of the deepest, the most secret caverns.

But without going immediately so far, and in order to begin at the beginning, a first task would present itself under our very feet: the catacombs of Paris, without bearing the solemn lessons of the Roman catacombs in their memories, have their secrets to tell us, and, above all, we have to acknowledge the admirable human work accomplished in the network of our Parisian sewers.

*

We have passed through the catacombs, indicating up to now only briefly our operative procedure, whose real difficulties will occur mainly in the metropolitan emunctory.

In order to follow a precise order, let us first proceed with a reconnaissance of the place and try to take note of its inventory.

*

Under the dim light of the lanterns and, from time to time, under the faint daylight which comes through the little "peepholes" intentionally open to the outside for the sake of tourist visits, we notice an endless gallery of cement and red millstone. One could almost say that humidity makes the stone rusty.

A narrow sidewalk borders on left and right a canal more deep than wide; this concentration of an impure liquid, with a thick surface, is fringed on both sides by a margin of rails on which circulate the little passenger cars designated for service and for visitors. Under the direction of the employee charged with doing the honors at the place, four escorts wearing high statutory boots, two on this side and two on the other, will act as locomotive for us, the hand already stretched on the grab bars of the little wagon.

Noteworthy is the irreproachable politeness of these workers, resigned to the most menial jobs, whose decorum could often prove useful to the gentlemen, junior or senior clerks, in our public administration.

We have hardly taken our seats on the little wagon when a long horn blast resounds under the arches to signal our departure, to be repeated from time to time, in front of us, as we advance, by other bell-ringers at their posts. Our four conductors have already pushed us forward—and here we are on our rails with all the speed of these eight legs, with a rumble of thunder, which, nevertheless, does not prevent us from hearing either the muffled roar of cars circulating above our heads, or the crush of the plates which fall again behind us, the one after the other, on the "peepholes" we have just passed. Across the whole line through which we have to run, both above and below, the orders are to watch over us.

It is high time we noticed that we were wise to have taken the precaution of bringing an extra layer of clothes. The moist atmosphere that we traverse at full speed has soon become icy: it could become murderous.

We were rolling so fast that we hardly had the time to distinguish, on the enameled municipal signs, with white letters on blue background, the names of the public roads under which we slid repeated here.

An enormous iron pipe, one meter in diameter, supported by substantial brackets and even fastened by securely sealed beams, keeps us company all along the wall. This is the main water pipeline of the City. A simple crack, happily impossible, to this pipe and we would be unremittingly swallowed up by the rupture provoked by the pressure.

From time to time a dirty cascade falls to our left or to our right through a predetermined channel: a group of sewer workers on the job arrange themselves against the wall as we approach, and, silently, watch us pass. Right and left we leave behind us many transversal galleries, arteries and arterials of this vast circulatory system, all of whose vessels put together do not measure less than sixty leagues.

Here we pass through a thick fog which clouds the reflector lamp placed in front of our wagon and the lantern held by our head crew member: this means that on top of our heads a washhouse liquidates its morning operations. Further away a smell invades us, which could be pleasant if it weren't so strong: we pass by the laboratory of the perfumer. This smell, a memory of jasmine spoiled by patchouli (one of the pseudonyms of the horrible artificial musk whose odor the Germans extract from bituminous coal), will be the only one we will recognize in our entire journey through this outlet of the infinite putridness of a great capital, thanks to the perfect ventilation and to the system of movable hatches, wagons or boats, which maintain in these open sewers a permanent movement: the "circulus" of the mud. Yet it should not be trusted too much either; poison, even if it is latent, is nevertheless poison. Microbes have their states here, they reign and govern.

*

But far off, quite a long way ahead of us, a bright spot appears, which advances with the roar of a typhoon: from there the signal of the horn resounds. There is another convoy coming toward us and there is no double lane. A derailment in this ignominy, caused by a collision, would be horrible! Fortunately, because of our counter call, the enemy slows its pace. We have arrived, by the measures taken, at a drift angle: our car veers to the right at a turning plate, and we resume our journey at full speed.

Not one rat; I wish only to say that we didn't notice any. I want to believe that the administrative care invites them to retire during these public visits in order to mitigate the anxiety of nervous people.

At some intersections our way expands unexpectedly into large domes. As these amphitheaters, a little excessive, do not appear to be precisely designed for conferences or concerts, it does not seem foolhardy to admit here the hypothesis of some strategic foresight. Certainly each of these clandestine Coliseums would offer quite useful points for the concentration of forces in some contingency, just as the interminable underground network opened an all-too-ready mine of thousands of galleries under all the points of the capital ...

This is a conception of the Empire, but the flash of lightning which annihilated the Empire did not give it time to realize it; it is even more difficult to explain why the leaders of the Commune, at bay, crushed, determined to do anything, did not use this formidable means of destruction while the troops were arriving, as many expected, having been persuaded that this would be the best course of action.[12]

But not all our destinies are achieved ...

*

In the meantime, we're still rolling and the vault, whose icy sweat falls drop by drop more frequently, crushes on us more and more and the cramped walls are increasingly closing in. At times, we must—warned by our conductors' shouts—bow our heads, especially under the large transversal stanchion whose iron, viscous and eaten away, weeps tears of rust. The high boots of our escorts clap in the horrible liquid, on the submerged sidewalks. The path descends, descends still more: the flood rises; and they sink to above the knee, to the waist in a moment, always running, and everything around us streams, puddles, flows, drips, oozes. The place has become totally sinister: by the thick miasmas that float, our dimming lamps seem to be fainting, ready to go out. Uneasiness is followed by shivers, shivers will be shortly followed by anxiety: we are at one of the most lugubrious crossings of the hypogeum, in the old sewer, there where no layman has dared to enter for almost sixty years now. There is nothing around us but vent holes, channels, stilts, siphons, waterspouts, deformed entanglements of sinks and tunnels to defy the imagination of Piranesi:[13]

This is the black meeting place of immense nothingness ...

There are different levels, stages in the fluid gutter. The hutch has its arrogance and its prerogatives. Whatever space remains, strangled between stone and water, is still further obstructed by unnamable, disturbing things, and competes for space with the drizzle. Enormous chains, all corroded, pull on a more elevated part of the arch, appearing to be heavier in order to accelerate the collapse; these pulleys, welded by oxidation, were they not prepared by a mysterious torturer for some horrible questioning? Among the crooked pillars, the saturated, peeling wall, and this monstrous scrap iron, our bewitched car cannot advance even an inch: would it be able to go back? ... This is the Barathrum.[14] And always, beneath, above, in front, behind, everywhere, the water, this sanious, infamous water, with all its voices—bellowing, hiccupping, splashing, spitting, rumbling ...

*

At last we retreat; the horror fled, and, liberated from these terrors, we roll through a new series of routes, sometimes straight, sometimes curved. At the turn of a tangent, they stop us.

We step off our cart and, in a few steps, we find ourselves under the arch of a major vault, next to a large canal. This is the final river, which unites all these tributaries, the supreme synthesis of all our Parisian life—the Great Collector.

A massive skiff, square in shape, welcomes us, and the last relay of runners—these will only be able to walk, given the heaviness of our convoy—tows us slowly on the sordid tide. We trace in this thick liquid a large furrow, while, at the same time, by our thrust, the action of our mobile van pushes in front of our boat the mud of the depths toward the stinking Seine.

In the history of sewers, writing with the brilliant pen of the poet and the philosopher, after this description that he was able to render more moving than a dramatic work, Hugo tells us that in China there is no peasant returning from selling his vegetables in the city who does not bring back the heavy load of a double bucket filled with these precious enzymes. The very interesting and very well-documented book by Mr. Simon, who lived in China for many years, announces this customary fact, which the author himself confirmed to me.

We, on the other hand, send ships to Peru to bring back to us, at great cost, what we disdainfully throw away here, very eager to get rid of it, while Barral, in his *Agricultural Trilogy*, estimates that our agriculture annually loses in natural fertilizers forty million bushels of wheat. All our agrarian economists, all the specialists, the Boussingaults, the Liebigs, the Grandeaus, do not cease to protest every day against such an incomprehensible insanity.[15] But we take good care not to listen to them, and even better care not to understand them, and our unfathomable human stupidity persists in losing, in Paris alone, hundreds of millions every year in order to poison our fish ...

It has been repeatedly said that in all order of things we will persist in walking on our heads, which is not the best way of doing things.

But let us return, in order to finish, to our underground activities.

*

Based on the trial and error of our first experiments in the studio, a practitioner quickly could have foreseen the difficulties awaiting us in localities entirely unready to receive us.

The first of our impediments was the cumbersome baggage of our batteries, successively distributed on one or two carriages. All combinations tested, exhausted, finally ended up failing, confronted with the narrowness of some of these underground paths, strangled in certain places like molehills ...

We were forced to leave this part of our equipment outside, on the public road, from where it could communicate with us through one of the small municipal craters, the catacomb pits or manholes. We would roll it from one of these holes to the other as we proceeded in our underground operations.

The supervision of an attentive staff did not always manage to protect the equipment sufficiently against the curiosity, the indiscretion, of the gathering passersby. The crowd is everywhere inopportune, obtrusive, and if Parisian idle curiosity did not steal its reputation, it is not because it is more childish there than everywhere else (we have encountered at least equal stupidity in all the cities and towns of all countries without exception), it is because Paris offers a denser public.

The remoteness of the home generator did not facilitate our operations. At every moment we were up against the slowness of the arrangements or modifications, against the forced intervals of the practical work, or against some unforeseeable incident. A number of times, from our burrows where time was already too long—"we grow old here!," an aide would say—, we hastily had to send a messenger through makeshift roads in order to get information about some sudden stop which was forcing us to painfully restart an operation, an already difficult operation, exactly at the moment in which it was coming to an end.

At certain points, the distance from the mouths of communication imposed on us an exaggerated development of secondary conductors, and, not to mention all the other inconveniences or difficulties, we needed at every move to test our exposure times empirically; now, some of these plates were found to require up to *eighteen minutes*. Remember that we were still using collodion emulsion, which is slower than Lumière plates.

I had judged it advisable to animate some of these scenes by the use of a human figure, less in order to render them picturesque than in order to give a sense of scale, a precaution too often neglected by explorers in this medium, sometimes with disconcerting consequences. For these eighteen minutes of exposure, I found it difficult to obtain absolute, inorganic immobility from a human being. I tried to get around this difficulty by means of mannequins, which I dressed in worker's overalls and arranged on the stage with as little awkwardness as possible; this detail did not complicate our tasks.

But I couldn't say how many times our work was interrupted, stopped, for one reason or another. Sometimes the weakened acids were not sufficiently replenished and we had to stand at attention during these unpleasant delays, suspending all operations. Twice I had to change the operator whom we had contracted to supply our light. Should we still talk about our disappointment, our anger, when, after many efforts to overcome a difficult problem, at a moment in which, having taken all precautions and eliminated or circumvented all obstacles, our decisive operation was nearing its end—suddenly, in the last seconds of the exposure, a cloud rising from the canal came to veil our photograph—and how many imprecations, then, against the beautiful woman or the good man above us, who, without suspecting that we were there, chose that exact moment to replenish the water in their bathtub!

*

We have to take into account that this nasty work, through sewers or catacombs, lasted no fewer than three consecutive months. I would not wish these three months of holiday on my worst enemy, if I had one. I had given much more than I could give and I had reached the limit of my patience. I stopped—with regret, however, since the work, as I had envisaged it, was not yet entirely completed. But, somewhat nervously, I was recalled to the studio by necessities that, after such a long absence, were even more urgent.

In short, I brought back a hundred negatives, most of them very good, some truly so perfect that they seemed to have been achieved *sub Jove, sub sole.*[16] In any case, they cost me a lot, but I did not regret anything.

I hastened to offer the first hundred proofs to the collections of the Ville de Paris through the hands of the eminent engineer of our underground constructions, Mr. Belgrand: our work testified to his glory. A few months later, he did me the honor of requesting a second collection with which I had again the pleasure of paying him homage.

Female and Male Clients

A couple, a man and a woman—it doesn't matter of what social status—, come to see their test proofs.

Nine times, I would even say eleven times out of ten, you will see that the wife is absorbed by the portraits of her husband, while the husband, no less hypnotized but by his own image, seems miles away from even thinking of the image of his other half.

This observation has been repeated too many times, and with mathematical precision, not to deserve to be at the head of these notes.

*

So good is everyone's opinion of his or her physical qualities that the first impression of every model in front of the proofs of his or her portrait is almost inevitably disappointment and recoil (it goes without saying that we are talking here of perfect proofs).

Some people have the hypocritical modesty to conceal their shock under an appearance of indifference, but do not believe them. They had entered through the door defiant, aggressive, and many will come out furious.

It is by no means easy to avoid this difficulty; the amateur photographer will suffer as much as the professional, even more, the poor thing! doomed in advance to all acerbities, and especially because he has the disadvantage of not being duly licensed. He had better get ready, then, exactly like the other one, and ponder the advice of experience.

Prophylactically, that is, before the act, entertain the eventuality of a "retake." The hope of this beneficial "retake" will appease everything, everybody will gain—since, you yourself, are you so certain that you cannot get something even better than this first proof?

Above all, when two models have come to you together, be sure to arrange for them to come together to get the photographs.

Never forget, then, to submit the proofs of the one to the other and those of the other to the first: what in billiards is called "playing off the cushion"—and, for a moment, escape!

Without fail the one will find the other very successful and the other will find the first perfect. As counterevidence, let them still debate together.

The inevitable first shock thus dissipated and reduced to a simple effect of the back and forth, you can then approach them without fear of being bitten.

Thrice happy is the operator who happens upon a client like my dear Philippe Gille (without an *s*!)—this well-read mandarin, always in such a good humor.

I had scarcely had the time to submit to him his first proof when, without even looking at the second one, the excellent man cries out:

— Perfect! And how nicely you have rendered *my good look, sweet, loyal!—and intelligent!!!*

*

We have attributed to women the reputation of coquetry—which, between us, they would be totally wrong not to merit; but this constant solicitude of the effect provoked by our physical appearance, this coquetry, is even more reproachable in man himself. This I have seen many times, and from the right place from which one can see it best.

Nothing in women can compare to the infatuation of certain men and to the constant concern about their "appearance" in the majority of them. Those who pretend to be the most detached in this matter are precisely the most affected.

*

I have found in men considered serious by everyone, in the most eminent personages, an anxiety, an extreme agitation, almost an agony in regard to the most insignificant details of their appearance or to a "nuance in their expression." It has been depressing, sometimes even repugnant.

One of them came back one time, early in the morning the day after his visit to see the proofs, all thrown off by a hair—I say *one hair*—which was sticking out past the part and which he absolutely wanted to see return to the line. "But wouldn't there be a way, Mr. Nadar? And wouldn't it be better to redo it? ..." And this is what this solemn man had come to ask me at dawn, dropping everything.

The whole night he had been unable to sleep a wink—and in full candor he confessed it to me.

*

But shall we contemplate masculine infatuation pushed to the point of madness? What more explicit demonstration than the inexplicable unconsciousness of some candidates, professional politicians who have planned, as a supreme, decisive means of persuasion, to send their photograph to their constituents, an image of the word-merchants that they are? What virtue of attraction, then, can these people assume in their shameful faces, where all baseness, all human ugliness flourishes, faces which exude baseness and ignominious lies and all the physiognostic signs of duplicity, lust, greed, depredation?

Is it not the epitome of egotistical monomania, this hallucination that has no qualms about winning the approval of all hearts with the presentation of such mugs?

And if Niépce had foreseen the parting shot of this discovery, wouldn't he have recoiled?

*

It has been shown that some professions more than others seem to develop, within the individual, the cult of the self and infatuation. Naturally the actor comes first here, and we should neither be surprised nor should we reproach him: it is a professional liability.

Immediately after the actor, it is the officer who presents himself.

The meticulous rigidity of order, which the incessant surveillance of the minutest details of the uniform imposes, is it not there to a great extent, too?

I myself have been in the position, for some forty years and more, to make these observations, every day, from morning to evening, and I must admit that, alongside perfectly dignified bearings, in the orthodox and virile unawareness of their image, I have happened to encounter, in some of our military men, disconcerting affectations and petty behaviors.

But I have also taken the portrait of a good number of foreign officers, Italian and of all nationalities, and I have quickly realized that these exotic iron-bearers have in their dress and appearance manners and bearings from which our men would still have much to learn.

*

But where I saw the insanity of male coquetry in its paroxysm is—though I must sadden some consciences—in two … Anglican pastors!

Never—ever! have I encountered in female creatures a similar science of arrangements and cosmetic strategy: disgusting …

How could I forget especially that one who came to me once in all the splendor borrowed from mother Jezebel,[1] so outrageously rosy-cheeked that I could not resist the temptation to check it out?

Under the pretext of removing from his cheek an atom of soot, I take my handkerchief, I touch, and I find—carmine!

My creature turned pale …

On the other hand, if many models are wrong to indulge in exaggerations of pretensions and affectations, others, quite on the contrary, demonstrate such an indifference, such a sidereal disengagement from themselves, that they manage to disorient all sentiment of probability.

*

Such was the one I noticed one afternoon in our "hall" at the time when the proofs are submitted to our clientele for their review, notably punctual at this daily appointment. Among the small groups, all absorbed by their respective proofs, I would go from the one to the other, giving my advice. When I came to that one:

—And you, sir, would you like me to help you to be critical? First of all, how do you find yourself?

— Not bad, sir. I'm satisfied.

— Let me see …

I look at the two proofs—I raise my eyes to the model …

It was the proof *of someone else* that he was holding in his hand—and with which he was "satisfied" …

*

Oh, well, I have seen worse: another time I killed two birds with one stone!

But we should first of all keep in mind that the sounding line has never touched, will never touch, the depths of—how should I put it? … —human naïveté.

For example, all those who have penned something in a newspaper were from the beginning made aware of the famous legend of the old subscriber whose sight is failing and who writes to the editor requesting that he get his copy in "slightly larger" print. Since his request is very exceptional, he assumes that it cannot be refused to one of the oldest subscribers to the newspaper …

And do not believe that this preposterous request was unique: it reproduces itself from time to time and even I myself have uncovered it in the offices of the first newspaper where I found myself seated at a desk.

I have, personally, dealt with a good lady who recommends "above all" reproducing the portrait on "good paper," and it is me that the good gentleman addressed, who offered with no prompting to pay "a little more" for his painted image, on the condition that it would be painted with "fine colors."

The Poet, himself, did not mince words. He said: "Stupidity belongs to man."

*

So then, two gentlemen, from the provinces, came together to have their pictures taken and returned together to see the proofs.

According to the invariable ritual, the employee gave the one the proofs of the other, and the other the proofs of the first one.

For a while they have both been staring silently at these images, each in his own turn ...

I intervene:

— Well, gentlemen, are you satisfied? Have you chosen?

Both equally say that they are content.

— ... Only, one points out to me, all timidly, it seems to me that ... I did not have a mustache? ...

I look at the image, I look at the man, I look at his friend ...

Each held the portrait of the other—and recognized himself there!!!

The order of things reestablished, here they are, then, the one and the other, a little more comfortable—and the one that, until now, had not breathed, said to me, timidly:

— I was thinking, too: it seems to me that there is ... *something that is not quite right ...*

You've had enough? Just a moment ...

But will you believe me? ...

*

This person enters (and I do not make them do it on purpose), he chooses the type of portrait that he desires, asks to pay his bill immediately, pays and: he disappears! We did not even have time to turn around ...

With great agitation, we exclaim: but where did the gentleman go? A second ago he was here! Run quickly: he did not even have time to get down the stairs! ...

We rush, we fly, we catch up with him, we bring him back:

— But, sir? What about your session? You must pose!

— Ah??? ... As you wish. But *I thought that this was enough ...*

*

Put a woman in a photography studio, as indeed in the neutral terrain of any other shop or counter, and you do not have a more sensitive and reliable instrument of precision than this touchstone to register, from the door, if the client who just entered is a gentleman or a badly raised man.

Still, we must point out that there are gentlemen and gentlemen. One of the most correct, he who "in his world" will always be considered irreproachable, can represent, in another world, a very uncivil man, and even a perfect bore: the one, for example, for whom a woman who is not from a specific class of woman is not a woman. This is primarily where the true gentleman stands out.

The affectation of the Anglo-Saxon stiffness has become, for those among us who set the tone, the paragon of gentility. Our habits have been infiltrated by the mores of the Market, a crude place par excellence, where, through the wild pushing and shoving for money and the Israeli way of having the hat fixed on the head, the brutality of the clashes and collisions has never afforded the time for an apology. The base level there is even lower than the offense.

Through all this our educational habits have changed. We are far from the days when, as children, we would hold our caps low even in the most humble shop, where we were told to take them off in order to give a penny to a poor man, and when Mom would refuse our pleas to replace our old hat, the whole thing being superfluous, because a hat "*is held in the hand.*"

"*Petit Bob*" wouldn't hear of it at all.[2]

Some old families still try to keep and transmit received traditions; but everything wears out, and very soon we will wonder what could well be the nature of that politeness whose evocation would find nothing to respond to it in the new order of things.

What a pity! Courtesy, amiability, affability, were not, in fact, other than delicate means, dilutions of sensitivity, of goodness—and this politeness which seems to be lost forever was not one of the least charms of our French race ...

*

But let us return quickly to our laboratories.

A little more often than the justice of the axiom merits, impertinent people repeat to us that people always get the government they deserve—which would be too offensive for many people, including us. We must nevertheless recognize that every artistic or commercial establishment will be treated by its clients in the same way as it treats them, and vice versa.

In truth, you would never be able to tame certain, often very charming monsters, whose naïvely ferocious egoism absolutely mocks everything that is not them. There are some who seem to derive a secret and intimate enjoyment from doing harm, for example, by disrupting the entire schedule of a workday with a delay, and turning all the appointments upside down, like a deck of cards.

Against these monsters, the profession itself will provide you with more than one sufficient riposte, if not to have everything turn out well, at least to neutralize their harmfulness. Hold on first, without any wavering, to a rigorous punctuality, and remain ruthless to all latecomers, whatever the cost. What you might have lost on one side will soon be regained on the other.

The whole question boils down for you into "*doing well.*" Always and still always look for the best, there and everywhere, and, preoccupied day and night with how to perfect your work, be stricter with yourself than with anybody else. Never let anything emerge from your studio that cannot defy the criticism of a rival.

To seek honor before profit is the surest means of finding profit with honor.

*

It was in the very early days of my being a photographer.

Night was falling, and in the garden of the rue Saint-Lazare which served as my studio then—a garden long since eliminated by municipal redistricting—, I was already putting in order, for the next day's work, the instruments, very basic then, of which I would try to make the most: the tools of the novice were as modest as his fortune.

The bell rings: two strangers, tall and with a nice air about them, attended by a beautiful lady who accompanies them, ask me to make their portrait. They both have to leave the next evening on the express train—they are officers in the army in India.

I refuse: the daylight is too dim; I wouldn't have been able to do anything good. Tomorrow?

Tomorrow, impossible for them, since their whole day is taken—and so much do they insist that, in order not to offend them, I end up giving in, but by reiterating to them that the proof, in similar conditions, will not be acceptable.

*

The two poses were taken:

— How much?

— But they will not be good.

— How much?

— It will be two hundred francs; but …

They still intend to pay; they put two bills on the table, without accepting a receipt—and off they go.

*

The next morning, I expose the two negatives without any conviction—and in fact all I obtain is two gray, blurry proofs—not deliverable.

If only my two obstinate clients could return during the day, I would send them, anywhere, other proofs than these! …

But no. It is only in the evening, like the day before, that I see them again.

*

— Well, you will realize that I did not mislead you yesterday. Judge for yourselves.

The two men and the beautiful lady examine the proofs, consult among themselves in English—and finally, in agreement:

— But we do not find these bad; they're even good.

— No!

— Yes!— and, moreover, these portraits suit us. Could you please prepare them so that we can take them?

— Never in my life! I do not deliver such things. You will begin all over again …

— Impossible.

— Then you will not begin again; but these will never leave my house. Here are your two hundred francs.

*

And I had already torn the proofs into four pieces.

The trio jumped!!! ...

— Excuse me, and please accept all my regrets for displeasing you ...

One of my two Englishmen is more than displeased, and similarly the lady: he's even pale ... A little nervously, he says to me:

— But, sir, you did not have the right to dispose of these proofs, which were paid for?

— Excuse me: here is your money: moreover, you remember that yesterday I refused to accept it. Didn't I tell you in advance, and repeat, that my work would not be deliverable?

— But you did not have the right to dispose of this work by yourself, even if it were bad. It partly belongs to us, since we wasted time and energy in order to pose.

The argument, even though specious, touches me here: I sensibly soften up:

— What you say here, sir, would be fair up to a point; but please bear in mind that there is nothing to worry about. Your money is good, beyond dispute: the work that I have to give you, in exchange for this money, has to be equally good and, indisputably, of equal value—or else the establishment you entered is not an honest one—, and thus it would not be I who receives you there. I can only reiterate my regrets to you.

It is necessary that they take a stand.

The trio exchanges a few words in English—and looks at me with curiosity.

Evidently, to them I seem like an eccentric, perhaps a madman. But all the excitement dies down, and, withdrawing, my Englishman says to me:

— You are a strange businessman, sir, and you seem to me to have adopted a method that does not lead to riches.

— Perhaps; unless, even further than Calcutta, Madras, and for a long time, you will keep the memory of a businessman, as you say, scrupulously fair, even at his own expense. If the case is quite uncommon and seems to you curious enough to be mentioned, then I will not have lost but gained. But this point is secondary, and there is another that comes first: you have your point of honor as an officer; why shouldn't a businessman have his point of honor as a businessman? ...

We part, almost good friends at last ...

*

What would my three English people have thought, had they suspected what, that day, their repudiated ten louis represented for me—at that so difficult moment of my poor beginnings—, when I lacked everything ...

But I persist in believing that it is in this way, and only this way, that *the best establishments are built.*

And this is what we must always demonstrate.

The Professional Secret

Surely, this man had been loved …

He was stretched out, already rigid, under the white sheets from which the top of the body emerged, aligning both arms on the upturned bedcover.

He had been dressed in formalwear for this unique, ultimate reception chez Death: the ritual, shiny new black suit, with strict folds; the white collar, the tie, the shirt front, the pale violet gloves, all of an irreproachable correctness; the razor had clearly just passed one last time over his dead face. The waxen face was set off from the brightness of the bedding and the porcelain starch of the underwear, by the opaque black of hirsuteness, thick hair, an ample mustache, and bushy eyebrows meeting like a large bar traced in ink above his beak-shaped nose.

This dead man had hardly had the time to glimpse his thirty-fifth year, at most. His features were of a classic, antique rectangularity. On his chest, an enormous crucifix stretched its arms, as if to preserve him, now and hereafter. The rest of the bed disappeared under piles of freshly cut flowers and the whole bedroom was still so strewn with flowers, sumptuous bouquets and wreaths, that one could hardly get a foothold among this profusion.

*

Yes, certainly, he had been loved, adored by everyone around him; the two maids, in deep mourning, who received us in the antechamber, fled immediately, suffocated by tears. Still other women—one, two, three, an entire family—all uniformly dressed in long black mourning crêpes, appeared silently one after the other, and all these somber eyes, burnt by tears, watched us with an anxious, jealous, almost hateful defiance, as if we had something to do with this death, as if we had come to rip this dear dead man away from them. ...

In this confusion, we had trouble obtaining two or three indispensable words in French: the whole household was Spanish, which we were at least able to intuit from a few muffled words, almost fading out of pious respect, crushed under ...

The sister of Charity who had remained kneeling at the foot of the bed finally stood, and, without turning away from it, disappeared.

We got down to our work ...

*

If there is a tiresome task in professional photography, it is the obligatory submission to these funeral calls—which can't be put off ...

It is not only falling, like this time, into the midst of suffering against which one cannot do anything—at times such cruel, harrowing explosions that, while they belong to someone else, they manage to make themselves yours without your being able to defend yourself; it is also the experience before long of feeling the recollection of personal sorrows evoked in oneself, suddenly finding old pains rekindled, ones that had been silenced, lulled asleep—badly healed wounds revive and begin bleeding, piercing ...

At other times, it is true, and how many other times! did we not, entirely on the contrary, find, behind the appearance of mourning and official regret, indifference icier than the dead body itself, bitter greed, the only devotee for the remains of him or her who has just passed away, long impatient desires finally relieved, vile calculations, falseness, callow lies maintained for so long—released and finally rewarded, having a hard time repressing the overflowing joy of victory achieved: a compelling argument against inheritance.

But here, we were far from this muck and, as in the prostration of these pains, so in the smallest details of what surrounded us, we felt an atmosphere of infinite kindness, of unbridled adoration that persisted, still beating warm and more than ever around this idolized being, frozen forever! …

What was he not worth, thus, for having been loved so much, what had he not given in kindness to receive so much in return!

*

We had been urged to hurry with developing the prints.

Indeed, the next morning, at the earliest hour, a lady in long crêpe veils came for news, one no doubt among the others who had spoken to us the night before.

When the employee brought her the two still wet prints on a sheet of glass, the lady lifted her veil and contemplated them avidly, leaning over the dear images. Long tears flowed down her cheeks, misting up her eyes that her handkerchief was unable to dry, until suffocating, nervous and terrified, she finally turned away, lowering her veil, to tell us that she had to take these prints with her, as they were, and that we should print others immediately.

We could only bow to her wishes: the lady had left with the two photographs rolled up in blotting paper.

*

Barely an hour had passed, when two other women, scrupulously in deep mourning like the first one, introduced themselves asking to see the prints …

*

What did this mean? Did these two people have no word of what had been delivered an hour earlier … ?

I examined them: the younger one had a long, regular face with the tan paleness of Creoles or Madrilenians, pitch-black eyes, encircled with bistre. These eyes had clearly cried too much to have kept a single tear; they were forever dry and hard. Anyone who has suffered too much at once defies all other suffering. Surely, there had been and there remained a profound, absorbing and unique passion here, which cannot and does not want to be consoled. From now on these eyes of Erebus could only look inward—forever fixed on the One who cannot be replaced …

The other one, manifestly the mother: a tracing of the girl's features with years added. But that was all. The morose seriousness, the attractive despondency of the young woman's gaze took on a bad, haughty, combative and singularly disagreeable character in the mother's steely pupils.

Next to the daughter, crushed under her pain, the mother would however have been necessary—the tender mother, who also suffers, who cries, who soothes what cannot be soothed …

*

The two silent women looked at the prints … We stood waiting, my employee and I …

The mother finally muttered toward the daughter, in a curt tone, a few words in the idiom that was foreign to us—and translating, the young woman said to me:

— Monsieur, it is understood that you will give these prints to me *alone* …

An obedient interpreter, she emphasized the word "*alone*."

I felt myself shudder … I had just begun to guess the truth …

This one was really the spouse, the legitimate spouse, without a doubt.

But then—the other?—the one who rose first this morning? …

A shiver passed over me, a premonition of the drama … What had I done!!! …

*

Suddenly, like lightning, the old woman fixed her gaze upon me, moved her head brusquely, first back then forward, the two in one beat: the viper's attack—and I heard her whisper in her daughter's ear—(oh! this time I understood her well … !)

He has already given some out!! …

— Have you already given these portraits to someone? … the young woman asked me breathlessly, each strangled syllable unable to come out.

My employee threw himself forward: he was of an imperturbable composure—a strong man, a born liar, it was like breathing to him.

— To no one, Madame, to no one! Not one print has left here—since this is our first trial printing! Moreover, and besides …

And he talked, he went on talking, he was talking too much—as those who want to deceive always do …

But the old woman didn't allow herself to be misled; her hellish gaze bore into me relentlessly. Under her dark glove of mourning, her long index finger, her thin hand, all of her was stretched toward me, accusing, denouncing, raising my agitation to its peak—and I could clearly hear the black viper whisper:

—HIM!—TO HIM, then!!!—Only speak to HIM!!!

There wasn't a mother here, in fact: there was only the cruel stepmother, the mother-in-law, eternal and implacable hatred—the only viper that does not reject non-living prey: this one was finishing off her dead son-in-law, gnawing with the same bites—and what did it matter to her loathing!—at her own daughter's heart ...

The young widow rose, and came right up against me, face to face:

— On your honor, Monsieur—as a man of honor, tell us the truth: yes or no, have these portraits already been handed out? ...

Why did I lack the strength to forget myself, to disown myself, seeing only the unfortunate woman standing before me, awaiting her sentence? Would I now dare to claim that I had never lied—and would it then be in order to save? What morality, which God would have condemned my lie?

But what! my agitation, this revealing, intractable agitation, hadn't it already responded too much, and how was I to refute this renunciation of myself by myself, when this truth that was being demanded of me was exploding, blindingly? Must a death sentence absolutely be uttered twice?

The ground beneath my feet stopped crumbling ... With difficulty, I muttered:

— You have already seen so much, Madame, that it is not possible for me to lie to you ...

I thought that she was going to fall: I rushed forward ...

But she straightened herself up, and, without a word, carrying the broken blade in her wound, she withdrew, followed by this mother, this executioner ... whom I had helped ...

*

Since then—for how many years already!—how many times have I seen her again in our Paris, the one woman to whom I have unwillingly caused so much pain, pain that I will never—intolerable thought!—be allowed to redress! A whole world of dear memories, an entire past of youth, love and confidence, shattered: instead of a bitter sweetness softened by the memory of beautiful days spent next to the beloved, there was inexorable resentment, the indignation of the betrayed, outraged wife—instead of respect and love, hatred and contempt forever …

How many, many times have I found her unexpectedly, at a street corner, at another, everywhere, suddenly focused upon me, an always living reminder of that atrocious hour—motionless and piercing me with her ashen eyes—which I still see …

Doctor Van Monckhoven

Among the essential readings, more and more rare, which can elevate the soul and strengthen the heart, few pages are so eloquent in their brevity, at times a little pompous, following the fashion of the time, than the few pages of the report presented by Fourcroy at the National Convention, on behalf of the Committee on Public Health—*On the arts that have already served in defense of the Republic and a recent discovery of citizen Armand Seguin.*

Whatever opinion one might have—and it is not even necessary to be French—, it is impossible not to experience a profound emotion before this document of the admirable effort of a people determined not to perish or to retreat under the universe conspiring against them.

"Everything was missing at the same time, men, materials, and time." It was necessary to create everything, "to overcome at every step the resistance of nature itself, the inertia of idleness and of carelessness, the obstacles of malevolence."

In this report, a real patriotic breviary, and quickly, since he himself does not have time to waste or to make others waste, Fourcroy declares that arms factories, improvised immediately and throughout the territory, have already responded to the first needs: Paris alone has provided or refurbished one hundred and fifty thousand rifles.

In nine months, twelve million pounds of saltpeter had been delivered, while on average we used to obtain barely a million per year. From now on, twenty-four hours are enough to make thirty thousand pounds of saltpeter.

Our steel, until now dependent on other people, emancipates itself suddenly and becomes national. Our manufacturing facilities multiply everywhere: we create cannons in cast iron.

The telegraph—"this new revolutionary courier"—inspires and impels in the same breath the movements of our sparse armies, at the same time that it imposes on us the study and the methodical fabrication of the flint glass that we used to borrow from our enemy, who, each time, found the right composition for it only by chance.

The aerostation school of Meudon builds balloons and trains students for aerostatic companies; each army corps will have its aerostation park just as it has its artillery park. In the plains of Fleurus, in the ramparts of Maubeuge, in Franckenthal, in Ehrenbreistein, everywhere, our balloons stun the enemy and prepare his defeat.

Hemp, tar, potash, all that is missing is substituted by something else: we braid the ropes with plants until now neglected, even with animal materials.

But the manufacturing of saltpeter absorbs all our potash and we will be forced to close the factories of glass, soap, bleach, etc.: immediately soda replaces potash.

So far we have paid for tar: from now on our coal, our purified peat, will provide it.

Even graphite was missing, until recently supplied by England alone: —Conté ("all the sciences in the mind, all the arts in the hand," said Monge), Conté, on his first encounter with our mountains, extracts the iron carbide from which he will create the pencils which our students still use today and which the English in turn will borrow from us

And this first, absorbing preoccupation of the war, far from being the obstacle, becomes instead the most precious auxiliary of the arts of peace. The military scientific commissions accelerate the study of all products useful for domestic purposes. An ardent youth rushes to attend public courses on all sciences at the Military School, at the Central School of Public Works, at the three Schools of Health, everywhere, and the progress of universal instruction, which must renew and improve the economic conditions of our existence, results naturally from the preparation for combat.

The fact that concludes Fourcroy's report is startling.

For the fourteen improvised armies assigned to the Republic—usually forgetting that of Santo Domingo, which nevertheless did not stay idle—shoes were needed, and right away.

If the annual consumption of each citizen of the Republic is calculated to be two pairs of shoes, the expenditure is a billion: for the armies alone, it is one hundred and forty million. At this stage, the expense comes to two hundred million, representing around fifteen hundred thousand skins of oxen, twelve hundred thousand skins of cows, and a million calfskins: all this "needing to pass, according to the report, through the chamois shop, the belt shop, the gelding clinic, the fine leather goods business, the tannery, the parchment shop, the leatherwear shop; and many other '*arts*' of no less importance that derive directly from them. These '*arts*' must therefore call the attention of legislators. Like those of primary necessity, they contribute effectively to the prosperity of the Republic and can give us, in the commercial balance of nations, a considerable advantage over all the powers of Europe ..."

We see that here everything is examined from above and from afar and that considerations of general economy do not get lost even in the face of the very serious preoccupations with the present war.

To confine ourselves to the present situation and to the only shoe repair store, in a pinch we have leather; but this leather, flushed and swollen by lime, by fermented barley or tan, must be kept for two years in tanning pits before it is delivered to us.

It is not in two years, it is in two weeks, in two days, that we need this leather.

We will have it.

At an invitation by the Committee of Public Health, Berthollet[1] comes immediately to present the process of Armand Séguin, who, treating leather with sulfuric acid mixed with tan, eliminates the barley, reduces the expenses by eighty percent, the time to nothing, simplifies and popularizes the operation to such a degree that every citizen can now prepare at home the leather necessary for his consumption—"more easily than he does his laundry." And this new leather, delivered on time, will be more supple, more solid and durable than the old leather ...

Never has the memory of these pages that one cannot read enough, repeat enough—the most beautiful pages that the human soul has dictated to human genius—, never has this memory come back to me without my immediately evoking my dear Monckhoven, just as my thinking of Monckhoven always evokes Fourcroy's report.

*

It is because Van Monckhoven was also one of those scholars from whom one can *order a discovery.*

He was truly worthy of being born in that heroic age, and he would have been one of the most brilliant in the pleiad of Condorcet, Lavoisier, Monge, Chaptal, Vauquelin, Lalande, Fourcroy, Bossut, Darcet, Conté, etc., as he remains one of the first today among Janssen, sworn observer of the sun, the brothers Henry who impose their *ne varietur* (let us not move anymore!) to the last nebula, marking the exits and escapades of the comets, and that incredible Marey who makes us see the invisible, and will soon, in time, make us fly like a bird.

Monckhoven had everything going for him: universal notions, a passion for research, unparalleled physical and intellectual activity, inventive acuity and quick understanding, precise vision, sagacity of observation, ingenuity of application, fecundity of means and resources, flexibility in front of the obstacle: add still to the dexterity of the experimenter perseverance pushed to the point of obstinacy.

His acquired knowledge was enhanced by incessant personal work—for, as one of the orators who spoke at his funeral said, "who ever saw him rest? From the time he became a man he was able to count his days by ingenious discoveries and fruitful research."

This productive man was in fact the exact opposite of the type that is all too familiar in a world in which, as elsewhere, the empire belongs primarily to the impudent; I refer to the pseudo-savant, the cryptoramic, or rather pedicular parasite, who more often frequents the antechambers than the laboratory, who adorns himself with all kinds of feathers that are not his own, self-important, pompous, richly colored, having no other resources than to walk on others in order to elevate his pettiness and to obtain honors to decorate his boutonnière, that is, to blow his own trumpet: a meddler on all committees or commissions, a hornet whose sterile existence is spent on busyness around the bee hole without ever entering it.

And if Monckhoven's work had not, in its full bloom, been abruptly cut short by death—he was barely forty-eight years old—, how much more could we not have expected from him who had already given us so much, still extracting from nature its secrets and popularizing them so passionately that he became an industrialist in order to better diffuse them.

Photography, having just been born, had immediately captured him. Direct heir of the Niépces, the Talbots, the Poitevins, addressing the practice, directly and in depth, as soon as the theory was revealed to him, he will never stop. Blow by blow, he gives us a *New Procedure for Iron Plates* (these "ferrotypes," which are presently still part of the daily life of humble families), the *Simplified Method of Photography on Paper*, the

Treatise on Collodion Photography, the *History of the Carbon Process*, the *Procedure of the Carbon Practice*, etc., and he condenses all his initial studies in his precious *Treatise on Photography*, whose successive editions will never stop. And, believe me, not like those editions of recent invention, published in fantastic quantities, but in reality different only on the covers. With each of these editions, he adds, he revises, with the zeal of an honest man, with his scientific conscience always restless, unquenched. I have seen him, every time, preoccupied, absorbed, feverish, as if he had given birth to a new child.

He goes on and on, enlarging his circle without ever losing sight of photography. He publishes *Studies on Nitroglucose*, *The Various Modes of the Production of Light*, *Gelatin-Bromide*, the *Treatise on Photographic Optics*, where he has explained so beautifully all the forms of adopted lenses, their qualities and their defects, that, in 1882, the great optician Steinheil declared publicly—and to his credit—that he owed the inspiration for his most important works to the teaching, to the scientific impulse, of Van Monckhoven.

Everywhere and in every new science, doing is as necessary as knowing. From invention and theory, Van Monckhoven proceeds everywhere and immediately to practice, to action.

He had already constructed, for enlargements, his own dialitic apparatus with a heliostat, superior to the best systems known until then.

At the first appearance of carbon processes, he takes the lead in industrial manufacturing and his papers replace all the others.

The same happened in regard to his gelatin-bromide plates, from which he created in Ghent a considerable industry, using, from the very beginning, over ten thousand kilos of glass per week, producing on average twelve hundred dozen plates per day—nearly four and a half million plates per year.

Model head of family, adored as much as venerated by his own, it is to the intelligence, to the activity of his closest relatives, to female hands, that he confides the management of his factory, a large patrimony put together for his daughters, which will have been created for the family by the family.

*

But, either in the private laboratory or in the factory, photography would not be sufficient for the curiosity of this universal and insatiable mind. Independently of the participating sciences that he continues to pursue and all the other problems to which he attends, it is to astronomy, his favorite, that he ceaselessly returns. And there where he felt the strongest, because of a special attraction and because it was his first course of study, it is there where, deplorably, he will not be able to display the true measure of his strength. By one of those contradictions which are encountered in more than one of our destinies, it is exactly there, where he is especially called upon, that he will be unable to go freely: other attachments, other duties, have claimed his attention and they will keep him.

You should have heard him talk about his passion for astronomy. You would say a lover was singing the charms of "*the person*," of the beloved person, inaccessible, unimaginable. Even I, despite my irresistible aversion to everything that is a number, despite my innate terror of anything that resembles the execrable number, I could not help but be touched by the tone of this passion, so sincere, so emotional, for the matters of algebra: at times I would feel as if I were myself rising with my friend through the ether, carried away by the inextricable cosmogony, in the contagion of an unimagined poetics where we were bound to see theorems rounding out to the rhythm of the periods and the mnb^2 flying away in winged strophes ...

But duty was there, strict, jealous. Astronomy had to elude him, and Monckhoven did not have the time to consummate this much-desired marriage, which could have been so fecund. His dream remained a dream.

Nevertheless, he found more than one moment to escape in order to pull over to that side. His superhuman activity knew how to reserve, here and there, precious leisure time to dedicate to his most fervent obsession.

He had an observatory built just for him, where he accumulated the instruments that only a nation can provide.[2] He did not know there, any more than anywhere else, how to count or how to bargain. Nothing was too expensive, and he himself built the telescopes, whose models were copied in the premier observatories of the world.

And these expenses, these efforts, were not, could not be sterile. When I was given the joy of bringing together two of my best, of my highest friendships, by reuniting for the first—and the last!—time Monckhoven and Marey, Monck (as we called him) trusted Marey to present at the Academy a thesis *On the Enlargement of Hydrogen's Principal Trajectories and on the Diffusion of Solar Rays.*

At the moment of his death, he had finished a work on *Rarefied Gases and Electricity.*

*

How did we meet, Monckhoven and I?

I had never seen him, until, on a clear and mild morning thirty years ago, my wonderful Ghemar dropped by, from his studio in Brussels to my studio on the boulevard des Capucines.

He was accompanied by two friends, the one a French chemist established in Berlin, the other a very young man, small and blond.

After the first exchange of pleasantries between Ghemar and me, he tells me, putting his hand on the shoulder of the beardless blond:

— I present to you Van Monckhoven.

— Related to the author of the *Treatise*?

— No. The author.

I looked, surprised, at this very young man, almost a child, pale blond, buttery-blond, the real Belgian blond. And as he, nose in the air, was steadily pointing at me the two carbuncles of his lenses, so shiny that you couldn't see anything through them, I ask him:

—*You*—it is *you* who wrote the *Treatise on Photography*?

—Yes!

—You are nothing but a little liar; it's your grandfather ...

Then, and continuously until his death, how many years—so quickly gone today!—of joyful, sweet, fraternal friendship, without ever a shadow of a cloud passing between us ...

*

He was blessed with the beautiful and joyous temperament that belongs by right to those with clear consciences, and he was, moreover, one of those wise people who are convinced that laughter is a characteristic of a healthy person. Always cheerful, restless and rustling like a silkworm butterfly in front of its laid eggs—and in fact wasn't he always there?—this Flemish man, this native of Ghent, had all the pleasant exuberance of the Walloon: Rops, Rops[3] himself was never more brilliant, more alive, from living the beautiful and good life of an honest man. Alas! of my poor Monck, and then of my very dear Rops, of all these joys, of all these achievements, what remains today? ...

*

He had the noble indifference to what can be possessed, the liberality, the generosity of great souls, and he could have adopted as his the Ravenswood motto, one of the most beautiful I know: "*The open hand*."[4]

When he constructed his enlargement apparatuses with heliostats, his first words were:

— I will send you one.

I declined the offer. I knew how much these instruments cost (three thousand francs then, I think) and however urgent it was for me to make this acquisition, it was not the right moment.

As he insisted, I ended up telling him the reason. He lost his temper:

—Are you kidding me, and did you think I wanted to make a "deal" with you?

It did not matter how much we debated: barely had he left than I received the instrument, with an affectionate word in place of the bill: we were, he and I, merchants!

It was necessary to give in—and await the hour of revenge.

It took a long time, but it struck.

On one of his trips to Paris (he never failed to stay with me, and what a feast for us, especially when he was with his family!), he told me of his intentions to buy a one-horsepower gas motor, which he needed.

I just happened to have one, which was not being used at that moment. It was two-horsepower, but the double power was not a great obstacle.

Immediately and without a word, the heavy machine was dismantled, cleaned like jewelry, packaged, piece by piece, with the most meticulous care, and dispatched to Ghent postage paid, as is necessary for all gifts.

My good Monck, more accustomed to give than to receive, appeared dazzled by the delivery, far more so than necessary.

"You give gifts befitting a gentleman," he wrote to me.

—A gentleman yourself, it was you who started it.

He had forgotten his first gift:

—Well, he responded, but an ox in exchange for an egg![5] ...

As if he did not know, he better than anyone else, that in friendship the one who remains in debt is the one who gives ...

*

Brave and dear companion lost so early! What affection lost, what fidelity, what loyalty! Affable, kind to everyone, severe only with procrastinators and stick-in-the-muds, from the beginning he found himself naturally in personal relations with anyone who was eminent in the domain of abstract science as well as in industrial science. These relations, that such a happy character could only strengthen more and more intimately, had become forever unshakeable. I find the most moving testimonials to this in abundance in the voluminous dossier collected by the devotion of his wife during the hours of the funeral, in that sad month of September 1882. The press of all countries, the letters, the telegrams, testify to the universal respect for the scholar, no less than to the highest esteem and affection for the man.

Free spirit, if ever there was one, noble soul, he has always lived outside of and very far from all official attachments, all conventions, all negotiations, wanting only to do good. His death was in accordance with all his life as an honest man. He belongs to the very small number of those who remain the Honor of a nation.

Yes, he had an assuredly clear look, and a far-reaching perspective, this son of his work, always free from all ties, who was able to see clearly the error becoming truth and the truth becoming error, from this or from that side of a stream, a stone, a pond, and who, meticulous observer that he was, so attentive and rigorously precise a calculator of both the infinitesimal and the great spaces, did not fear, when the time came, to proclaim human liberty and his own faith by this transcendent affirmation, which sums him up:

NEITHER IN THE SCIENCES, NOR IN THE ARTS,
NOR IN MORALS, ARE THERE FORMULAS.

Obsidional Photography

I was again reading and rereading the exquisite pages where Legouvé[1]—a man, a poet—still very moved and filled with gratitude, recalled the unforgettable benefits of postal photography during the cruel days of the siege.

And it was painful for me to think that we don't even know to whom we owe this precious assistance. We don't even know the name of the one who at last came to soothe and sustain so many "*souls who were hungry and thirsty after so many long days*" ... Wouldn't someone have dared to usurp such glory?

For it is like this: when it's not a lacuna, it's an inexactitude. And seeing every morning the most inconsequential street incident, which happened yesterday before our very eyes, reported by our newspapers in so many different and sometimes even contradictory ways, what can we believe of what is transmitted to us from past centuries—and what is History worth?

While I am still on the subject, at least I can establish the origin of a very interesting fact in the legends surrounding the siege of Paris and bear witness to the one whose too rare selflessness encouraged us to remain ignorant of a name which we should "*admire, love, thank, and bless*" ...

*

So, when it was a question of supplying in Paris the mail intercepted by the German blockade, the small aerostatic material that, from the beginning and with our private initiative, we had installed in Place Saint-Pierre in Montmartre, was all ready. Is it necessary to repeat that, by implementing the service, we primarily had hoped to resume the precious tradition of military aerostats, lost since Coutelle and Conté,[2] but our persistent entreaties were never able to wring this decision out of the government, also known as the National Defense—even though every day during those four rough months we were claimed as emergency forces at three critical points of the main defense of Paris, which were being struck down by an invisible enemy ...

For lack of other longed-for destinies, I at least had the patriotic satisfaction of organizing and inaugurating the Airmail Service by launching, over the German lines on the 25th of September, the first of our postal balloons, the *Neptune*, mounted by Duruof.[3]

Soon other departures of balloons followed almost daily,[4] carrying in full bags and tied bundles precious news to distant families. This was for our besieged both a relief and an encouragement.

This mode of thwarting the siege was not, on the other hand, to the liking of the Prussians, whom it seemed to disappoint beyond their expectations. Their threat to consider a spy and to shoot on the spot every balloonist who fell into their hands, this threat, decreed beyond all sense of measure and all human rights, would have been sufficient testimony to this, even if their bad mood had not left an indelible and vengeful trace on the pamphlet in which Wagner gave us the last kick. It is in fact precisely there—without mentioning the generosity of every human soul before the defeated enemy—it is precisely in this *Song of the Scalp* that the gall of the great composer has ingeniously concentrated all the subtloty, all the Attic grace and svelteness, all the spirit of his race—a race already renounced by their "liberated" Heine, from the time when the victor revealed himself in front of the disarmed legions.

From a personal point of view—and since there must always be a "little piece" next to the big one—, there was some comic element to our sudden importance.

Certainly never, after passing through diverse professions in our life, never would we have imagined our latest incarnation under the aesthetic of a varnished cockaded hat and a mailman's bag on the belly. And yet, without any other title here except the unique obstinacy of our personal initiative, without nomination, without promotion or official qualification of any sort, and, above all, without salary! (this first integral condition, constitutive of every bureaucratic mentality in the city as we imagine it ...), not having even the rations of the soldier which we would have considered a delicacy, but which nobody thought of offering us and for which we did not think of asking, we became de facto, in these first hours, in the flesh, the real "*director*" of the Central Post Office, responsible for the departures section—that is, of the whole Post Office, since there were no arrivals.

It was to us, in fact, to us alone—and to whom else, at this hour?—to whom were addressed, in every instance, directly or through elaborate presentations, the *registered* letters of our highest officials, politicians, magistrates, major financiers, the Rothschilds as well as the Pereires, and above all—what strange reversals and coincidences in this world—our railroad directors, for the moment *suspended* and on forced strike, all begging us to confide their missives to the mailbag of the balloonist, designated by us for the day's delivery. I have kept a good part of this correspondence, strange enough to want to reread it today. What more can I say: at the head of these eminent supplicants, more urgent and eager than all the others put together, was the Postmaster himself, the titular, the official, the real, since it was He, the man in charge of the fees—who would run to ask me to insert his family letters into the personal satchel of my crew member ...

But these memories must find their place somewhere else.

*

To send news from the inside was already something; the question now was how to receive news from the outside.

A number of projects emerged: messengers on foot, resolute but risky; hermetically sealed metal balls dropped between two currents of the Seine to be collected by our stretched nets, etc.

None of these means presented itself with the character of certainty, method, and continuity indispensable to a public service.

We had already received the suggestion of a good pigeon-fancier from Batignolles who, introduced by our old friend Lucien Puteaux, would put his pigeon house at our disposal. Every balloon would carry a basket of these Parisian pigeons, who would swiftly bring back to the pigeon house the awaited messages.

The principle was established, as much as it could be. But how much weight can the flight of a pigeon support, and what was this puny resource in the face of so many needs? I was certainly not the only one turning and tossing in my head this question of such great importance ...

*

We would generally sleep on Place Saint-Pierre, where we were finally able to obtain from the office of Mayor Clemenceau a few bundles of straw under two sheltered tents. It immediately became the meeting place of all the stray dogs of Montmartre that we had not yet eaten and to which we offered a fraternal welcome. When feet are cold, good natural foot muffs cannot but be accepted with respect and gratitude.

I generally strove to get away during my work break, at dinnertime (? ...), to run home and get news of my family. But it was never without the apprehension of coming across, at the entrance of my house, a full litany of inventors who were resolutely waiting for me there, bringing with the most laudable willingness in the world the wildest but always infallible projects, of dirigible balloons and other "flying fish."

In one of these escapes—and precisely that evening I was more than ever absorbed in my preoccupation with the most serious problem—, a man introduces himself, a most distinguished-looking man, who, without beating about the bush, tackles the question by asking me directly if I have found something that will make his visit useless. Upon my negative answer, my visitor explains himself.

An engineer, employed, if I remember correctly, by a large sugar factory, and since he had never been engaged with photography, it was with all possible reserve, and with his good will as excuse in case he is wrong, that he brings to me, on the off chance that I might be interested, the theory that had crossed his mind.

Since the question, he says, is how to transport by pigeon the most considerable quantity of messages, I presume that in every major postal center—Lyon, Bordeaux, Tours, Orléans, etc., or even, if necessary, concentrating all services in a single point—everyone brings to the office of outgoing mail his correspondence, written on one side only, with the recipient's address at the top, written as clearly as possible.

A special photographic studio is installed there under an experienced practitioner.

All the letters brought are placed alongside each other on a mobile surface, in a number to be determined, a hundred, two hundred, five hundred, a thousand. A two-way mirror keeps them in place by pressing them down.

This set, once completed, is then adjusted vertically to be immediately photographed at the minimal reduction possible—to the hundredth, the thousandth, what do I know?

Only that, instead of photographing on glass or paper, as with ordinary shots, the operation must be performed simply on collodion, whose substance seems to me the prototypical entity, thanks to its lack of grain, transparency, flexibility, and, above all, thinness.

This micrographic image of an almost zero weight is mounted on one of the quills or claws of the bird, under the usual conditions of dispatch by bird.

Once at its destination, the counter-operation: enlargement of the micrographic image of every missive, amplified to its current format, in order to be cut immediately, folded into an envelope, and addressed to each recipient.

Suddenly, the light dawned: the solution was there, in the benefit that comes from these pellicules—and I remained struck, admiring the ingenious simplicity of the process no less than the modest reserve of the man who was explaining it to me.

— I congratulate you for rendering such service to your country, sir, and I thank you for the honor of your communication. Your idea seems to be very rational and readily implemented: to the implementation now, as soon as possible! You have only one thing to do: without losing a second, run to the Ministry of Postal Services and ...

— This, sir, no! I am satisfied that you think that my idea is applicable: do with it what you wish, but in no way do I intend to put myself forward or to boast about a chance discovery. I am independent by position and choice; I do not need anything, I ask for nothing, and I want nothing.

I took his hand and squeezed it ...

— Even better, then! But if you will admit that it cannot be right for me to go, without you, to present a project that is yours, why would you refuse to just accompany me tomorrow morning to see the person who can make it happen? We will, you and I, be seen early tomorrow morning at the Post Office by the head of the Cabinet, Mr. Mercadier, who is substituting for Steenackers, who has left, and there, you will explain your system much better than me.

He finally gave in and we established that the next day at dawn he would come to pick me up, since he had a carriage and I did not.

*

He was there at the crack of dawn.

Before reaching rue de Grenelle, I point out to him that it might be good to first get in touch with a photographer familiar with the work of micrography for confirmation: we had to go quickly! I had thought of a practitioner called Dagron, whom I did not at all know personally but whose special notoriety recommended him to us.

We soon arrived at the rue Neuve-des-Petits-Champs, at the corner of rue Louis-le-Grand, and we rang the bell to wake up the household. The project explained and approved, I ask my colleague if he is disposed to take, at a moment's notice, any route that will lead him to Tours in one of our balloons. He accepts immediately. As he was leaving us:

— You have understood, I told him, that I do not bring you a "deal": you will ask for a reimbursement of your expenses—and that's all! Our poor France is not rich at this time.

He seems to agree wholeheartedly.

At the Ministry, an immediate and excellent welcome; Mercadier is elated, and even more so when I tell him that we have already come to an agreement with a specialist, who is ready to leave at the first call. Everything is, as we say, "mulled over." Mercadier wishes me to follow the operation with a micrograph and insists that this is, as he tells me, "in my own interest." I manage to make him understand that I would be useless there, since I have never dealt with what had been the principal study of my colleague—and that, since I was not doing business, especially at that time, I had other things to do elsewhere ...

(Can you believe that, awaiting my military observation balloons from Trochu, I remained obstinately attached to my first idea? ...)

*

So, Dagron left on a balloon. As soon as he arrived in Tours, he installed there, with all his competence, and put into place in the best way, the precious service that had been entrusted to him. Our Paris, strangled by its anxiety over its absent ones, finally breathed! ...

I haven't seen again, since that one time, the excellent micrographer Dagron, whom I had so rightly chosen and appointed. But I do not doubt that his civic sense would have reminded him that at a time like this you do not make "deals."

And I am no less convinced that, in the report published by him on his mission in Tours, he paid the deserved tribute to the very modest inventor whose sole initiative had shown him the way.

*

And that initial inventor?

May I myself be forgiven! ... In the center of the furnace in which we lived then, personally absorbed in the pursuit of these military observations that I was still trying very hard and beyond all means to obtain from those who were refusing them to me, torn day and night between the duties and preoccupations with my postal balloons, with my life away from home, feverish, tormented, panting, finally falling exhausted—I even misplaced the business card of that gallant man who vanished from view as soon as his service was rendered ...

May these lines reach him, and may one of his close relatives wish to finally reveal to national recognition the name of the glorious and anonymous man who, as our dear Legouvé so eloquently says, "*refueled with bread the souls of those whose hearts were hungry and thirsty after so many long days!! ...*"

The Primitives of Photography

The *daguerreotypists*: Chevalier and Lerebours. — Richebourg. — Vaillat. — Legros. — Thierry de Lyon. — Claudet de Londres. —The caricaturist Randon. — The *photographers*: Bayard. — Poitevin. — Paul Perier. — Bertsch et Camille d'Arnaud. — Gustave Le Gray. — Moitessier. — Taupenot. — Fortier. — Olympe and Onésyme Aguado. — Édouard and Benjamin Delessert. — Edmond Becquerel. — Bareswill and Company — Van Monckhoven. — Léon Vidal. — Adam Salomon. — Numa Blanc. — Hampsteingl, of Munich. — Mayer and Pierson. — The painter Ballue. — The brothers Bisson and their operator Marmand. — Marville. — Adrien Tournachon. — Alophe (Menut). — Berne-Bellecourt. — Louis de Lucy, Lafon de Carsac, Mathieu Deroche. — Carjat. — Bertall. — *Photosculpture*: — the printer Lemercier. — Disdéri. — Warnod. — Lazerge and Dallemagne. — Braun, of Dornach. — Lewitzski, Lejeune, Joliot. — Luckhard, of Vienna. — Alessandri, Daziaro, Abdullah. — Séverin, of The Hague. — The brothers Sarony. Ghemar, of Brussels. — Silvy. — Walery. — Nadar.

We are in an era of exasperated curiosity that explores everything, men and things; in the absence of the great history that we no longer know how to produce, we pick up the crumbs of the small histories with such zeal that our attention becomes wide-eyed in front of a stamp-collector.

More justifiably, then, the extraordinary researchers of the past perhaps will have an interest in receiving certain indications, even in summary form, of our primordial practitioners, workers in the first hour, whom we have known or only encountered. This task falls on the one who, because of the modestly enviable benefit of accumulated years, finds himself today the dean of working photographers, and he carries it out while there is still just enough time.

*

So the Daguerreotype would cede its place to Photography, but not without having had its moment of glory in the hands of the engineers Chevalier and Lerebours and also of the optician Richebourg, who never failed to add to his signature the Masonic Δ: it seems that this was a title in those days. Other practitioners took no less advantage of the silver plate: the excellent Vaillat and the ineffable Legros, that flamboyant man, wearing secondhand gowns, would galvanize the last beautiful days of the Palais-Royal, whose local region never managed to fall out of love with them and would finally be extinguished with them. In the meantime, the Rhône and the Saône were still in raptures before the plates of the good Thierry from Lyon, and even the caricaturist Randon had touched on them in passing. But the daguerreotype was finished with the advent of photography and, as they said then, "This would kill That."

In the movement of this first period of photography and in the avant-garde of the small, still sacred contemporary battalion of Niépce and Daguerre, I detect Bayard through the haze of the horizon, brother of the prolific collaborator of Scribe and uncle of the late artist Émile Bayard.[1] Beside this noble father of photography—who came to photography, as the legend has it, from fruit farming—there appears to me, no less correct in every respect but more enduring, another amateur and precious researcher, Paul Perier, Casimir's nephew. Then, small and lean, showing that he is somewhat fragile, Bertsch, who first applied photography to the micrograph and megalograph, as precise and meticulous when observing planets as when observing microscopic insects, in his tiny attic in the rue Saint-Georges: we did what we could! And even though this garret was narrow, and cluttered with stacked bowls and bottles, there was still room at Bertsch's elbow for his inseparable and equally ingenious collaborator, Camille d'Arnaud, who, irresistibly drawn to the new phenomena, had for them abandoned the management of Houssaye's journal, *The Artist*—the good Arnaud, who wished to be and was my master.

We will find more than one other in this elite, abandoning everything in order to march toward this new star: Tripier, the son of Codes, whom we called "the Baron," the alter ego of Leclanché, nicknamed "Farouchot," the translator of Cellini; Gustave Le Gray, leaving painting behind in order to propagate the method on paper that our benefactor, Poitevin, had just invented; and other zealots still, Moitessier, Taupenot, Fortier (a dyer), and the two brothers Olympe and Onésyme Aguado, no less passionate and indefatigable than Édouard and Benjamin Delessert and my dear classmate Edmond Becquerel, who had not yet sat at his father's chair at the Institute which he would pass on to his son; all dedicated researchers, clearing our path and offering us new processes every day, improvements that Bareswill and Davanne modestly and carefully registered, noting the part in the game that the others played.

The push was universal. Not to mention the wonder that could be satisfied only by producing images that had never gone through a School of Design, the most summary apprenticeship was more than sufficient to produce mediocre results: it was up to the more refined to look further. With regard to expenses, the initial outlay was insignificant and the earnings were so much greater since they remained optional, entirely dependent on the manufacturer's discretion. There were no expenses except those of the laboratory, Adam Salomon not yet having reported from Munich the costly retouching of Hampsteingl, as necessary as it was harmful, as detestable as it was indispensable.[2]

So everyone unqualified or wishing to be qualified called themselves a photographer: the professional student who had neglected to appear on time on payday, the tenor singing in a café who lost his voice, the concierge seized with artistic nostalgia—they all called themselves: *artistic!*—Failed painters, unsuccessful sculptors, rushed in, and we even noticed a glowing cook: Hasn't it been said that cuisine is itself a form of chemistry?

But it's not just a matter of this little world, which happens to be a very select flock—*egregium pecus*[3]—with which we are concerned. Let us evoke these few glories of a day in which each passing hour ends by thickening the dust of oblivion …

*

Gustave Le Gray[4] was a painter, a student at the then celebrated workshop in which "Father Picot" continued, the last to do so, the traditions of the School of David, Gérard, and Girodet. "Father Picot" was numbered among the constellations in the gray sky of Mr. Paul Delaroche and of the other "father," Father Ingres—"this Chinese," as Préault said, "wandering in the streets of Athens." It was the time of what we called—Oh, great gods!—"*The Historical Landscape*," and while we booed Géricault and reared up against Delacroix, Father Picot held as appropriately as others his place in that fuliginous galaxy in which stars were called Alaux, Steuben, Vernet, and other glories of the Versailles Museum. The Impressionists have swept all this away, and who could blame them, even if they were sometimes wrong? If there remains someone decorated by this St. Helena,[5] still resistant in front of the open-air school, if there is still a last one whom our good Manet, first so scorned, still frightens, let him console himself by contemplating again *Oath of the Horatii*, *The Rape of the Sabine Women*, and *Atala on the Tomb of Chactas*.

But the School would remain obstinate, standing firm, and Le Gray was ill at ease there. The food was insufficient for him and the robust stomach of this little man with the restless spirit wanted something other than the perennial boiled turnip in marshmallows. This all-too-young father of a family, struggling tirelessly between the obsessive need to produce, the embarrassment of material life, and intimate sorrows, this agitated man was annoyed to be wasting away so unproductively in the same spot in his workshop on the covered walkway of the Barrière de Clichy.

He had always been attracted to chemistry, and painting had not kept him from the laboratory where, next to his workshop, he pursued the secret of making definitive, immutable colors, the fabrication of which, according to him, was too often left to the greedy indifference of merchants. It is on this stage of the road to Damascus that he was suddenly illuminated by the first ray lit by Poitevin. If there was one among us that the wonderful discovery of Niépce had seized, it was him. Photography whistled for him. Le Gray came along, and almost immediately he published the first, I believe, *Method of Procedures on Paper and Glass*. The die was cast: what remained in him of the painter was taste exercised by study, a habit, a science of form, the practice of the effects and dispositions of light, not to mention our old knowledge of chemical agents and reactions, all to the profit of the photographer

And it was high time that Art came to intervene a little bit, because this recently born photography was already threatening to go wrong.

Paris and our provinces knew only one house: Mayer and Pierson; from everywhere, people were gathering there. But the two men who had created this house, who were indeed smart, found themselves, by origin and because of their earlier trades, total strangers to any aesthetic.

Their portraits factory installed in the center of the boulevard confined itself very profitably to a single style and even to a nearly unique format, singularly practical for the small spaces of our bourgeois households. Without somehow dealing with the disposition of lines from the point of view most favorable to the model, nor with the expression on his face any more than with how the light was illuminating all this, they would install the client in an invariable place and would obtain from him a single shot, dull and gray, any old how. The proof, just washed, would pass immediately onto the table of the painter working in the shop, who had taken notes, summary notes like those of a passport: regular complexion, blue or brown eyes, chestnut or black hair, and the thing—paid for in advance—would be delivered entirely framed and tied up, in an envelope. We scarcely had the right to open the package before being shown the door. Claims were not permitted, except, as an exceptional favor, when a client had received as her portrait that of a client unknown to her; otherwise, it would be impossible to return. In this revival bursting with everyday cares, we did not have the time to dwell on such trifles.

The specialist painter who earned a good living by making these miniature portraits was a good little man, very gentle beneath his mischievous and even formidable bearing. His name was Ballue and he was not without some worth. To relax from his workdays and to take revenge on the gray watercolors of Mayer and Pierson, he rediscovered himself as a mad colorist, and inundated the Jouffroy passageway (which had just been opened) with ferocious small pastels, with rabid "Díaz-like" paintings of women in pure carmine in fantastic landscapes with pistachio terrains, under blue trees and nacarat skies.[6]

But with all this, if photography strictly speaking was not involved, she ran the risk of having everything to lose. The painters who had welcomed her with distrust would remember their first apprehension and did not have any difficulty treating her with supreme disdain.

It was necessary that without any further delay photography be freed from the Infidels, from the inflicted travesties, and that she show herself exactly as she should let herself be seen, without veils, as truth.

Le Gray had appeared just at this moment and simultaneously with him the Bisson brothers, Adrien Tournachon, and a fourth of whom we will need to say a bit more—and soon the sculptor Adam Salomon, Numa Blanc, the painters Alophe, Berne-Bellecourt, Louis de Lucy; the caricaturists Bertall, Carjat, etc.

*

In this first hour of enthusiasm Le Gray had easily found a rich sponsor, the Count of Briges, who, in order to house him, rented, at a high price, a determined cubic volume of ambient air over our Parisian zone.

I'm not kidding. This intangible volume, suddenly converted into the most palpable and resonant material, was encountered on a roof over a large building in a chicken coop, inadequate only in relation to all the houses of wealthy Paris, sumptuously constructed in carved stone.

*

But this house, which is not a house and which is so much better than a house, this fateful hut deserves its little page of history.

It was inexorably devoted to photography.

Such that, as in tragedy, and in relation to this Greek temple of the Odéon, it would suffice to turn it inside out, like the skin of a rabbit, in order to obtain unrestricted access, inside, to the classic décor dear to the three unities.

The architecture in question, which did not exhaust the imagination of the architect, stands in a very interesting perimeter at the corner of boulevard des Capucines and rue Saint-Augustin—just the place that would be occupied in 1848 by the Ministry of Foreign Affairs, in front of which, on the evening of February 23, the shot was fired that brought down the throne of Louis-Philippe, despite its apparent solidity. It is true that what remains linked to appearance is not worth much.

At that time—and this will appear surprising today—at least sixty years ago, the Madeleine quarter was not frequented very much, and some shops were as modest as window-shoppers were rare. The vast area was subsequently bought, as they say, for a piece of bread, and no less economically the purchaser, an old baroness who understood business well, decided to establish there in the most summary way a series of shops, identically positioned on a single level divided into cube-like compartments.

It was exactly then that the aforementioned expansion of Paris toward the west happened. In these things, as in all others, both the rise and the fall accelerate according to the accumulated speed. From good, the area was becoming excellent. There was an extension measuring some tens of meters and, on the first floor above the mezzanine, a terrace due north that photography could not resist eyeing up first.

Almost simultaneously two major studios started up there, including that of Le Gray, leaving between them room for the photosculpture that arrived with Mr. de Marnhyac, while on the Bisson brothers' ground floor, sponsored by Dollfus de Mulhouse, a sumptuous boutique opened in which, before an enchanted audience, the beautiful prints from the library of the Louvre and views of Switzerland were showcased in dimensions previously unknown. Only Marville (still a painter!) was able to match them in the very remarkable collections he left to the City archives.

It was the first period of the wet process: one who has passed through the acrimonious moments of the collodion process still remains amazed in front of the impeccable execution of these immense shots. The Bisson brothers had succeeded in discovering and giving form in the laboratory to a simple municipal guard who, with his arms stretched, covered completely—without any alteration, without any streaks, without any blowholes, without a speck of dust—a glass plate one meter by eighty centimeters. This good man, who had his hour of relative fame, perhaps deserves to have his name retained in this legend: he was called Marmand.

The Bissons' boutique was all the rage. It was not only the extraordinary luxury and good taste of the window display nor the novelty and perfection of the products which made passersby stop: they would find no less interest in contemplating through the glass of the store windows the illustrious visitors who followed each other on the velvet auricula of the great circular divan, passing from hand to hand the proofs of the day. In truth, it was like a rendezvous with the intellectual elite of Paris: Gautier, Cormenin Louis, Saint-Victor, Janin, Gozlan, Méry, Préault, Delacroix, Chassériau, Nanteuil, Baudelaire, Penguilly, the Leleux—everyone! I saw there, at least twice, another amateur fairly eminent in his field, Mr. Rothschild—Baron James, as he was called—, quite affable, incidentally, and already managing not to look young anymore. And all these splendid people of high status, coming out of the Bissons', finished the rounds there by stopping by the studio of the portraitist Le Gray.

*

But all that glitters is not gold. This public so brilliant, of the highest order, usually pays with a different currency than the current one and, except for Rothschild, is not exactly the one who puts the coal under the pot.

Now, while upstairs the excellent Le Gray, generous like all poor people, exhausted his products and his packing materials to shower each of his visitors with free prints, downstairs, the good brothers Bisson did the same—it's so good to give!—so well that the two sponsors, both in the store and on the roof, manifested a certain agitation and the beginning of an anxious fatigue from always shelling out and never receiving. The installation costs had already exceeded the normal estimates, since the building where we met justified more than any other its name of building. In fact, in the boutiques, as on the only floor, nothing had been done except the plasterwork of the four walls behind the windows, which had been chosen most economically. Tenants were free to clothe these naked walls with rich papers, that is, draperies, to replace the Saint-Gobain glass, to buy themselves fireplaces, if they were sensitive to the cold, and even, they say, to dig cellars if they needed basements. A more than strict management, a true school for landlords, confined itself to renting out the place to them: nothing else. It was a "principle"—and every mind firm in its intentions knows what a principle is. Moreover, no one had the right to complain: no one had really been forced. Each tenant had been in the position to understand if the hand he was going to shake was too tightfisted—each had the right to opt, perfectly freely, having sniffed the place, to enter or to flee.

As for Le Gray, he had been even less favored than our Bisson brothers. He did not even have to wipe the plasterwork since for him there wasn't any; he had to provide it himself. On this virgin roof, he was renting only the space to put it—a square of atmosphere, of open sky, where he had to build his home—, with good and valuable materials, please, well and duly weighted by the architect of the property, a ruthless eye!

These initial impedimenta, and even these formidable installation costs—which will pursue us and hound us until the end, implacable as any original sin—, it was perhaps still possible to escape them, but under the firm condition of possessing to a high degree this je ne sais quoi, this mundane and divine gift, called the commercial spirit. It is precisely that spirit that was lacking in the good Le Gray and in the equally excellent brothers Bisson—as in some others still, whom I know ... And in this case the lack was so pronounced that, while Le Gray was wearing himself out cramming his prints, free of charge, into the crook of his visitors' arms (just as later the munificent Le Pic loaded the biceps of anyone leaving with his canvases), the two Bissons, totally intoxicated by the sudden exhilaration of the new situation, immediately had thought of building on Saint-Germain, on the bank of the Seine, two charming twin cottages, from which they would arrive in the morning and to which they would return in the evening, in a carriage with two horses. Thus I saw them one morning, by the Bois de Boulogne: the elder Bisson very appropriately adorned the carriage with ladies; the younger Bisson, on a sorrel horse, covered the door.

It was beautiful, I admired it; but I got frightened. Photography on horseback! One must know how to behave well …

*

And meanwhile, from everywhere, every day other photographers emerged, full of ardor and no less apt to prove through their work that they, too, knew how to see and render nature.

Then, a decisive blow: the appearance of Disdéri who, with his business card, offered twelve portraits for some twenty francs, when, until then, one could pay fifty or a hundred francs for a single portrait.

It was a rout. One had to submit, that is, to go with the flow, or resign. Le Gray's primary interest in art had pushed him toward photography; he could not resign himself to changing his studio into a factory: he gave up.

His very well-equipped establishment was unlikely to remain empty even for a moment in this house dedicated to the arts. Le Gray's name was immediately replaced by that of another artist, Alophe (Menut), known for his innumerable romance titles in lithography.

It would be unjust here to forget in this memento a lost lithographic work by Alophe, a lithograph that had enjoyed a popular success equal to that of Vigneron's celebrated *Convoy of the Poor*: under a gray sky, a dog all alone following a third-class hearse. Under the same inspiration, Alophe had drawn, in a miserable attic—with sketches and palette against the wall, brushes scattered—a dog licking the hand of its young master, dying or dead on the bed, thin as is indicated in such cases, but combed and smoothed with the impeccable exactness of Alophe himself. Title: *The Last Friend.*

And while the Bissons, finally unseated themselves, too, abandoned the heights they would never find again, Le Gray embarked for Egypt, even more tired after his last fruitless attempt, overwhelmed with grief of every kind, on the verge of despair …

He was nevertheless still fighting. Without saying his final farewell to photography, he took up painting again and was appointed Professor of Drawing at the University of Cairo by the Egyptian government. The very curious newspaper *l'Intermédiaire* in which everything ends up was telling us just yesterday that Le Gray had been chosen to give lessons to the Princes Tewfik (later Khedive), Hussein, Ibrahim, etc., whom we have seen for a long time in Paris.

But bad luck seemed to plague Le Gray. He broke a leg in a riding accident and finally died around 1882 in a distress that was certainly undeserved.

He was an industrious and remarkably intelligent researcher, a generous soul, above all an honest man. Such men do not all have their own houses and do not know how to become rich by exploiting others or simply how to fish for annuities in a marriage contract.

*

I just mentioned Disdéri.[7] But in evoking his name, which nevertheless has raised for a quarter of a century more ruckus than that of a general and especially more than that of a benefactor of the people, I feel myself halted by doubt: I wonder if these retrospective notes on departed personalities, special here but often rather secondary, can have any interest for others, except for our professionals—and even for them?

On the other hand, I think of so many other personages, major or great, word-merchants, sellers of air, dealers of healing potions and meager nourishments, political wheelers and dealers, and other traders, about whom we hear continuously, day after day: very illustrious, but whose entire life's work will not amount to that of a board planer or a laboratory assistant—but let's skip all of this: my reader will be able to do the same, as he pleases.

*

Disdéri has left, even outside the world of photography, the memory of the most considerable fortune made at a time that could be called the golden age of photography. In a single year, he made what would be sufficient, even at the present time, to secure the future of a family, and this prosperity seemed never to run out or slow down.

Finally, this man, who had acquired many millions, passed away some years ago in profound distress near Nice where, sick, helpless, he had finally ended up, living only thanks to the help of some colleagues who knew his situation.[8] Having become almost completely blind and deaf, he died on the threshold of the asylum where Public Assistance was going to receive him …

*

A certain intuitive genius had pushed Disdéri, among the first, toward the door that photography had just opened to all those without a profession.

Of an evidently more than modest origin, deprived of elementary instruction and even of the most basic education, ignorant of even the ordinary forms whose use convention indicates and imposes, forms even more important and unequivocal for him because of his appearance, since all in all he was scarcely attractive, even repulsive—but of a real practical intelligence, well served by special natural gifts, active and quick by nature, imperturbable in a faith that does not doubt anything and especially not himself, he might have just as well, with the same aplomb, the same certainty, the same specific verbosity, and most likely the same success, manufactured and even sold an entirely different kind of "*article*" and played to completely different audiences.

One of the coincidences of Parisian life led him to meet with the designer Chandelier, the inseparable close friend of Gavarni. Just at that moment, Chandelier happened to inherit from an uncle of his, an old country priest, but a friend of savings, the sum of eight hundred thousand francs. Even though he was renowned for his defiance, Chandelier allowed himself to be taken in by the irresistible sales pitch. They teamed up and Disdéri began to work straightaway. But his first attempt led to a bad end; a judge even had to get involved ... Let's move on.

But Disdéri was not one of those whom a disgrace can bring down. We do not know or we have forgotten if he had tried his luck again, somewhere else and with someone else, until the day he was installed at the boulevard des Italiens, where his fortune awaited him.

The really extraordinary success of Disdéri was actually legitimately due to his ingenious idea of the carte de visite. His industrialist intuition had come up with the right idea at the right time. Disdéri had just created a real fashion that would infatuate the entire world all at once. Even more, by reversing the economic proportion established until then, that is, by giving infinitely more for infinitely less, he decisively popularized photography. Finally, we must recognize that the number of these small images produced with prodigious speed in front of the endless parade of customers did not lack either a certain taste or charm.

A singularly unexpected, exceptional (Disdéri had to say: *exclusive!!! ...*) circumstance appeared one day to give the final push to this already unprecedented trend: Napoleon III, passing with great pomp and ceremony along the boulevards at the head of the army corps leaving for Italy, stopped short in front of Disdéri's establishment in order to be photographed (this gesture, in itself, wasn't it already more like the model than his photograph?)—and behind him the whole army, the ranks massed on the spot, weapons at hand, waited for the photographer to take the shot of the Emperor ... With this coup, the enthusiasm for Disdéri became a delirium. The whole universe came to know his name and the road to his house.

It would be difficult to assess the number of millions who passed by his cash register during these years of overabundance, and it was certainly Disdéri who was least aware of it. People talked about nothing else but luxury then, about Disdéri's country houses, his stables (ah! The poor little horse of my poor Bisson brothers! ...). Passersby, stupefied, stopped at the sound of his horse carriages, à la russe, which he drove himself, since he naturally had a taste for spectacle, for excessive pomp—and he must not even for a moment have doubted that this triumphant spontaneous beginning, without precedent and without limits, would last forever.

*

But, our parents would teach us, this is not the way to build good houses. There is no treasure that does not run out, and profusion always ends up creating a vacuum. So quick was Disdéri's ascent, and it reached such a height, that he was dazzled by vertigo. Still under the sway of his fascinations, Disdéri had for a long time disdained to follow the progress of the photography to which he had owed so much, even though every day would bring us something to learn from it.

From then on, the man was lost, like his establishment. The fall was as rapid as had been the rise. Already his clientele was disseminated across other established or new institutions, more concerned with the dignity of their work, more organized. Disdéri had to abandon his house in Paris and to sell even his name.

Courageously, but in vain, he tried to return to work a little everywhere, and this is how many of his former clients saw again with astonishment, in boutiques or even in stalls in Cauterets, Biarritz, Monaco, etc., that name so brilliant yesterday. But everywhere he failed: the talisman was broken.

Fortune is a woman, and she does not forgive someone who misses an opportunity.

*

We can say, in modern parlance, that a thing is "launched" when caricature becomes aware of it and targets it. Among all its other very essential roles, caricature today retains that of the ancient character who mocked and jeered behind the triumphal chariot. It is the supreme consecration of every glory.

The time had come in which photography could not escape it. There was not even a corner of an illustrated newspaper where the impertinent pencil did not occupy itself with our heroes. Needless to say, all these games could only be and only were benevolent. Nothing *against*, everything *for*.

Thus, in the abundance of his everyday work, without peace or truce, the greatest of our athletes, inordinate genius, brilliant as Benvenuto even in the most frivolous little detail,[9] Daumier sculpted daily on the lithographic stones of *Charivari* various scenes from our studios.

*

Nothing more was needed for the apotheosis of Photography—nothing but a first general Exhibition for which, just born yesterday, it was entirely ripe.

This first Photography Exhibition took place in 1855 at the Palace of Industry. It was wildly successful.

Certainly the luxury of the installations, through which habit has rendered us indifferent today, had no part in this success, which was justified even more by the novelty of the surprising invention. The public would throng with an almost breathless curiosity in front of the innumerable portraits of well-known people whom they did not yet know, of beauties of theater whom they had been able to see only from afar, and who were revealed to them in these images where thought itself seemed to live.

While the initiates, the specialists, were examining the indelible proofs of Poitevin, Moitessier, Taupenot, Charles Nègre, Baudrand, and La Blanchère, and the lithographic transpositions of Lemercier—anticipating through the breakthrough of these first paths the limitless immensity of the domain henceforth secured for photography—the multitude of the other bystanders crammed, like bees at a bee hole, at the entrance of a mysterious small dark cubbyhole, where you could go in only one at a time, and where, fleeing daylight for an artificial, almost hieratic half-light, the famous parrot of our dear Becquerel already prophesied that photography would one day victoriously take on color reproduction. People would throng in front of the display windows of the exhibitors, and in truth they had never seen anything like them—I wouldn't even hesitate to affirm that, since then, we have not seen anything superior to the great expressive faces of the mime Deburau junior by Adrien Tournachon (another one who escaped from painting)—, to a marvelous 30 x 40 live portrait of Frédérick Lemaître, by Carjat, wide like a Van Dyck, deep like a Holbein, to many others still, among which we should not fail to acknowledge Warnod's impeccable positives on glass. What is more: Warnod was an eminent aesthete, a writer of real worth; Carjat, first an industrial designer, became a portrait designer: the eye that has been through such an education knows how to see. We have not forgotten the qualities of observation and technique of the numerous caricatures magnificently drawn by the pencil of the good Carjat—who was moreover an orator and, what is more, occasionally a poet.

*

It is important to note here that the perfection of these exposed proofs was and has remained all the more interesting since it owed nothing to the touching up of the negatives. The proofs themselves were not corrected by the brush or the pencil—at most they were retouched in one or two spots where a speck of dust had managed to perforate the layer of nitrate.

Yet the touching up of negatives, excellent and detestable at one and the same time, like Language in Aesop's fable, but certainly indispensable in numerous cases, had just been envisaged by a German from Munich, named Hampsteingl, who had hung against the light, at the end of one of the galleries of the exhibition, a retouched negative with proofs before and after the retouching.

This negative opened a new era in photography, and I assure you that the curious were not slow to come and look. The approval was general, especially from the most interested, the "professionals." We immediately realized how useful the blessed discovery of this Hampsteingl would be for us, a resource for which everyone had yearned but never known, as everyone had imagined it without naming it.

*

In addition, two steps away, the demonstration was made complete by the sculptor Adam Salomon's show, crammed with portraits of various notables from politics, finance, from the world of fashion, in which all the negatives, not to mention the proofs, had been retouched according to the new method, which, more sensible and more diligent than us thanks to his Israeli blood, Adam Salomon had taken the trouble to learn from the Bavarians.

The retouching of these negatives, constrained by a prudent reserve, worked wonders there, and if people thronged in front of other exhibitions, in front of this one they crushed, they suffocated.

No less practically, Adam Salomon had adopted a unique format of small dimensions, from which he refused to depart under any circumstances. In this restricted space, at the same time that his prudence enabled him to avoid deformations, disdaining the vain glory of triumphing over them, the smallness of heads would leave the field open for him to develop the bodies, with which criticism has the least to do, and for the arrangement of costumes and draperies, dear to all sculptors.

Moreover, the ensuing unity of the format would finally give the entire and very considerable production of the photographer Salomon the character, the respectability, of an Oeuvre.

Under the concurrence of such conditions, and with the powerful initial benevolence of the brothers Émile and Isaac Pereire, it is not surprising if, from the very first day to the last, and for many years, Adam Salomon kept fashion conquered in this way.

Fantastic and whimsical like Hoffmann's Master Coppelius, under the alluvium of his overcoats and superimposed scarves, even more exaggerated by the narrations of the legend that, among all of us, he was the best suited to stay alive, this little man, all dried up, frightening in appearance, even a little sinister with his small eyes lost in the depths of his bony cheeks, hoarse with a falsetto voice like a castrated rooster, and remarkably unbearable for his logorrheic flow of puns, was known moreover for at times mistreating quite brutally his aristocratic female clientele—who did not seem to get discouraged by this.

The fact is that what repairs and erases everything—affability, graciousness, the exquisite distinction of a superior soul and spirit—was right next to him.[10] And it is not only in the Jewish family that the man must bow before the supreme, benevolent, and incontestable superiority of women ...

*

Let us also recall here the photographic work, transient but very interesting, of two other artists, painters of merit, Lazerge and Dallemagne.

Gil Blas observes somewhere: "Every little man is decisive"; yes, certainly, and it is necessary to say "decorative" when the little man is in the Arts.

Indeed, we see almost certainly that, sculptor or painter, the smaller in size the artist, the more he tries to rise by working on a large scale. In our time, the homunculus Meissonier, obstinate in his pedicular painting, from which he was never able to depart, would be, I think, almost unique, the exception we usually invoke to confirm the rule. But if he painted on a small scale, at least during the siege he made up for it with the immense boots into which he disappeared, swallowed up, atop a horse from the largest cavalry. Short arms seem to be born for grand gestures. The entire universe, part of which is the episcopate, knows that such a valiant diehard photographer is great mainly through his works: well, from his studio, a portrait would never come out in which the owner of the hardware store in the corner would not have the majestic look of a Saxon marshal or the haughty gesture of the Grand Condé throwing his baton into the enemy ranks.[11]

Lazerge, taken by a sudden passion for photography, did not have much trouble sharing his enthusiasm with his colleague and friend Dallemagne. A special workshop was immediately installed in the quaint little Hôtel Dallemagne, behind the Invalides.

But born "decorative," due to his lack of stature, Lazerge would certainly have remained unsatisfied with the pure and simple reproductions of his contemporaries, given the banality with which they were produced elsewhere. He had gone digging in the grand epochs where, as Veuillot would tell me: "... *we were given* one architecture per reign! M ..."—and he had chosen various models of highly tasteful décors, Louis XIV, Louis XV, Louis XVI—especially Louis XIV: Lazerge would naturally get along better with Louis XIV.

In the copies of these paintings, executed on a large scale, every model which presented itself was willy-nilly stuffed into one of these backgrounds, standing in a pose of felicitous majesty, and through the foliage, the embossments, the vermiculations, he found himself heroically crowned in laurel or more modestly under an oak wreath.

At times, in order to give the final touch, Lazerge, on tiptoe, would throw onto a corner of the painting an ample velvet curtain that seemed to fly in the wind, as in the large paintings by Mignard or Van Loo.

The sincerity of our current taste, simplistic in appearance, might seem to suffer from this excess of pomp; we must nevertheless recognize the real artistic sentiment and the beautiful allure of these compositions. A few months ago, we experienced true enjoyment when we saw the curious collection of Lazerge and Dallemagne, where we came across, with great emotion, in a pomp that was not at all displeasing to us, many beloved faces among these celebrities of the preceding generation …

*

If something was missing from Van Monckhoven's first encounter with Léon Vidal, our other master, it was certainly not the comic element.

Van Monckhoven, always lying in wait for anything that concerned his beloved photography, was beside himself after seeing Vidal's early works. He had only one idea, one obsession: to see, to get to know Vidal!

Many kilometers separated him from this desired Vidal. But decisiveness was one of Monckhoven's cardinal virtues. He writes to Vidal that he cannot wait any longer, that he is about to devour the kilometers. Departing from Gand the night before, he would arrive the next morning at the train station in Marseille, where Vidal should wait for him.

I have talked on another occasion about the extreme youth, the almost childlike look of this Monckhoven, already famous in the photographic and even scientific world. As for Vidal, another child prodigy, I do not really know whether our two antediluvians together reached any more than fifty years between them.

In the confused disorder of the station when the train arrived, Vidal looked out for the famous doyen whom he was waiting to welcome in full reverence, while Monck was peeking in every corner in search of the other veteran, this Vidal to whom the acquired notoriety attributed by right gray, if not white, hair.

Since neither the one nor the other found the person they were looking for, tired of waiting, they decided, each on his own, to leave, with all the bad mood of the disappointed, when Vidal noticed Monckhoven's name on the suitcase carried by the last exiting passenger, a blond adolescent:

— Is this Mr. Van Monckhoven's suitcase? ... Vidal asks with hesitation and caution.

Receiving an affirming nod, he presents himself. At that point, Monck continues, no less coldly:

— Sir, your father was not able to come?

— But my father was not expected to come. I am Léon Vidal!

For a moment, they measure each other up, their eyes wide open—then they burst into laughter:

— Only the devil knows why, says Monck, but imagine that I was filled with the idea—I was convinced, I would have bet that you were an old gentleman, an old merchant retired from his business and devoting himself to photography to keep himself busy during his free time! But let us go quickly to see what you do—and to have lunch!

And until the so lamented death of our dear Monckhoven, the closest friendship reigned between these two noble men, an unwavering friendship based on mutual esteem and respect. It is to Vidal that Monckhoven reserved the honor of the dedication of the seventh (and last!) edition of his grand *General Treatise on Photography*, as if he had wanted to designate, with this glorifying preference, the most worthy, not to replace him, but to succeed him.

*

Léon Vidal actually seems to be the most suitable person to inherit such a noble legacy and to represent, after the One who is no longer here, the science and interests of photography.

If, in our chronology, hardly rigorous after all, Léon Vidal cannot be properly counted among the "primitives of photography," he at least will be included in the top ranks of our forerunners. Since 1851 in fact, and far away from the Parisian center, he worked on processes with inert powders when Poitevin's great discovery had just been reported. Devoting himself from then on to the study of photography with all the fervor of a consecrated neophyte, he would soon found the Society of Marseille, he would invent the *photometer* for negatives, publish first *Calculation of Exposure Time*, and later, one after the other, a series of books and brochures which together would constitute a practitioner's essential library: *Practical Treatise on Carbon Photography*, *Practical Treatise on Phototypy*, *The Art of Photography Considered from the Industrial Point of View*, *Photography Applied to the Industrial Arts of Reproduction*, *The Practical Manual of Reproduction*, *Photoglypty*, *The Tourist's Practical Manual*, *Photography for Beginners*, *Practical Manual of Orthochromatism*, *Photography at the 1899 Exhibition*, etc. At the same time in Marseille, and later at the Sorbonne and everywhere in Paris, he held courses and delivered widely attended lectures, he took over the technical management of the *Monitor of Photography*, manufacturing, after his *Autopolygraph*, the *En-Cas Vidal*, the first manual device invented after the appearance of bromide gelatin, and founded the *Photographic Union*, inspired by the model of the associations created by our most beneficent, admirable Taylor.

In addition to all this, evidence of an incessant laboriousness guided by a remarkably perspicacious intelligence and by the purest love for science, who among us could forget the amazing results that Léon Vidal obtained with his *Photochromy*, a process that covered colored backgrounds with a photoglyptic proof. Never had such an ingeniously simple idea produced such striking effects. The wonder was universal in front of these reproductions of ceramics, textiles, paintings, jewelry, copied, when necessary, with stereoscopic relief in prestigious trompe-l'oeil, "... rendering," according to Paul de Saint-Victor, "as no brush could have done, the matt glow of the pearl, the dark blue of the sapphire, the intense red of the ruby, the turbid colors of the opal: assimilating, as in the baking sun, the milky whites, heavenly blues, rutilant flames, bright or diaphanous colors of porcelain; the glossy enamel, the clear-cut décor, the metallic reflexes, the endless nuances of the majolica, etc."

It has been for many years now that, with a perfect disinterest equal to his popular success, Mr. Léon Vidal has run his public course on photography at the School of Decorative Arts. Besides his great and unquestionable scientific value, he has something that is extremely rare: character.

Mr. Léon Vidal has never been decorated ...

*

This incomplete list of the "primitives of photography"—today almost an obituary—will soon come to an end.

When I have recalled Braun from Dornach, with his splendid balloon views of Alsace and Switzerland, and the Russian Lewitzki, a technician of the first order, a man distinguished from every point of view, who appeared in Paris only to found there the Lejeune House (later Joliot), when I have mentioned our first enamel photographers, Louis de Lucy, apprentice at Paul Delaroche's studio, author of a method which is still in use today, Lafon de Camarsac and the Mathieu Deroches, the latter always standing and attending to his work, I will no longer know whom else to mention except for our veterans abroad: the French Claudet, daguerreotypist in England, the master of masters Luckhard from Vienna, Alessandri in Saint Petersburg, Daziaro and Abdullah in Constantinople, Séverin at The Hague, the Sarony brothers in Brighton and New York, Ghemar from Brussels and our compatriot Silvy in London.

There is no photographer of a certain age who has not held in his hands some photographs by Luckhard, Alessandri, Daziaro—the classics—, and did not admire the perfect results, due to the precision of the execution—no less than the originality of the poses and the audacity of the effects produced by the Saronys, unparalleled painters and draftsmen.

*

Like the Saronys and many others among us, Ghemar was a painter, and particularly a portraitist. A precise and fast pencil, like the calligrapher's pen, he was an esteemed colorist even in that noble land of Flemish art, and also a passionate and polyglot traveler; the *high life* of the entire world flowed into his palette.

He could not resist the attraction: one fine day the painter renounced his clientele of kings and queens to modestly declare himself a photographer and to found in Brussels, under the precious counsel of our dear Monckhoven and with his younger brother, endowed with all the complementary administrative skills, an establishment with which nobody even dreamt of competing.

His benevolent availability, his generosity, his radiating good humor, a little too loud for these placid parts of the country, had long won everybody's sympathy. Through his fecundity of imagination, exceptional and quotidian at one and the same time, of burlesque and, most often, comical improvisations, always picturesque and decorative, with which he never failed to entertain the crowds, he managed to create for himself a real popularity which remained faithful to him until the very end. In his sometimes immense, spontaneous gaieties, this little Brabantian who was exemplarily sober, but who looked instead as if he had been made ruddy by all the wines of Burgundy, combined the mocking vivacity of an urchin of La Villette with the ardor of a son of the Cannebière.[12] In this land of the kermesse,[13] there was not a mayor who, a little worried about his cavalcade, would not seek a consultation with Ghemar, from which he would return quickly and triumphantly to his constituents. In amiable countries where the creators of spectacles decide Constitutions, the good Ghemar was rightly appointed and acclaimed director of Public Joy.

His last phantasy was his crowning glory.

Ghemar had announced with great fanfare that he was

about to paint, all by himself, an entire universal exhibition, and let's be clear: an exhibition of the major works of contemporary art, in which all the masters of all modern schools would be represented by their principal works, not in a format meanly reduced, but in the same proportions as the originals.

Despite the precision of the terms, everyone expected a formidable trick, in the style of the "*humbugs*" familiar to Master Ghemar.

But very soon, one could see in the center of Brussels, like ants on an anthill, architects, carpenters, construction workers, gathering within the wide perimeter chosen by Ghemar for the improvised site of his exhibition.—On the scheduled day and at the scheduled hour, the doors opened up for the besieging crowd ...

There were three large halls: 1. Square Hall, 2. *Hall O*, and 3. *Hall T*—this last hall was marked as unsuitable for families, something like the "hell" of a library. A note in the catalog, signed by the *editor*, warned with the utmost seriousness: "If the mother wishes to take her daughter to *Hall T*, it is at her own peril." I am quoting; but we must pass through these pranks and other innumerable non sequiturs, experiencing their *terroir*, in order to reach the very serious side of this gigantic farce.

For the first time, the brush replaced the pencil in the animated satire of these paintings. Ghemar had kept his promise and, of all the contemporary painters I know, he was the only one who could keep such an audacious promise: the works of our masters were reproduced with their defects and, even more incredibly, with their merits, with such perfection that the illusion was produced and that, from a certain distance, you could have believed that you were indeed in front of the original.[14]

There actually were—and in their best rendering—the colorful kaleidoscope of Isabey, the explosions of Díaz, the furious mixture of colors of Decamps, the attractive veilings of Corot, the sun of Marilhat that cooks the stones, the moon of Daubigny which refuses to eat them, the dark and striking coarseness of Millet's proletarian exhortation, the exquisite preciousness of Fromentin, the pre-Raphaelite nobility and linearity of Puvis, the cruel and charming precision of Millais and Mulready, the deep fogs, mists, and rains pierced by the gaslights of de Nittis, the pale yellow palette of Clays, and the good humor of Jongkind, and the chlorosis of Hamon, and the elegant modernity of Stevens and Wilhems. Couture, the man of "process," yields the presidential baton to Offenbach in the grand supper of our French Decadence, Troyon moos, Palizzi bleats, Jacque clucks and grunts next to the stove in which Rousseau *revives* his foliage between Courbet's trowel and the bitumen bath where Robert Fleury drowns, while Doré, a Genius at times, gets lost ...

They all meet there, beginning with Géricault, whose "Trumpet" becomes—naturally—"*Jericho's* trumpet," up to Caillebotte with his violet Place de l'Europe "*as seen leaving Manet's studio*."

To make sure that nothing is missing from the madness of his tour de force and "de farce," Ghemar has modeled symbolic frames, analogous to the subjects of his canvases. He does not fail to nail nails, real and enormous nails, under the soles of Horace Vernet's zouaves; elsewhere he amuses himself by fixing a real oar, a wooden oar, to the edge of a boat, and in *The Horse Fair* by Rosa Bonheur he makes a stallion's mounted head stick out, with hay between his teeth.

Do we need to say that the proceeds of this "Ghemar Museum"—of which, more than twenty years later, people were still talking from Brussels to Ixelles—had already been straightaway predestined to charity?

As for the expenses, apart from his personal work, Ghemar was happy to get away with two hundred thousand-franc notes on the table. He had entertained others and he had himself, as they say, taken his share.

Vicissitudes, human failures! Eventually this amazing collection of the "Ghemar Museum"—which caused quite a stir in its time, and which it would have been of the greatest interest to preserve as a whole—was dispersed a few years ago, abroad, quietly, incognito, in an auction without an echo, in a virtually empty salesroom.

Ghemar was no longer there: suddenly, after that apotheotic explosion of the most ingenious incoherence, that burst of laughter was forever frozen in an unfathomable sadness—and the "*poor Yorick!*" so good, so cheerful, so lively, so open and welcoming to all brilliant ideas, was wasted, somber, his temples tightened by the screw of the atrocious black idea ...

*

Entirely different from these memories of Ghemar—always present—the figure of Silvy, whose works and at least as much his personality perturbed London's "Nobility" and "Gentry" for several years, appears in our recollection.

There are some people who seem to constantly attract public attention, which persists in following them, independently of what they do or do not do. Silvy was essentially one of these.

He was a member of the diplomatic corps and had already secured a brilliant career when, following an inspiration which was very unexpected, but very understandable at the time, he quit everything to establish a photography studio in London. A photographer and a business that, as we shall see, were unparalleled.

From an excellent French family, Silvy revealed obvious Italian origins in his mask of the young Michelangelo, in the utterly academic rigor of his statuary and the classical purity of form that makes the graciousness, the eurhythmics of the gesture. In the mornings at Hyde Park, which a man of such elegance could not fail to observe with liturgical punctuality, in the continuous comings and goings of horsemen and Amazons whose "snapshots" have been provided by the indefatigable pencil of Guys, Brummel and d'Orsay would have recognized at first glance in the fugitive from the Parthenon, riding a thoroughbred which provoked the envy of more than one lord, the perfect *sportsman*, the impeccable, the last follower of a dying dilettantism. With a very personal originality, whose impeccable taste in clothing would be horrified if it were to be confused with eccentricity, this "*sensational*" man moved the crowds without ever appearing to notice it.

What lines of long and deep looks, petrified by the ravager's passing! How many long-dreaming *misses* and entranced mothers! On certain occasions, wasn't Silvy led to complain to the press because of some unfounded, legendary rumors which had distressed him, and which eventually could have cast some discredit on him?

It is not surprising that the afternoons, following these mornings, did not furnish enough hours to satisfy the aristocratic clientele that all came running to Silvy, and never tired of coming, and even less of coming again, requesting weeks and months in advance the inspection tour that would permit the lucky ones to find themselves for a few minutes before the charming Master in strictly formal attire, with white cravat—and, on the entrance of each client, he used to throw his pair of white gloves, somewhat negligently, into an already full basket, only to pick up another, brand-new pair ...

Moreover—and why would this glory count less than all our other glories?—everyone was sure to find his or her name the following "Christmas" printed in the golden book of the customers of the year which, with the same regularity as that of the Gotha almanac,[15] Silvy addressed with the most generous courtesy to all his followers! What an attraction, especially for the little world of the "Gentry" in this "Vanity Fair"!

The wait, to which everyone in Silvy's salons was tenaciously resigned, could be long, but not boring. The establishment—if I dare to use this commercial term—perfectly arranged and furnished, occupied a wide perimeter, in the very center, near Hyde Park, within that area of London where land is measured in banknotes. At their discretion, the customers, men and women, could be distracted by watching the parade of equipages, the aristocratic male and female equestrians, who, one after the other, passed endlessly before the camera lens, always ready to shoot, or by admiring the decorative riches generously laid out in the galleries with irreproachably good taste and with a profusion of limitless sumptuosity. In the details, layout, and selection of the furnishings in this exhibition, singularly limited as it was, the astonished Englishman could get a glimpse of the Latin genius. I should say, however, that it was in Flanders that this gorgeous tapestry of the time of Charles the Bold had blossomed, woven with gold and silver, which I could not stop admiring …

Silvy, though, had made at a certain point a concession to British quiddity: THE QUEEN'S ROOM!—furnished, exceptionally, in the purest English style.

Every visitor, in his or her combined trajectory, inevitably had to pass this room with its two open doors, but defended from all public access by a high wrought-iron gate, a beautiful Florentine work of the sixteenth century. Across the room, on the central fireplace, an equestrian statuette in pure silver for which Silvy had paid thirty thousand francs in cash, a considerable amount of money then, to the favorite sculptor of that epoch, Marochetti: THE QUEEN!!! … To this apparition, all good Englishmen, all purebred English ladies, bowed in respectful silence, only daring to satisfy with a furtive glance the terrible, I do not dare say the beastly need for objective curiosity, one of their national characteristics.

No one was allowed to enter the QUEEN'S ROOM—except for THE QUEEN—and no one ever did:

— … Not even the Queen, Silvy told me, laughing, in fact I'm still waiting for her … But it doesn't matter: *it looks good!* …

One can see that the perfect gentleman, the artist and the man of the world, had a certain greedy intuition about "business" and its procedures. This has probably already been understood.

And he was thus able to accumulate enormous sums. I assume that he also knew how to spend them generously, given that his aristocratic manners were not a vain affectation. He was born with open hands, and his delicate spirit and friendly face were also open.

In one of those moments of fatigue that we all know very well, Silvy was taken with the idea of giving away his English house. He came to Paris to talk with me about it, and at his invitation I went to visit him in London.

But had he already abandoned the idea he had just conceived, through one of the oddities of his restless spirit that seemed to give him an additional graciousness? Whatever the case, he did not speak one word about it during my brief stay in London; I maintained the same silence as he did, and we parted very amicably, without having breathed a word on the matter. This characteristic was very typical of Silvy: perhaps it was of me, too, a little bit.

But it seemed to me that his tactfulness made him feel uncomfortable about the unnecessary trouble he had caused me. At the moment of saying goodbye, he absolutely wanted to offer me a casket containing the only known daguerreotype of Balzac, which he had received from Gavarni. Obviously, no gift could have given me more pleasure.

What became of that house of such great renown then, whose name is now no longer even mentioned? What became of that radiant and triumphant Silvy? In whose hands did all this splendor end up? Where is the rich tapestry of Charles the Bold? Where is Marochetti's "*Queen*"? Where is Marochetti himself? ... The death that mows us down at least concedes more time to things ...

*

In this nomenclature, very approximately chronological, of our "primitives" and of our lost ones, that I try to evoke, without any documents, with only my memories, I have surely forgotten more than one deserving person. I ask for forgiveness in memory of those who have passed away, and from the survivors.

One of the last to come and the last to leave, Walery, has left recent and above all too many good memories for his name to escape us.

Walery—by name Count Ostroróg[16]—was born in Russian Poland, one of the three partitions that exiles call "the Poland of the Kingdom."

Like several other remarkable personalities of the successive emigrations of these courageous people who will never consider themselves defeated, Count Ostroróg was initially educated in the Corps of Pages, in Saint Petersburg.

We will find him again, during the Crimean War, captain of the Polish lancers serving in the sultan's army, and already producing daguerreotypes while he was in the Warna garrison.

At the same time, a talented musician and a researcher into everything, he receives a gold medal for an invention related to the percussive elements in organs.

But it is above all photography that fascinates and attracts him: around 1864, he opens his first atelier in Marseille, on the boulevard du Musée.

Soon after he secures his success, he sells his business in order to create another one in Paris, on the rue de Londres.

Walery's indefatigable activity, his always lively ingenuity and his general intelligence for everything artistic, his practical spirit, his personal distinction, his gentle manners, above all his constant presence on the ground of everyday struggle—a real presence, a precious quality in every industry leader—all these elements ensured the great success of his creative activity.

But when, after barely four years, the establishment was growing and prospering, Walery no longer found any stimulus for his still relentless work. He had to go even further, elsewhere, in order to create something else. He wishes to sell, to sell at any price; he sells his studio at half its value, returns to Marseille, hurries to Nice, and, without wasting too much time, after two unsuccessful attempts, finally arrives in London where, after passing the inevitable test of the initial slowness and hesitation of all the Anglo-Saxon public, he reaches the heights of Silvy and Sarony, when brutally, all of the sudden, an aneurysm strikes, with a complete and definitive victory, this indefatigable fighter.

Walery had the most and the best of the native charm of the Polish people, a charm that was immediately attractive despite a hint of banality, and it is especially regrettable when the man of intelligence and action is at the same time a man with a heart. He never harmed anyone and he only did good.

*

Let's conclude.

In this chronology, I need to say a little about the one who is writing these lines and who remains, he believes, the doyen of French professional photographers, as long as his eighty years do not prevent him from being the first in his studios every morning.

Thus, a fortuitous accident transformed me from the journalist that I was when I was young into a sketch artist. I mean sketch artist *without knowing it*, as people used to say in the age that was so dear to Veuillot,[17] the age of the grand style that we will leave there wrestling with good French. I had never taken a single drawing class: the thousands of sketches published under my *N* confirm this confession all too clearly. I just took advantage of a certain attraction, perhaps a certain, more than limited, native aptitude toward aesthetics, and an inexhaustible fecundity of themes and legends in these times of militant politics.

Lack of technical training and talent was no problem at that time thanks to the indulgence of an era so different from today's, in which the whole world is talented; but it was still necessary to respond to the inexplicable and encouraging interest expressed by publishers and the public. Now, demand greatly exceeded our production. Art having nothing to do with this, and all the glory being awarded elsewhere, the camaraderie of the pencil eventually created a sort of social cause, a union, as one would say nowadays, whose brand was that prolific *N* of which I found myself to be the managing editor, and which emerged in the overwhelming majority of illustrated magazines of the time. Real artists, Nanteuil, Gavarni, Couture, Voillemot, Bayard, Foulquier, Darjou, Béguin, Prevost and others still, occasionally dropping into our studio, did not disdain to leave their sketches in pencil, and some of them even stayed longer.

When we had the idea of the *Panthéon Nadar*, which was meant to contain in its four serial pages a thousand portraits—writers, playwrights, painters and sculptors, musicians— and which withered soon after the publication of the first issue, the importance of the endeavor made us think.

There were many reasons to do so.

To be honest, the first significant difficulty was resolved. Nothing was actually easier than making all our models come to that home to which each of them knew the way; by a singular grace, I had friendly relations—intimate or benevolent—with all the illustrious people of the time.

What remained was the execution of the work, the *hic*: to transfigure those hundreds of different faces into *comicalities*, while preserving for each the imponderable physical resemblance of the features, the personal bearing—and the character, that is, the moral and intellectual resemblance.

To underline, for example, in the so sympathetic face of Dumas the father, the most popular of all at the time, the lineaments of the exotic race and to force the simian analogy of a profile that seemed to provide immediate evidence that Darwin was right, especially by accentuating the dominant note of the person's *character*, that is to say, the extreme, infinite goodness: to flatten the nose, too thin in the model, enlarge his delicately etched nostrils, make his eyelids' benevolent smile more oblique, exaggerate, in the manner of Mesopotamia, that fleshy lip always jutting forward to kiss, amplify the power of that proconsul nape, without neglecting to make more frizzy, more flaky, what Jules Janin used to call "*his mop*" and, not to forget the last detail, to further minimize the pinna of his microscopic ears.

But if it is possible to encounter those with whom, as we say, everything runs smoothly, nature already having arranged everything to our benefit and having worked on our behalf to such an extent that one no longer knows whether the model is the portrait or the portrait is the model—as, for example, in the case of Champfleury—, it is less easy to maintain a glimmer of resemblance by altering the oriental beauty and Olympic tranquility of Théo!

Is there not, all the same, something there that resembles an impiety, an irreverence worthy of a Scarron or an Offenbach,[18] of which one has no need to take any account?

And there are many others still for whom the impertinence, whatever it be, will never be enough. How can the clumsy, boorish pencil ever translate, in the most vulgar language, the delicateness, the exquisite finesse of Branville?[19]

And, finally, how to infer the individuality, so personal, and the strangeness, so ingenuously and perfectly sincere, of that complicated man Baudelaire, born, indeed, in the land of the Hippogriff and the Chimera?[20]

Photography, which was just being born, offered, at least to my lack of ability, the virtue of not exhausting the good will of my models for too long, even as it opened paths of which I had hitherto been unaware …

An old friend—although then we were young—, Camille d'Arnaud, who had quit the board of d' Houssaye's magazine, *The Artist*, to share the research conducted by the practitioner scholar Bertsch, offered to train me in the trade.

At this time in which jobs, today so simplified, were so difficult and complicated, with such a loving patience, never exasperated, this excellent man committed himself to educating the reluctant animal that I was, inattentive, with my mind elsewhere and my wandering look, always unbearably impatient to see the end before the beginning!

How many mornings, for hours and hours, with implacable and methodical good will, did he insist on making me hold the glass plate between my thumb and index finger—up to thirty times in a row—following the ritual, before allowing me, in one go, to throw the colloidal layer upon it, as people used to do in those heroic times!

But only in this way are good fingers created, and it is, above all, good fingers that build good houses; and it is this result that, doing my best, I have been trying to achieve, maintaining a touching memory of my beloved master who passed away before me …

The New President of the French Society of Photography

A house around the middle of the rue de l'Ancienne-Comédie, on the even-numbered side of the street, almost in front of the old Café Procope familiar to the Encyclopedists of the eighteenth century, where Diderot, elbows on the table, occasionally managed to make Rameau's nephew speak.

We had to climb to the roof to reach the huge attic bathed in sunlight, turned into a laboratory by the young and already celebrated professor; but having arrived, we did not regret the climb, because it was impossible to get bored there. It smelled of work.

Laboratory, yes, and also menagerie: the place was memorable. It is one of those memories so engraved at first glance that it will always appear when it is recalled, trembling, like a proof still wet with some nitric acid, and freshly printed.

In a beautiful irreproachable order, without which every laborer who does not have time to waste feels uncomfortable, among apparatuses and scientific instruments of all sorts, traditional or just devised yesterday—new tools for a new science—, cages, aquariums, and beings to populate them. pigeons, buzzards, fish, saurians, ophidians, batrachians. The pigeons were cooing; the buzzards were not breathing a word, perhaps for fear of being reprimanded for their quality or reputation as buzzards. A frog, having escaped from its jar, was jumping in front of us like crazy, with exceptional recklessness, in order to avoid caressing the ground. Full of gravity, a tortoise would proceed without vain haste but with tenacious perseverance from one corner to another across various impediments, indefatigable in its task, as if possessed by a fixed idea in search of some problem and with the security that comes with a clear conscience, assisted by a foolproof shell. Under the mesh of the trellis, the garter snakes with their yellow necks would stretch their spinal muscles unnervingly, enjoying the warm temperature, and in the neighboring compartment the small alert eye of a gray lizard would keep watch, just in case, for the passage of some imprudent insect, visible to it alone. Everywhere, in every corner, Life.

Around the study tables, in front of the bodies of complicated machines, a swarm of young men, some barely adolescent, asking for explanations, correcting the functioning of some gears, or researching some formula in the texts. Their clear faces are illuminated by their inquisitive and noble passion. From side rooms with revolving doors against the walls, like hive cells, other young people come out, come, and go. And all of these glances, all of these steps, converge in the center, in order to be called by the wonderful silent conductor of this orchestra, the beloved MASTER, still almost as young as them.

But—unforgettable appearance—first of all, above all, a woman who has reckoned with age but is nimble and keeps an eye on everything, discreet, almost meager in her solemnity, her clothes having remained faithful to the simplicity of her native soil, comes toward me, as if wreathed with an aureole in the particular halo that follows her, and hurrying along silently without disrupting or disturbing anything, with this youth who reveres her: I bow before this ingenuous and real creator, unassuming and venerated, of everything produced there—the Master's Mother.

And even yesterday, after these last thirty years on her shoulders, which put her well into her nineties, I had yesterday the sweet emotion of finding her just the same, always watching over her son who had grown so much, alert as always, as if she lived forever by the benefit of some deserved grace, reading her newspaper without glasses, indifferent in front of the clock which counted so many long hours for her and is still in our debt ...

*

How did I go there the first time, I, particularly uninitiated, not to say undeserving, in this sanctuary of applied, exact science, I, the impractical one, the rebel against every form of cogitation, deduction, of any coherence, born recalcitrant to all calculations, even to primitive rhabdologies, irresistibly fleeing everything that is not immediately payment in cash?—That is why I have to repeat one more time what I had to say again and again so many times.

It is 1863. I had dared to ask the aerostation if I could take photographs of the planisphere. After a few somewhat rough descents, some clashes and scrapes, where, with even the slightest wind, we happened to break trees and walls, I had to conclude that it was definitely crazy to claim to direct, against the wind, what we were unable to even stop with the wind and that, as a consequence, what we persist in calling the navigation of balloons was a pure chimera. On the other hand, considering that, like the animal, man has the right to go up there, it didn't take me long to conclude that, like homeopaths vis-à-vis allopathy, we needed to reverse the proposition, that is, following the example of the bird, of the insect, to be "heavier than air," more dense, if you like, in order to impose ourselves on the air, to command it. (And to think that for some people, this still needs to be repeated, even today! …)

All illuminated, transported by the discovery that seemed to me essential, I had with a certain ruckus sounded the bell to call all those who know more than me toward this path, whose endpoint my personal incompetence would prevent me from achieving alone …

My manifesto raised a general *outcry* in the then very populous tribe of the "flying fish" breeders. The clamor was deafening; especially great was the indignation against the ignorant, impertinent one, who was sticking his nose where it did not belong. Decidedly, Banville was right:[1] I was born to always be ready to meddle in what did not concern me. For that reason, naturally, I suffered many insults. In addition, not knowing how to commit to anything casually or how to stop once having started, given that the bottom of my purse had suddenly disappeared, including even the money that was not there, we can assume ... No! we can never assume such cruel troubles and such long sorrows ...

Today, when there is in the world, for those who look and see, no other *credo* than aviation, when the humble little clan of the first apostles, our trio of Anabaptists, has become legion, and when all researchers are hence concentrating on the unique problem of the "heavier," there is no reason for anyone—except perhaps for me—to recall this little personal corner of its earliest history.

At the height of the battle, at the nastiest moment of the ordeals that I have just described, quite an unexpected turn of events happened to me: the honor of a spontaneous visit by the academician Babinet, whom I was seeing for the first time. He was coming to tell me:

— You are right!

I needed something more than an approval, but the encouragement did me some good.

Another, just as precious, did not make me wait: the one I had not yet met and of whom I today have the glory of being a friend, Professor Marey, came unexpectedly to my house. He was giving a course at the Collège de France on comparative animal movements, and he had not, he told me, devoted a slot in his syllabus to human flight.

— But you have caused such an uproar in that area that it was impossible for me not to look into it, and here I am with you. *What can you teach me?*

— I—teach Him! ... Ah! if he, he above all, wanted it, if he could turn away from his absorbing work, how sure would I be to have finally, before my last hour, the ineffable joy of seeing man plowing the skies, in full possession of this last domain—which belongs to him!

How could I ever forget this arrival of Marey—so precious, so sweet amid the bitterness of that time!—which led me to my first visit to the rue de l'Ancienne-Comédie?

*

Certainly, in this great scientific century, Marey had to be born at the extraordinary moment in which the phonograph would transform, from the imaginary to the real, Rabelais's fantastic chapter—picking and laying out synoptically and synacoustically on paper, without thawing them out, all the words caught in flight and fixed in the air by congelation.

From the beginning of his medical studies, he had estimated his abilities and judged it more worthy of him and more useful to others to devote all his work not to clinical medicine properly speaking, but to research into physiological phenomena that would illuminate the path and apply its laws to therapy.

He felt imperatively called to these meticulous investigations by a thirst for knowledge, a methodical mind, the need for absolute certitude, an acuteness of perception, generous mental resources, an extreme ingenuity doubly served by a taste for mechanics, and by the very special gift of dexterity. Reserved, always defiant, even in the face of evidence, resolutely active, relentless in verifying what is certain through what is indisputable—the proof of the proof—, Marey was destined to be the future director of the École *a posteriori*, the ark of the science of father Chevreul.[2] Like the stubborn centenarian, when he has seen, he will want to see again. And besides, he will not agree to accept with his eye alone and without all due reservation what his hand will have confirmed and his ear guaranteed: legitimately on guard against our illusions of sight, touch, hearing, all of which often produce unreliable results, he will want to trust decisively only the automatic, unmistakable sincerity of the instrument from now on charged by him to see, to touch, to hear for him, even as it at the same time is commissioned by him to mark impeccably, *ne varietur*, what will be seen, touched, heard.

And since for this so jealous, so easily offended lover of the incontestable, the use of a single instrument can always leave an opening for doubt or suspicion, he understands that—where his word, that is, his honor is at stake—other instruments besides the first will control the first one, instruments collated in their concomitance, monitoring and denouncing each other, functioning as police and counter-police for each other.

*

And here we are in front of the inexhaustible, imaginative, interminable, surprising litany of all the machines of investigation, apparatuses of observation reproducing life outside of life, recording mechanisms, schematic equipment of the micrographic instantaneity in the animal organism, tactile, optical, acoustic: only the olfactory will be allowed to sulk in its corner. Anything that looks, touches, listens, counts, weighs and measures has been requisitioned, set up and framed like the equipment of the besieger—dynamography, chronography, densigraphy, hypography, calorigraphy—all the graphies. There are only probes, springs, cogwheels, tubes, coils, pedals, release mechanisms, connecting rods, gears, cylinders, *id est* headache of all sorts: Pandora's box is wide open to migraines; but Marey does not care. The instruments that are not there, he creates: those which are there, he perfects, always advancing one by one, deaf to the fanfare of his discoveries, always unfulfilled in his quest for the better over the worse through sphygmoscopes, sphygmometers, sphymographs, sphymophones: what else? Then our hyperproductive man imagines gathering all these services into one, and he creates, by way of a general warrant officer, his polygraph, which includes and enhances the ensemble: the transmitting sphymograph capable of exploring the pulse of the heart and arteries, which will demonstrate what Bouillaud called "*the missteps of the heart*"[3]—the pneumograph that can collect the curves of respiratory movements—, the chronograph able to classify the durations and intervals of registered events.

Is it over?

Never!!! On his polygraph, he superimposes another, a new one—a pocket one, this time—, charged to verify the controls of the first. And he continues to push ahead, always searching, always finding, less breathless himself from its overzealous proliferation than we from its enumeration. But when will he stop? When he has thought up his ultimate trick, the one that will finally keep him quiet? We are not there yet.

*

We have seen that having begun at the beginning, this man has oriented the direction of his earliest research toward the phenomena of circulation. We would not be able to follow him, through the particulars of the body, into his inquisitions and requisitions of the heart, the arterial and veinal systems, the liver, the nerves, locomotion, the arteries, etc., investigations sustained all the way to the capillaries and even to the smallest animals, through all the idiopathies, from hyperemia to anemia, from febrility to algidity, spying even on the cadaver and obtaining the explanation of its final caloric loss.

We do not doubt that this scrupulous investigator of the positive, this very fine hunter and bloodhound of the absolute, will beat the bushes, scrutinize the last furrow, to track down the secret of things. We will confine ourselves, in the brevity necessary here, to a summary indication of the principle, which is like the point of departure of his general method: *a lever set into motion by vital beats inscribes its oscillations on the turning cylinder of a hymographion.* Thus, to take the pulse, the rubber phial replaces the doctor's finger pressing on the radial, and the resulting sphygmogram, ratifying the indications sent by every thrust of the blood waves, comes, in one more line, to add its testimony to the endless collection of documentary evidence.

*

I had examined with lively interest, during my first visit to the rue de l'Ancienne-Comédie, these grand synoptic pages, barely framed tableaux, which could be opened and turned with the finger in a folio colligated on a pivotal binding mounted at the height of the eye, on a pedestal with three legs, so practical, so ingeniously easy. I did not find them again at the charming Villa Maria of Posilipo, where—always present at his work like an incessant fire in a blast furnace—the Master will spend his winters, at times descending from his laboratory in order to contemplate dreamily, but still studiously, the slow advance of sea urchins climbing a rock through the transparent and cerulean depths of the Neapolitan gulf. But nobody is in any doubt that the accumulation of these fundamental archives, true coins of our modern science, should be preciously guarded in a collection worthy of them, continuing to be enriched every day.

They are of an absorbing charm, these sheets where, in white lineaments on the funerary blank of the tableaux, the infinite variations of the hymn of life, that is, the lament for our misery, are delineated. Men and women, children, adults, old people, healthy and sick, all have put forward, in their own way, a signed testimony under an oath that can never be broken. There are only waves, curves, steps, trepidations, leaps, jolts, sudden ascents and precipitous or gradual falls, twists similar to the jagged peaks of some volcanic chain. Amid these symptomatic diversities of the stigmata of our existence, rhythms of all human suffering, every disease, every poison has its own personal gamut. The choppy spasms of lead poisoning are not the thrusts of typhoid fever, the effect of belladonna is marked differently than that of curare. The pulse of the child vibrates, soars, frolics: in that of the old man, the lifeline, significantly diminished, settles, crushes, as if, responding to the call, the dying man wished to hug this earth, which summons him, in order to bury himself there ...

From these images, the most pathetic, the most striking, seems to me that in which, at a glance, we can read the last breath, the final temperature of a man with cholera: I have never encountered a staging, a painting, or a written page as dramatic as the unique filament of this diagram in its lugubrious simplicity.

As if it were more brilliant at the very moment of its extinction, the agonizing man's life-rocket launches itself in a final thrust, the vain effort of a desperate resistance, tracing its convulsions through the black void in frantic zigzags, until it reaches its zenith—from where, suddenly, it falls obliquely, like a star that spins and returns into the night of the icy horizon …

*

We admire the magician of arts and crafts who was able to make unthinking matter talk in this way, and to draw from it such eloquence for us.

But it's about time I noticed that an ancient, always dear attraction, maintained from some early studies, has already made me spend too long on the biologist, when it is the photographer who should occupy us here. The new President of our French Society of Photography cannot wait.

The automatic method applied by Marey to the observation of animal movements could not fail to claim photography as one of its most precious adjuvants.

Already in the inaugural pages of the collection *Paris-Photographe* we find an interesting presentation in which the Master illustrates the application of photography to the analysis of all movements. Figures complete the explanation of the text.

Here is the sequence of changes in a baton thrown with a rotating impulse; there, the consecutive images, seven in number, of a man who jumps, crosses an obstacle, and falls again; then, that of a horse with a disjointed trot; then twenty-four images presenting the phases of the lunge in French fencing, compared with twenty others of Spanish fencing, the twenty-four having been obtained in two seconds. Finally a series of small photographs of a fly apprehended as it flies, moving its wings.

In the photographic world, we have not forgotten the emotion caused by the first snapshot photographs that reached us from San Francisco. Muybridge sent twenty-four successive shots of a horse in the act of galloping. Arranged in a zoetrope, father of the cinematograph, these twenty-four shots of a periodic action managed, through rotation, to give the illusion of movement itself. Muybridge will keep this honor.

We must nevertheless acknowledge that a lot, almost everything, was still to be done, in order to progress from this empiricism to the creation of a positive science, to the snapshot photography of precision, that is, of the rigorous, absolute precision imposed for scientific observations. Marey began by doing away with the ploy of Muybridge's twenty-four lenses. Tolerable under certain conditions for large models and long distances, this system was inadmissible for small distances and small subjects.

Once the twenty-four lenses had been replaced by a single lens, Marey's *chronophotography* endeavored to establish, first in the take, the indispensable equidistances. Having abolished the condition, originally imposed, of white models standing out against black backgrounds in full sunlight, soon he managed to obtain sixty images per second, and, still involved with his microscopic studies, enlargements of 1 to 1000. It was only the beginning.

We cannot present here the series of experiments through which Marey had to pass in order to constitute this new science of documentary photography, which will remain his. The practitioner will find in his *Graphic Method*[4] and in a number of his essays the interesting history of his trials and conquests. As the first *positive* analyst of animal mechanics, he translated the movements of locomotion into real geometric diagrams. Having reached the indefinite in the division of time, until then divided into milliseconds, to the point of disdaining the unnecessary exaggerations of speed set to his liking, he caught movements that the eye could not seize.[5] While Mach follows and records the ballistics of the bullet from Vienna, Marey optically demonstrates in falling bodies the law of the uniformity of acceleration, and he even manages to get the better of latent phenomena when he captures movements in liquids and gases, etc. In the *etc.* for the past, let us add here the *etc.* for the future, expected from this indefatigable man.

*

Too often we regret not finding the character of extraordinary people to be at the same level as their Oeuvre. In the case of Marey, simplicity and cordial ease seem to be in perfect agreement with modesty, I would say with the effacement of the role chosen by predilection: a role apparently minor, but in reality major when the brilliant scorekeeper is the one who really leads the match and wins it for us.

Around him the dedication, the solicitude of the assistants, justly proud to work under such a master, respond to his benevolence, paternal and fraternal at the same time. Pushing to an extreme the loyalty of the inventor, it is with an almost cumbersome profusion of names that he likes to enumerate the sources from which he found himself drawing, and what is especially moving is the effusion with which he acknowledges his principal collaborators or students, his friends Chauveau, Lorain, Demény.

The high respect with which Professor Marey is held in the universality of the intellectual world testifies to the fact that neither our enthusiasm nor an old and dear friendship will have induced an exaggeration in the one who has not forgotten, who would never forget his first visit thirty years ago to the attic-laboratory of the rue de l'Ancienne-Comédie …

From its founding in 1854, the French Society of Photography has had as successive presidents before Professor Marey, elected unanimously, by acclamation, on the 1st of December 1893, the following:

1856 to 1867: Regnault;
1868 to 1876: Ballard;
1876 to 1880: Peligot,

and finally the great investigator who in 1870 gloriously flew over the German lines in order to observe the passage of Venus—Janssen, who lost the title only because of the limit imposed by the new regulations.

The Bee Tamer

His business card had just informed me: his name was not only "Maunier" but also, if you please, "de Flore"—"Mr. Maunier de Flore," who could only be a rustic …

And I saw coming into the room a pure, solid Provençal, a little above average height, with broad shoulders, valiantly squared, his clear look straight into yours, with a frank, good-humored face; I am not made for inspiring melancholy either: we might get along.

Immediately, cutting short the formalities, and with a singing and sonorous cadence, which always charms me and which comes from the Pays d'Oc, from the Pays d'Oil (there is always garlic),[1] he asks me right away:

— Sir, do you know bees?

— Sir, yes; but I know them—without knowing them.

— Not enough, not enough, sir! You must come to know them, and that's where I come in. We have given them the reputation of being difficult, which they do not deserve at all: they are sheep, sir, real sheep! Yes, I know: there are people who wear gloves to talk to them, gloves and masks; it's a shame! I never use a mask, sir, I never use gloves—and I live with them all the time! And I take it upon myself, I who am talking to you, I take it upon myself, listen to me clearly, Mr. Nadar, to plant you in the midst of an unleashed swarm—with you beside me, sir, with me! And both of us together, we will open, turn, return, tamper with—on our knees, if you will—a hive at work, without you having to suffer a single sting! And we will photograph this, for sure! If this whole thing suits you, I am your man: does it suit you?

*

They have always been alluring for me, these kinds of expeditions: it seems that the adventure whistles for me ... — and then once again, as my friend Banville would say, it is so much fun to get mixed up in something that does not concern you: and what's more, well, my tempter appeared to be so sure of his business, of our business ...

But this time, let's not get carried away too quickly! From here, I can already hear *THEM* scolding me (*THEY* worry about everything!) and yelling at me that adventures are not for someone my age anymore (as if I needed them to remind me of that, alas! ...). And all of a sudden, I remember the legends of so many people getting sick, really sick, indeed, from those creatures: just the other day, in the newspaper, there was the story of that porter who was attacked and did not recover ...

And without going further, how could he not come to my mind again, the man whom we call the *Monster*—you know, my neighbor in the countryside, that animal of a landowner, so unpleasant, so miserly, that, according to Karr, he pushed stinginess to the limit of prodigality—, the one who had a hive installed in his garden "*in order to utilize*" his flowers. And so the bees, these brave little avengers, would have eaten him alive rather than allow him to show his face on his own footpaths unless he was enveloped in green gauze from head to toe, like municipal barometers in the countryside. This same "Monster" whom I can still see, I can still hear, shouting at me one morning over our trellis, raising his hands veiled with gauze toward the sky, of which the Monsters claim their part, too:

— Neighbor! MY flies have eaten MY honey!!!

Good! But to me, to me, truly, have they ever brought any shadow of prejudice, those vigilantes of that Pharisee? And

God only knows if these born communists cared about our individualistic trellis, and if they minded rummaging through and multiplying in my home as if they were in theirs!

*

In the meantime, our good Mr. Maunier—and even de Flore—was waiting for my answer, with a question mark in each eye, both fixed on me—and always looking sure, but so sure, of himself, of us! ...

We should not, however, always be in a hurry to criticize others: let's see, what would you have done in my place, you yourselves who are reading this? And we wouldn't really say that this is about lions and rhinoceroses! First of all, if there was a risk in this, would this good man engage me and would he engage himself beside me in such a venture? Yes, yes, we should go! But let's be smart: we will not breathe a word, in order not to disturb the family, since these good folks are always afraid of everything—and we will sneak away ...

— And so! Mr. Nadar?

— And so! Mr. de Flore, when you wish.

— Do you have time today?

— No, but I will make the time. Right now?

— Right now.

So I slip out, and we jump into the carriage that is waiting for us. The driver, at a signal, goes away.

— Are we going far?

— Not far at all, to the Prado.

*

I must tell you—I had forgotten—that we are in Marseille, in this bubbling, stunning, dazzling and so lovable Marseille which fascinates me and which I will never forgive myself for having discovered so late ...

On the way, my companion explains to me in detail that, because of its geographical position, its clear sky, its sun, Provence is par excellence the land of flowers and that, who would believe it!, it is precisely where the smallest number of beekeepers is found.

— But this is intolerable! and you are a hundred times right. Quickly, quickly, let us make hives!

They did not wait for me: the South, in the end and in the face of such evidence, could not fail to move, as they say. It is moving, and not half-heartedly, as it had just created, at its initial and only blow: first, the Apiarian Federation of Provence, the Alps, and the Rhône Valley; then a monthly journal (here is the first issue) on the activities of the Federation; and finally the first Fair of the Apiarian Federation of the South, with competitions, competitions for everything: competitions for live bees (?), Italian, Cypriot, Carniolan; competitions for honey in honeycombs, in boxes, in cases, in pots; competitions for candles, in honeycombs, in bricks, for meads, honey liqueurs, beers, vinegars, preserves with honey, waffles, chocolates, opiates, soaps, etc.—all with honey!—then the industrial competitions, then the agricultural competitions, with prizes and awards, beginning with the best hive, fixed or mobile—and finishing (number 46) with the best remedy—"*for the healing* (aye!) *of bee stings ...*"

— Ha, ha! here we go! They sting, then? ...

— Yes, sir, the maladroit creatures—and they are right!

Good de Flore has suddenly become a bit harsh: let's not press the point ... Moreover, we have arrived.

Flags, as many as are needed—the modest trappings of a rural festival, whose simplicity at first wins us over. The place is very well chosen, and the gay sun has all the liberty to rejoice in its clear sky, on top of this vast space framed, with its front gate, by three large galleries. Greetings: we are at the first Fair of the Apiarian Federation of the South!!!

*

Everything is methodically arranged and laid out in the best order, each exhibitor on the lookout in front of his stall, trying to catch your eye, flyer in hand, the tap of eloquence poised, ready to spout on a gesture, on a glance, on nothing (take a step and you will see! …), and the visitor is stupefied to see all the things he could never have assumed to belong to the world of bees—and all the things that come to us from it.

Quickly, my guide, who seems to me to be the soul of the exhibition, does me the honor of showing me all these things, here and there shoving in my pocket a bottle, a jar, or a soap of honey, but visibly speeding up our visit … At last:

— To us, now! he says—and he passes his hand under the spout of a fountain, then dries them with a very white cloth. Mr. Nadar, three essential points: never have any odor on you, even the slightest, never, ever, a sudden movement, which might frighten or worry them; and, finally, above all, trust and do not be afraid! Are you afraid?

— I am not afraid.

He passes in front of me, and, having returned to the main courtyard, we enter a reserved enclosure, guarded by an elbow-high barrier, an indispensable obstruction for the general public.

In fact, it is there that Mr. Maunier de Flore should not be disturbed at all during his demonstrations, which take place throughout the day.

Here is his hive, a hive of his own invention, which looks nothing like the hives we know, and which, I can see immediately, leaves them all well behind.

*

Imagine a sort of parallelogram, in white wood, approximately one meter by one meter, placed on the corner of a low stand. On the ground, close by, a plate containing a colorless liquid.

Under the direct Phocean sunlight, the hive is in all-out action, at the center of the buzzing swarm of *all*[2] the cellos of these laborious workers, who, without end or break, come and go, each absorbed with her own business …

Similarly absorbed in his own business, our beekeeper, passing in front of me without looking at me anymore, as if I did not exist, has lit and inserted something that smokes in a small bellows that he moves slightly, but not without some majesty, from right to left, all around him: in this way, a masterful magician draws in the air the Kabbalistic circles of incantation …

I followed his lead and installed myself effacingly against the hive, below and above which he blows two or three more times with his little instrument: then—now is the moment!—softly, he uncovers it, by raising the partition which serves as a cover …

*

So, as delicately arranged as it was, the movement in the swarm of winged personnel became violent passion and intense pandemonium accompanied by a formidable crescendo of the music.

The whole garrison comes out, but it goes on coming out and never ceases to come out: and of the twenty thousand militia women that every hive contains, this time, when there are no longer any more, there are more.

We find ourselves enveloped, obscured, blinded, lost in the midst of these myriads of sword-bearers, titillated everywhere, faces, necks, hands, by these moving effervescences—an immersion into a universal touch—, as when, in a balloon, you enter the thickest part of a cloud and encounter against your cheeks the lifeless caress of the mist or the freezing breakage of so many thin, invisible needles of ice …

But there is nothing that refreshing about the present needles, and the fact is—if you come to think about it—that if just one of these little "natural histories," suddenly seized with vertigo, decided to get angry and to give the *tone* to the others … brrr!!!

And, thinking of what our nebulized duo, collapsing under these multiplying proliferations, could offer to the already focused lens, a memory from Commerson's old *Tintamarre* obstinately comes to me,[3] this photograph, riddled with black points to such an extent that you would barely be able to distinguish the lamentable subject: *Spanish family pockmarked by bugs ...*

*

But, lo and behold, in the midst of our living cloud, always impassable, like an Olympian god, Mr. Maunier turns toward me, brandishing his cover with one hand, as in a demonstration:

— Well, well, well: you took a chair, did you, Mr. Nadar? Pretty smart!

— In fact, yes, Mr. Maunier: my old legs do not like standing still for long ...

— And you did the right thing. Well! You see that I was right and that there is no danger with me. Now, please note all the advantages of my hive, the disposition so comfortable, so propitious to everything and for everything, of my honeycomb in layers, which in effect I flip like the pages of a book—and how easy it is for me to consult them at any given moment, front and back, laden as they are with honey, wax, brood combs, and with workers so absorbed in their work that all my maneuvers cannot make them raise their nose from what they do. And you also see with what ease I detach at will and put back in their place each of my small flaps, like you with your new mobile bindings ... Am I not telling the truth? Have I exaggerated? You are my witness!

I indeed had to recognize and proclaim that never had something announced been more accurately accomplished, a rare case today when every program has become as much a lie as a profession of faith. And I congratulated and thanked the worldly beekeeper for initiating me—especially admiring the fact that this tamer of hymenoptera was, like you and me, but a simple and modest apterous being ...

As we were parting, he seemed to want me to understand that, quite apart from the prudent reserve of his movements, inspired by his prolonged practice with the bees, he attributed their innocuousness mainly to the small plate where he put a pinch of salt in a few drops of water ... Finally, he announced to me that, since his exhibition in Marseille was drawing to a close, he was about to bring to Brussels the curious teachings with which he had so invaluably gratified me ...

*

So now—since he has left—let's betray him!

Between you and me—if I understood correctly—I hardly believe that either the water or the salt on the little plate count much in the case, for the first time I did not see even one bee visiting the said plate. And the second time—since I asked for and was granted permission to repeat the experience—, the plate itself was absent, but that did not by any means prevent the lovable bees from behaving in perfect discretion toward us—and even against us ...

I would much rather believe that it is the indescribable something which burns in the little bellows that stupefies the bees—not enough to interrupt their operations—, enough to render them indifferent to any idea of combativeness.

But then, if that is the case, why doesn't the excellent man say so?

This, for the moment, seems to concern him alone ...

1830 and Thereabouts

I was born as those times of innocence drew near when a minister would not steal more than a hundred thousand francs: in addition, they went at it in twos, as if to make their arrest easier[1] and, even more strange, their condemnation. The customs were gentle, the hearts simple. A murder would last us for two years: the conversations around it were satisfying. Two years for the Beautiful Oyster Seller of rue Montorgueil killed by her fireman, two years for the murder of the Shepherdess of Ivry, since in Ivry at that time one could still find a shepherdess; we have changed all this. There were people who shouted "Long Live the King!" when the King passed by; there were others who would not shout at all. Vines yielded grapes with which to make wine. We would wear linen pants at Easter, because all the twill merchants had not yet been transformed into merchants of radiators. The four bronze lions who guard the entrance where one does not enter the Institute would receive submissively, at each new season, their administrative light-green wash—and the good semi-salted butter from Isigny was commonly sold for fourteen cents a pound.

*

In the first volume of his *Misérables*, Hugo—hail to him!—paints a brilliant picture of the year 1817, so alive, so bustling, that the characters obstruct the background somewhat: the Spirit first blames beings before things, just as the wide-open hand lets gathered things fall. The Master hardly gives us time to understand: "a thing which smoked and clattered on the Seine with the noise of a swimming dog went and came beneath the windows of the Tuileries, from the Pont Royal to the Pont Louis XV; it was a piece of mechanism which was not good for much; a sort of plaything, the idle dream of a dream-ridden inventor, a utopia; a steamboat. The Parisians stared indifferently at this useless thing."[2]

1817 is already a long way from this 1830 where my childhood and my adolescence merge, and around which time, with a melancholic sweetness, I find myself thinking back to actors and landscape. A little before, a little after, in the indistinct pell-mell of facts and dates among which my birth remains particularly blurred, they emerge clearly, detached from the mist of the faraway ...

First, we hold it, this vapor, in strict obedience. Stephenson has cut down the protruding notch, the legs which he had first thought of adapting to his wheels in order to protect them from the desire to skate on the rails, the human spirit always proceeding from the complex to the simple. The first railroad of the Pereire brothers already rolls on Saint-Germain at the time when Mr. Thiers at the tribune affirms from the heights of his platform that "the wheels will slip without ever advancing," then finally, without budging from his position since he cannot be wrong, that these "modes of transport" could be used only for "short distances."[3]

As if from an enchanter or from a stagehand, the first whistle of the first locomotive gave the wakeup signal for everything to begin. A whole new world is moved in this universal April, it feels, it stirs, it grows uncontrollably, it stops in order to find where to set foot next: everything is again put into question. Paris, heart and brain, is on fire.

One encounters religion on every street corner, following closely behind the extinction of the pterodactyl and of the plesiosaurus which have just overturned Cuvier and now disconcert Genesis, despite the admonitions and commandments of bishops. It is the moment when we absolutely want to believe in anything whatsoever, and to sincerely not believe in anything is still believing in something. You can find everything here, even the grotesque. On rue de Bondy—exactly next to the house where our admirable Taylor will begin earning the statue that Coquelin will not raise for him—, on rue de Bondy, at the back of the courtyard, behind the removal company's carriages, the abbot Châtel, who is not yet called Mr. Loyson, not even Father Hyacinth, says the Mass in French, evidently the only way for it to be understood. The Templars themselves were just resurrected—Jacques Molay is dead! Long live Jacques Molay!—with doublets, singlets, small toques, and a dagger in its gilded copper sheath dangling nobly on the left thigh; the ladies (there are ladies) bear in their fists something like stuffed falcons. But these good Templars do not pay their rent and there are still other little things that do not go as they should; the police evict them.[4] The Temple is for rent. In Ménilmontant, the aborigines treat the Saint-Simonians a little too vivaciously, throwing stones at them, because they are too coquettish, they wear low-cut clothes like female dancers, the chest is squeezed under the ritual style of tight-fitting redingotes, wide open at the neck, the tight pants are strapped up by the stirrups of the polished boots: Enfantin displays on the white breastplate of his thorax the word "*FATHER*" in black capital letters.[5] Making passers-by turn their heads, and being such serious people who will soon achieve everything!, "misunderstood as a poet, misunderstood as a reformer,"[6] Charles Fourier looks for a place to plant the foundations of his phalanstery, and Cabet thinks of sending his stubborn initiates, "returning from Texas," to Icaria.[7] There was also on rue Saint-Louis-en-l'Isle, next to our good Jean Wallon, who was a child then, another magnificent man, God Cheneau, called *Ma-Pa* because his religion put the *Mater* before the *Pater*, the woman before the man, waiting for Girardin to rescue matriarchy.[8] In this crowd, they were not after all, in the final analysis, that crazy, those two ...

*

We lived as if in a warm mist and in the atmosphere there were sudden surges of a burning air. I need only close my eyes to see, from the little bridge of the Hôtel-Dieu, under the last gunshots of the July Revolution which are fired joyously in the air on its victory, the large gilded armchairs from the pillaging of the archbishopric floating on the Seine at the mercy of its eddying motion, head up, head down, with the brocades of the chasubles, the whites of the surplices and the feather bed of Monseigneur de Quélen[9] ... But, after all, apparently, what's new?

The ideologues of yesterday, who the day before yesterday were called "the blues," are today called the republicans, in order to be called the socialists tomorrow; they will then be called the anarchists, until something better comes along. At the gate of the Tuileries, there are no longer Swiss guards in red uniforms to prohibit any package, even a book under the arm, from entering and even from exiting. How wonderful when it was "elegant" for the petit bourgeois to make their children wear mourning for the Duke de Berry; I did. But if we have now earned the right to read in public gardens, it is still forbidden to smoke there, freedom, as we are beginning to say, not being license. We would draw attention to ourselves, if we did not call Russia the "colossus of the North" and England, naturally, "perfidious Albion." We definitely mistrust these two. Las Cases, with his *Memorial of Saint Helena*, provokes a lot of tears over the monster who killed more than three million men, and even twelve-year-old children clench their fists at the name of Hudson Lowe, the distinguished dispenser of justice.[10] On the other hand, we adore "sweet" Germany, and romanticism arrived just in time to complete the infatuation.

Waterway transport is in full swing. Everything comes by water. The apples—what apples!—and the rest are loaded in dumpcarts around "la Rapée," at the Quai du Mail, which is no longer large enough to accommodate the arrivals; Paris's mouth opens wider than that and it has been protesting for some time: the administration conveys its concern. The genius Haureau, this sweet Haureau who will die coming back from the floating docks, without ever knowing why, without blaming anyone, without even thinking of complaining, this Haureau has not yet created the architecture of the future, in iron and cement; he hasn't yet given either the blueprints of the Sydenham Crystal Palace to Paxton, or the plan of the Halles Centrales to Baltard.[11] Thus the Parisian belly is limited to the Marché des Innocents, on the ancient cemetery not yet expropriated in favor of the catacombs. There is not, in the entire city, a single florist shop: just a market once a week, on Saturdays, at the Quai de l'Horloge. The giraffe just brought to Europe for the first time is all the rage in the Jardin du Roi, which is now called the Jardin des Plantes, because one goes there to see the animals. Fashions, signs, everything is "à la Giraffe." The "Osages," six or seven Redskins of the country dear to Cooper, followed next, not without some glory, but it is not the same thing anymore. Success always for the marionettes of Mr. Séraphin, *The Broken Bridge*, pyrrhic (?) fires and arabesques, at the Valois Gallery, near the Café of "the Wild" and that of the "the Blind," two holes under the corner near the Passage Radziwill: here, a man dressed as a savage from La Courtille, with a beige shirt, and multicolored feathers on his head and belt, beats furiously on a series of differently sized boxes; there, four poor devils, blind or pseudo-blind, scrape or blow monotonous tunes. Each of these two "caves" has its enthusiastic audience. These diversions are the crème de la crème of Parisian distractions. Apropos music, a conductor just invented an instrument about which everyone is crazy: the cornet. In front of the Palais de Justice, in the new small square where we soon will go to jump into the hall of the Prado d'Hiver, and which will later become our boulevard du Palais, once a week, on Thursdays, a roughly squared scaffold stands about ten feet high, with poles planted on the platform. The maid, somewhat adventurous, one day made me pass by there and through the thick crowd I managed to glimpse three men and a woman, in shirtsleeves, as we say, tied to these poles. They are the ones condemned to "exposure" and "branding." They vociferously exchange ignoble gibes with the crowd. On the platform, two other men, free from ties, those over there, the one holding a flaming coal stove on which there are two mysterious tools, with wooden handles, the other a bucket where a large sponge floats in vinegar water. This is for the branding: TF, forced labor for a determined amount of time, TP, perpetual labor.[12] One of the two men suddenly discovers the left shoulder of one of the tied ones and, rapidly, he presses the red-hot iron on it. A cry: the flesh sizzles, the odor reaches even to us, while the man with the vinegar, bathing the open wound with his sponge, has already moved to the second patient. I put my hand over my eyes and fled, full of horror. The frightful spectacle haunts me ... It is in front of the Hôtel de Ville, at the Place de Grève, where they guillotine.

We make a lot of fun of certain "civilians" who have now begun to wear a mustache as if they were in the military (why am I even bothering with this!) and mainly we are indignant against store clerks, the "*calicos*" who appear to be the most daring. We have staged plays about them, and there are even disputes about them. But the best way still is to grow a full beard in order to get knocked out at the first street corner as a *bousingot*.[13] There is a riot every day. The students, children of the bourgeoisie, fraternize with the workers, and the workers believe that their time has come. We also rely heavily on the students of the École polytechnique. The national guards have the job of repressing: those of the suburbs beat the hardest. Puteaux, Courbevoie, Saint-Ouen—I say Saint-Ouen and its municipal counselors at the head—are particularly ferocious at beating up the rioter.

They have just closed the gambling houses of the Palais-Royal and of the Frascati, at the corner of boulevard and rue

Richelieu, and at the same time they are inaugurating the new Bourse near the new Passage de Panoramas. As this Bourse and the synagogue have not yet decreed the fashion of the hat fastened on the head, and as there are fewer parvenus than there will be soon, the old French politeness remarkably still prevails. It is about who will give way; we say hello to each other on the stairs—we would rather go up the stairs again, absentmindedly—and we teach young boys to take their tasseled cap off as they enter a store. Mother would be upset with me if I neglected to take off my cap as I hand a penny to a poor man. A penny, and even less, because a penny is already a lot. If a gold coin is almost a curiosity, payments being made in coins of a hundred pennies in bags made of strong, gray cloth, we have coins of thirty pennies, of fifteen pennies, of six liards, all flat, and of one liard. Now, a penny is four liards, four units, each one of which can represent for us perfect bliss: a choice of four gingerbread men or four glasses of coconut juice. Not to mention twenty beetles: twenty! sold in the streets by children who announce at the top of their voices their teeming merchandise in an old refrain: here are twenty beetles, twenty beetles for a liard! ... Yes, life is sweet ...

So no one blinked when old Aunt Maillet, dismissing us, puts a penny in my hand for both of us, and addresses her sacramental recommendation to us.

— Go, children, have fun, and don't spend it all, because money's expensive!

It has been said that tastes are simple. People work everywhere, and hard. The offices of lawyers and of notary publics are statutorily open at eight o'clock sharp, and if the boss is not already the first at his desk, it is because he is dead or very sick. And people go to bed early. Everything is closed, without exception, and sleeps at midnight.

On the Quai de Gesvres, downstream, upstream, and vice versa, the secondhand clothes dealers have invaded all the stalls like bedbugs of old linden wood. In front of each door, the female shopkeepers hail and harpoon the passersby; they all wear on their head a tall man's hat. It is atrocious. It is still women, hands all oily, who clean during the day and at night light the streetlamps which they take down and put up again with a rope stored away and locked in the gallows during the day, waiting for natural gas, which, for years now, has been blazing in the smallest English villages. The oil and oil lamp merchant do not want to hear about it at all, and they have immediately secured the support of two commendable writers, Mr. Charles Nodier and Mr. Amédée Pichot—the academician Tissot is not involved this time—, in order to denounce and elaborate upon in an in-octavo all the inconveniences and perversities of gas, including the danger of our total subversion, by explosion, if it were to fall into the hands of criminals. But that doesn't matter, and we have just affirmed our initiative by a first demonstration on the rue de la Paix. Every night, the whole of Paris goes there, to admire it.

Meanwhile, we would not venture, once night has fallen, into the darkness of the Champs-Élysées whose dusty zigzagged rows stop at the Barrière d'Octroi, which opens up in the circular wall, just in front of the Arc de Triomphe. Avenue Montaigne was called L'Allée des Veuves: it is occupied from one end to the other and on both sides by vegetable growers. There are also vegetable growers in three of the four big holes which isometrically break up the Place de la Concorde, all supported by the same row of stone balusters; the fourth hole, in front of the Garde-Meuble, is populated by a small menagerie, poultry, guinea pigs, turtles, parrots, monkeys, from the "monkey woman." It does not smell very good when one leans over there from above. The animals, moreover, rule throughout the city. There is no fruit or coal shop in front of which a hen does not nibble in total freedom, a rabbit does not quibble, a magpie does not hop, going from time to time to have a drink at the hydrant that the municipality has recently installed in all the streets in order to splash passersby at midday, and on which absentminded people cruelly bang their shins. Water carriers go there to fill their two buckets, united by a loop, which they take to all the floors. Two pennies per trip. It is from the parapet of this "monkey woman" that, sitting with the companions of the institution of this excellent Mr. Augeron, we soon will see the obelisk brought yesterday on the *Louqsor* by the Prince of Joinville go up.[14] There is a nervousness, because of rumors that certainly do not reassure the engineer Lebas, who has been given the job of erecting it: the English, always jealous and of what?—would have paid a traitor to saw the interior of the cables: oh! these English ... Therefore, when slowly, slowly, the cables, lifting the huge needle set in wood, managed to install it in a vertical position, what a relief, what bravos! Soon, when the four large holes have been filled, we will see there on the asphalt glaze the first velocipedes being tried, which will be called velocifers, made of wood and with no need for pedals, since it is from the ground itself that the feet get their boost; followed by the other inventor who will demonstrate roller skates, postponed until later.

*

From the Place des Magasins du Louvre, right up to the Carrousel, there is an inextricable maze of dangerous little streets, suffocated, dark and humid, Pierre Lescot style,[15] from the Doyenné, cenacle of the Romantics,[16] to the rue de l'Échelle, where the printer Auber founded the valiant dynasty of Philipon and Martinet-Hautecœur. The Place du Carrousel is not paved. Between the pools of stagnant water and the mounds of trampled mud, at times a good meter high, there are wooden stalls where one can find everything for nothing, sixteenth-century trunks and credenzas, marriage chests, first edition Dürers and Rembrandts, armor nielloed in gold, and one, extremely rare, of the four little faience candlesticks from the service of Henry II, purchased there for a few dimes, for which Strauss will pay the hotel, later, fourteen thousand francs in cash, waiting for something better, etc.: treasures pell-mell, on the ground, under the rain. With forty-penny coins, Dusommerard and Sauvageot are there to equip the Museums of Cluny and Carnavelet. All around, wine merchants with large insignia, daubed in a military style, grenadiers with majestic leather bonnets, quaint lancers with yellow breastplates and amaranth schapskas.[17] From every door of these wine shops, on the lookout like spiders from their hole, military bloodhounds exercise their profession as recruiters, buyers and sellers of men, attracting the gullible with a description of the delights of military service, so tender that it could make you cry.

People walk for the most part, even though here and there one encounters a big carriage, painted chrome-yellow, awe-inspiring, and even a two-wheeled cabriolet where one sits by the driver who never lets the conversation drop. (A young expeditionary assigned to the offices of the civil list, Alexandre Dumas, of whom people have begun talking, pulled a pretty good short story out of it.) But it is to the Place de la Concorde that one must go in order to find the cuckoos,[18] still yellow, whose drivers shout themselves hoarse to attract the Enthusiasts: "Saint-Cloud! Saint-Cloud!" Saint-Cloud, at that time, was Dieppe, it was Trouville. The carriage will always leave immediately, at once; but we will have to wait an hour for the last traveler who can complete the cargo, and who will become wedged between the other two passengers already tightly packed there, "like rabbits," next to the driver.

Broussais[19] bleeds, the whole school bleeds over, overbleeds, pushing to a neurosis the anemic generation that will follow. At the ball, not even one bare arm of a young heiress without the vesicatory stigmata. Young Beraud, Anthony Beraud the playwright, strong like the rest of his dynasty, sees Frédéric Soulié undressing for the bath and, in pitying amazement, exclaims:

— Gracious me! You don't have any cauteries!

This is essential, constitutive, a badge of membership. Offending Humors. Garlic is the substance of alternative medicine: despite Orfila,[20] the name Raspail fits perfectly with the rhyme,[21] and his intuition in regard to helminths opens the invisible path to the microbes of Pasteur, Grancher, and Roux. "Abraham genuit Jacob," and Brid'oisin has said that we are always the sons of someone.[22] In all the shops, as is customary, the oak counter is embellished with false coins of any metal and any format, mercilessly screwed to the spot, like birds of prey on the door, indubitable proof of the scrupulous honesty of the merchant. Big fusses made of a certain market Gisquet-Perier, an arms market. The *Nain jaune* calls, with finesse, the Chief of Police, Delessert, Chief *Je-les-serre*,[23] but it is generally agreed that at least this Chief is an honest man, and this still means something. There is always an academy, even academicians, which does not prevent the prefecture from insisting on putting up every time a heat wave is approaching its "order concerning dogs AND bulldogs," as article 21 of the regulations of the Chamber of Deputies, piously copied by that of the House of Lords, persists in stipulating: "In discussions, speakers speak alternatively for AND against." Bulldogs, we even see too many of them at the Barrière du Combat, where my cousin Randon, who never misses a performance, just took me, near the Montée de Belleville. This show is all the rage with butchers, butchers' assistants, and "gentlemen amateurs." It is a matter of bringing one's most ferocious dog, there where they tear each other apart and maim each other. The little blue poster, permanently displayed at every intersection, shows the champion of the group distinguished by the strength of its jaws, under a crown of firecrackers. But the real celebrity, the star, is "the ass Martin," who, tied up, defies all the huge hounds they can bring, and, with a vertiginous rapidity, breaks their mandibles with each kick. I come out of there, nauseated, and filled with sadness! ... and I have not thanked my cousin. Shouldn't we prohibit these things?

The Englishman Perry has just brought us iron feathers a revolution that makes a clean sweep of goose feathers and penknives. It is not yet the case of friction matches which will appear soon under the name of German chemical matches, although they were invented by a Frenchman; but the friends of progress who have renounced the flintstone and the tinder lighter soak special matches in a small bottle of sulfuric acid and asbestos. The entire apparatus, in a small, red, cardboard cylinder, is sold for three pennies at Fumade—one of these small boutiques in a semicircle with a small round dome which, as in Florence, on the Arno, rest on columns on one of the platforms of the Pont-Neuf—, just to the side of the other half-rotunda where those apple fritters boil, engulfing passersby in fragrance. The female sellers with small carts shout "beautiful Chasselas grapes from Fontainebleau, twelve pennies a basket." There are three good pounds in there, and very nice-looking, too, amid the ferns of each basket, put together in a rush. Eggs, as many as you want, "three for six white, the red and the white"! Six white cost six liards: a penny and a half. There is no need to deprive yourself of anything. In the winter, the less well-off go to Pont-au-Change to eat potatoes, too, in the snow: a penny a pound, and the merchant adds the salt for you, in a bit of paper. At the same time, we warm our fingers on the steam from the stove. All this is good. People sing mainly three songs:

> Guernadier (*for* grenadier) how much you afflict me
> By ifnorming (*informing*) me of your departure, etc.
> Look, here are four shirts, etc.

And then:

> You will not have my rose, (*three times*)
> For you would destroy it.

And, in a lively mode:

> You who know the hussards of the guard,
> Don't you know the regimental trombone?

There is great enthusiasm for "The Marquis," a street singer, gallantly dressed as a Marquis of yesteryear, with a powdered wig, ruffles and cuffs flowing, thighs firm under his white tights, truly unparalleled, unique, since having sung his couplet and tucked his instrument under his left arm, he throws, with infallible accuracy, a coin wrapped in a sheet of music (the "*HEAVIER THAN AIR!*") toward the upper-floor windows, where the maids rush together, in a frenzy. But a rival soon appears, a second Marquis, no less powdered in frost, no less spruced, no less virtuosic, no less impeccably dexterous in his act: a century of competition, all the careers overcrowded! There is no doubt that Mr. Villemain's "performance" is "charming," but, when it comes to "depth," it is Mr. Royer-Collard who wins; Mr. de Rémusat can go on waiting. This one is called "Mr. Charles," as in the "Rendez-vous bourgeois."

*

Cafés and bars close exactly at midnight; rigorously, albeit statutorily, at eleven o'clock in the evening, there is not even a single girl wandering in the streets of Paris, even in the Galeries du Palais-Royal where the throng is such, especially at the end of the day, that one can no longer move, and the crowd walks on the spot, amid the brouhaha. We measure the prosperity of the shops by the profits accumulated in the Public Treasury. At the Galerie Valois, they have even just arrested, for his unkempt appearance, "the man with a long beard" who for years has been one of the curiosities of Paris for obstinately walking his rags through the shop. We know now that this tattered and mysterious peripatetic is a certain Chodruc-Duclos, from Bordeaux, formerly, legend has it, very rich and at one time intimately connected to Mr. de Peyronnet, the current minister. There are rumors that, by exhibiting his distress in this way, this man wants to avenge himself for his old friend's abandonment of him. And, by the way, as for clothing, this is what is new in the windows of the linen stores: until now we would see shirts with collars, now we see collars without shirts.

We used to change shirts when it was necessary, even if, strictly speaking, this meant that we would turn them inside out until we could get to Gascon's laundry: now we hide the dirty shirt with a fake clean collar. And why not soon use fake fronts and fake sleeves? I do not have a taste for these falsehoods. I prefer what has just begun in some streets and by the boulevards: Madame de Staël wouldn't recognize herself any longer in her rue du Bac. The streams which spilled somewhat liberally in the middle of the road itself, and rolled during heavy rains like impassable torrents, are now divided into two half-streams, one on each side of the street. But would it not be better still to channel them immediately under the sidewalks that we have started to install everywhere? One encounters a number of people with schapskas in the street. Each insurrection in this brave Poland that does not want to die brings us new waves of Poles. We are so crazy about it that the government, despite its fear of Czar Nicolas, must help the refugees with a subsidy; fifteen francs a month for the soldiers; for the officers, thirty-five francs. That is not enough to live on, but enough not to die on. On rue Mignon, near rue Hautefeuille and rue Serpente, there is a Polish table d'hôte where refugees can dine for thirteen pennies, with as much bread as they like. Old senior officers, whose appetite is the greater for having skipped lunch, wait for it to open, seated on the stone bench at the door of the printer of the *Monitor*. We just invented the word: *brat* (?). There is talk of major construction projects in the vast wasteland—there is space for an entire city—which extends from the top of the rue de Clichy to a small village named Courcelles, veritable steppes abandoned to the bramble and the nettle, where people go to dump demolition waste, refuse, and dogs and cats. In fact, it is perhaps time to take a little look at this part of the city. Toward the area called "little Poland,"[24] in the Plaine Monceaux, which has become a real plain of Arbela,[25] a pitched battle took place even yesterday, with slingshots and all, between the students of the Friars and those of the Mutuelle, both sides decidedly enraged; many children were seriously injured. Of note also is the increasing brutality of street brawls, punches, kicks: will we soon take to stabbing, like the Italians?

There are currently three Dupins at once, the Dupin brothers. In contrast, we go to admire the beautiful Ms. Véro-Dodat in her delicatessen, near the passage, at the corner of rue Montesquieu, and the blonde Ms. Véry at her counter in the Palais-Royal, but on rue Vivienne, Mr. Gibus, the hatter, finally irritated, has just decided to put green curtains on his windows in order to prevent the crowd from cluttering up the sidewalk to catch a glimpse of beautiful Ms. Gibus. He has nevertheless allowed a lithograph to be made from his wife's portrait for the publication of *The Beautiful Women of Paris*, which has just been started by a young man named Arsène Houssaye. Of this news, our Collège Bourbon is aware, as one can imagine; but for the moment it is perturbed by a very different event. The headmaster caught wind of our newspaper *The Schools' Press*, a real newspaper, printed and written by students and founded by a great man, Ferdinand Dugué, trained since birth in the Romantic *tutti*. *The Schools' Press* will expire after its third issue. It's a pity: precisely in this third issue, after the feature article was so supremely disdainful of the university and of its cursed pawns, there was another article, nicely sensual, approved of by us all: the history of the author himself (he is in third grade), trying in vain to restore goodness to one of these cubicular creatures who are angry about our temperament. The article was titled, simply: "*And yet she was born virtuous …*" We go to a shack to see, in the Filles-du-Calvaire, an indefatigable bulimic, the polyphagous Tarare, who swallows forthwith everything that is brought to him, including loads of cider apples. Dr. Venette is very proud to have reported this case in the *Dictionary of Medical Sciences*.

ʎ

The omnibuses everyone has been talking about have just made their appearance, to the lively dissatisfaction of the *fiacres*—coachmen and carriages have the same name—who stop the horses and thrash the drivers. Generally people doubt their success and many predict a fiasco. Yet a competition is already being created, the "White Ladies," which depart from Quai de la Monnaie, in front of rue Guénégaud, the street of the glassblowers, near Rodot's wine store. These carriages are painted all in white, and the coachmen, dressed in white under a varnished white hat, play with their foot on bellows the aria from the *White Lady*: "The White Lady looks at you ..." The public also looks and experiences great pleasure.

Mr. de Pontécoulant writes his Mémoires. He has a nice story about the Duke de Richelieu. When he appeared to assume his title and to receive the top personnel of the Ministry, where the King had appointed him, the Director of Accounting Services presented to him, with strict deference, a full envelope explaining that it was the thirty thousand francs allocated to any new Minister for his travel and moving expenses. Whereupon the Duke, returning the envelope without opening it:

— You will immediately pay the thirty pennies to the agent who will bring my trunk, and you will bring back the change.

We must always wait until the end of things; but this gesture is exemplary.

We currently build buildings everywhere. The hand is there, but not the brain. This reign was definitely destined to break the glorious chain of reigns: unlike its predecessors, it will not have merited its architecture. Here Piranesi is called Davioud.[26] There are three trendy restaurants: Véry and Véfour at the Palais-Royal, in the very center of Paris, dear to the provinces, and "The Suckling Calf," at the Place du Châtelet, not to mention Bonvalet for wedding dinners, over there, beyond the boulevard du Temple, near that new Turkish coffee shop where you sit on couches. We will go to admire this innovation. The principal cafés, Tortoni, Lemblin, Procope, have just tried another. They have written on their windows: *Rice Pudding*, *Bouillon Rice*, a summons to opulent debauchery. It's successful. On leaving the theaters which finish early, the dispersing audiences rush in a hurry to get there before they close—midnight sharp, or you get a fine!—to have a nightcap, and they hope they are seen. There has also been for some time now a new fashion in restaurants, that of asking for the "check," instead of the bill. This inevitably makes everyone turn around to look.

In theaters, it is Mr. Scribe who holds the rope—"the rope with which Gérard de Nerval hanged himself," Méry will later write to the good Audebrand. It is still fashionable for plays and books to have two titles: *Victorine or the Night Brings Counsel*, *Thirty Years or the Life of a Player*, *Pamela or Virtue Rewarded*. There are plays that go on for sixty performances. We never tire of dashing colonels who as a matter of course find young and beautiful widows to marry who have "an annuity of ten thousand pounds." But Mr. Guizot, Protestant and austere, has offered to raise the prices, formulating in a two-word axiom the new *Credo*: "Enrich yourselves!" In an entirely different Gospel, the wife of the chancellor of the Hospital had said: "We take only what we have given."

The Italians are at the Odéon, where in *canary*-colored gloves they go wild applauding Pasta, Malibran, Grisi. Every female singer is called "The Diva" and, in music, after Rossini, there is nothing else; on this point, for example, everybody is quite in agreement, except for one, but he is only a greenhorn, who no doubt wants people to notice him, a certain Berlioz. It is at the Opera, on rue Lepelletier, where Taglioni swirls, while in Naples Nourritt throws himself out the window on hearing about the triumph of his successor Duprez. There is, at the corner of the rue Grange-Batelière, a wine merchant associated with little father David, the promoter, who gives you for thirty-six pennies, on days when you are rich, a "single" entry to the amphitheater. You have to order at least two days in advance, when "it is Duprez." Another attraction, another fascination, at the Porte-Saint-Martin: the incomparable, prodigious Frédérick, the genius in a bottle of blue wine; at the

Funambules on boulevard du Temple, next to Petit Lazari, the flowered face of Deburau the father Gallicizes the pantomime of Pulcinella and Dom Nicolo. The Variétés presents Vernet, Odry, the two Lepeintres with Miss Ozy; but the Gymnase has Bouffé, a weeper dug up by Jules Favre. We just buried Ms. Calineau, the very authentic Calineau large as life, who, invited by Fontallard and his companions to follow the funeral procession, responded with dignity: "I only go to the funerals of people who go to mine." They say that Mr. Guizot will replace Mr. Thiers at the Ministry. The cigar shop, which the Duchess of Berry had authorized, can no longer satisfy the demand for tobacco, which is definitely replacing snuff.

People talk vaguely about the imminent creation, by a certain Émile de Girardin, of a newspaper that will cost forty francs a year instead of eighty. Many are incredulous and, in effect, it seems improbable to those who do the accounts seriously and to those who are competent; but there are people who can never stop, and there are others who are now talking about selling newspapers in single issues, as if there were already too many subscribers! And then, there will be shops especially for this trade? Good! But the buyers, where will you get them from? ... We must be a little reasonable, nevertheless! As for newspapers, they say that *The Caricature* will cease publication. Charles Philipon, this great Lyonnais who is not afraid of anything, the creator of *The Pear*, has received this year alone fifty-two jail sentences and fines for his two newspapers, *The Caricature* and *The Charivari*. Mr. Thiers is decidedly inexhaustible and will never be taken by surprise. This devilish little man knows everything, understands everything, for example, *The Solitary One* by Mr. D'Arlincourt.[27] He even just proclaimed that electrical telegraphy, with which we are thinking of replacing Chappe's optical telegraphs, "will never be more than an interesting *amusement* for people who are *curious about physics*." Horace Raisson, of the *Gazette of the Courts*, publishes on the same day *The Art of Wearing a*

Tie and *The Art of Dining Out in the City*. This tour de force of a double strike of such powerful fecundity could not fail to make a splash. All the painters' studios are *topsy-turvy*, as Balzac has just decreed à la Celte,[28] and we prepare kilometers of paintings for the Musée de Versailles, which will be the grand idea of the reign. The King sees only through the eyes of Father Pingret, the darling child who, together with Mr. Horace Vernet, has a great deal of influence here. Still also around are Father Hess, Father Heim, Father Couder, Father Picot, Father Ingres—still Fathers, at this time!—and the Scheffer brothers who produce, fraternally and flagrantly, the same kind of painting for "aesthetically minded ladies who revenge themselves for their leucorrhoea by playing religious music,"[29] while the jury is in ecstasy over Delaroche. Nothing matters: the Ferris wheel always turns and advances, there as elsewhere. The boom is at its peak: Pleiades of stars everywhere. Not everyone has talent, as will become clear soon, but everyone would consider it beneath him not to try, at the very least, to be a genius. Géricault just passed his palette to Delacroix, whom the jury in vain tries to brush aside at the door of every salon: Beyle, Hugo, de Vigny, Balzac, Gautier, not counting Musset and the others, provide us with a masterpiece every day that everyone fights over in the office of the good Mother Cardinal, on rue des Canettes, just left there by the rushing distributors, still wet like every newborn, the flesh redolent of good fresh printer's ink: a beautiful night for our little corner!

Mr. Comte, "physicist-in-ordinary (? ...) of the King" and Director of the *Theater of Young Students*, at the Passage Choiseul, just died. The number of people one encounters with the Cross of the Legion of Honor seems to increase every day. This gauge of super-excellence, which could once be awarded only extraordinarily, in certain particular and exceptional cases, is distributed now in series and by climatic cycles, like inundations during the rainy season. It is what we call a series of "waves." At the last "wave," Lireux said:

— They decorate here and there a few who deserve it

because it is through the mixing of the species that the beauty of the race is perpetuated.

There were four public balls, the Chaumière, the Prado, the Boule-Noire, and the Sauvage à la Courtille, not to mention some "bagpipes" in the neighborhood of Saint-Marcel or the Ranelagh of Passy, provincial areas after all, and these balls were authorized only on Sundays; subsequently, they were allowed to open on Mondays. It seems that the permission will be extended to Thursdays and that other balls, luxurious in other ways, will open at the Champs-Élysées. Good, good! The renowned sagacity of Mr. Thiers is still growing; one cannot foresee how far it will go. This eminent Statesman, who seems to combine prescience with omniscience, has just even delivered a very remarkable speech—"a ministerial speech," as *le Constitutionnel* so delicately put it—where he irrefutably demonstrated the impossibility of a Republican government, destined to fall after a few hours into "imbecility or blood." It is not surprising that such a man always wins the tug of war; it is thus announced that Thiers's new Cabinet will succeed the Cabinet of Guizot. The very notorious banker and purveyor of bankruptcy, Ouvrard, has just been released from Clichy prison; he will be reunited with his sheltered millions and enjoy in peace his fortune, henceforth liberated and purified by three statutory years of detention during which the detained man lacked nothing by way of entertainment, not even day release. As for this imprisonment for debt, the House has just rejected a last petition for its elimination, and by a large majority. The petitioner was basing his argument on the fact that we could not find two real traders, two serious lenders, among the hundreds of incarcerators, only buyers of shady loans. But the reporter efficiently and promptly did justice to "the Puritanism of the Order." He was highly congratulated as he descended from the Bench, and the House immediately went on to the order of the day. Another new word, "*advertisement*"; will it fare well? The legitimist newspaper *la Mode* just stood trial, that is, it was condemned; the artificial argot has, it seems, one word for the two things, a suggestive word: to be *screwed*. There was a small incident and a huge scandal. To the question addressed to the manager by the President, following all the protocols: "Coëtlogon, have you ever suffered an afflictive or defamatory sentence?", Mr. de Coëtlogon responded: "No, Mr. President. And you?" The response had its expected effect, and Mr. de Coëtlogon got "*screwed*" to the max.

The session has now ended and, as usual, the President of the Council read out the message from the King who, according to custom, gives the country his full assurances.

This time, too, as in all previous closing sessions, Deputy Isambert did not fail to create an atmosphere of general hilarity (he is decidedly a mental case), requesting our immediate evacuation from Algeria, still under the same pretext that this colony, more fertile than ancient Egypt and at our door, ever since we have occupied it, regularly costs us around a hundred or two hundred million a year. As if France was not rich enough to "pay for its glory" and not to have to negotiate on a question where "our honor is at stake"! And how is it that Mr. Isambert is so blind to the general sentiment that he does not take into account the civilizational benefit that our Arab offices offer to these barbaric populations! Moreover, isn't Algeria, as has been said so felicitously—always by Mr. Thiers, I think—, the first, true "nursery" of our generals for our first serious war? Mr. Isambert should be more patient: he will soon see them at work! ...

The carnival was splendid this year: the whole of Paris was in costume. Everyone wanted to see who could hold his breath the longest in order to shout his tirade in rhymes of the market, Vadé style,[30] the loudest. Shouters circulated through the crowd, selling: "the art of screaming in society without anger." Unimaginable throngs on the boulevards, everywhere, and overflowing universal joy, remarkably benevolent; but many hoarse voices became voiceless before the evening. Abandoned carriages of piled-up masks moved at a walking pace, with forced stops at every step. Lord Seymour, widely known by the name "Milord the Ruffian," dressed as a coachman and, as in other years, drove his six-horse carriage, but this year, instead of ordinary confetti, the carriage was filled with huge bags full of brand-new four-penny coins that lackeys in full livery were throwing to the crowd by the handful. We also recognized among his servants, despite his false nose, Baron Hope, the celebrated financier; he was very amused by the jostling kids under the wheels. There is a change in the Ministry; it is Mr. Guizot's turn to replace Mr. Thiers ...

Etc., etc., etc.

The conclusion?

Draw it yourselves ...

For my humble part, from this pandemonium of people and things, these effervescences, these eruptions, from this dross where disconcerting irrationality and the absurd float together, I will limit myself to a point that particularly strikes me: there is no more Respect for anything anywhere.

Respect is dead, dead as a doornail, together with the Honor that begat it. From above, even more than from below, everyone has dutifully, if not consciously, done his best to throw it into the gutter, and it is remarkable that those who have been most responsible for its death, people we respected yesterday, are exactly the ones who moan most lamentably in order to lay claim to it again today.

And yet, despite everything, we still point at a rogue when we meet him: I seriously fear that tomorrow it will perhaps be more difficult to find an honest person to point to ...

Chronology

1739	Ignace Tournachon born in Lyon.
1770	Ignace, now married to Jeanne-Marie Molin, daughter of the bookseller Alexis Molin, launches the Tournachon-Molin Press in Lyon.
1771	Birth of Victor Tournachon.
1793	Victor begins practicing as a printer.
1812	Death of Ignace Tournachon.
1817	Victor takes over the name "Tournachon-Molin" and joins forces with Hippolyte Seguin in Paris. They publish Félicité de Lamennais's *Essai sur l'indifférence en matière de religion.*
1820	April 6. Birth of Gaspard-Félix Tournachon to Victor Tournachon and Thérèse Maillet in Paris.
1822	Nicéphore Niépce begins his experiments with photography.
1824	The Tournachon household moves to 41, rue Saint-André-des-Arts.
1825	Victor Tournachon's press continues to be active but is running a deficit. August 26. Birth of Alban-Adrien Tournachon.
1826	November 11. Marriage of Victor Tournachon, aged 55, and Thérèse Maillet, aged 32.
1830	The press has financial difficulties.
1831–32	Félix is enrolled at the Pension Hubert in Versailles.
1833	Ruined by the high cost of publishing the *Dictionnaire universel de droit français*, Victor is forced to close his press.
1833–36	Félix studies at the Collège Bourbon and lives at the pension owned by Mr. Augeron.

1836	Victor Tournachon, ill, retires to Lyon with his family. Félix leaves the Collège Bourbon. Ernestine Lefèvre (future wife of Félix) is born to Édouard Lefèvre and Amélie-Elisabeth Planques at Épinay.
1837	Death of Victor Tournachon.
1837–38	Félix begins the study of medicine in Lyon. He contributes to *L'Entr'acte lyonnais* and *Fanal du commerce.*
1838	Félix returns to Paris and audits courses in medicine at the Hôtel-Dieu and Bicêtre. He works as a paste-up artist at the *Journal des dames et des modes.* He also writes for August Lireux's *Revue et gazette des théâtres.* Félix takes "Nadar" (sometimes "Nadard") as his nom de plume.
1839	Félix meets Karol d'Anelle. With Polydore Millaud he founds *Le Négociateur*, then *L'Audience.* With Léon Noël and Alfred Francey he launches the *Livre d'or.* August. The Académie des Sciences makes public Daguerre's invention of the daguerreotype, a photographic image made directly on a metal plate.
1841–42	Félix frequents the "Society of Water-Drinkers," Henry Murger's band of artists. He signs himself "Nadard" in *Les Papillotes.*
1842	Nadar contributes to Millaud's *L'Âge d'or*, publishing one of his early novels there. His first sketches are published by Martinet. July. Nadar is elected to the Société des Gens de Lettres.
1842–43	Nadar meets Charles Baudelaire through his friend Théodore de Banville.
1842–45	Nadar works at the republican daily *Le Commerce.* His actions are watched by the police.
1844–45	Nadar publishes *La Robe de Déjanire,* "L'Indienne bleue," and "La Vie et la mort de Lequeux."
1846	Nadar begins in earnest his career as a caricaturist; he works for the satirical journals *Le Corsaire-Satan* and *La Silhouette.*
1847–48	Niépce de Saint-Victor develops a method for making photographic negatives on glass coated with albumen, soon replaced by wet collodion.

1848	Nadar contributes to the *Voleur* and to Charles Philipon's *Charivari*. February. Revolution breaks out in Paris. *Pierrot ministre*, a pantomime written by Nadar, is performed at the Théâtre des Funambules. Champfleury and Nadar argue and nearly fight a duel. March 30. Nadar and Adrien join a volunteer military expedition to win independence for Poland; are arrested, imprisoned at Eisleben in Prussia, then released, and return to Paris June 1. Nadar is sent by Jules Hetzel on a "secret mission" to Prussia. September. Nadar is back in Paris, contributing to Alphonse Karr's *Journal*.
1849	Nadar draws and writes for Hetzel's *Revue comique à l'usage des gens sérieux*. May. Nadar does his first work for Philipon's *Journal pour rire*, and a long friendship begins. September-November. Nadar is in London.
1849–62	Nadar collaborates closely with Philipon. The drawings from his atelier are widely published, especially in Philipon's *Journal pour rire* and the *Petit Journal pour rire*, and also in Auguste Commerson's *Tintamarre*.
1850	August. Nadar is imprisoned in Clichy, for debts.
1851	London International Exhibition; the Crystal Palace draws crowds. Nadar goes to London in June. He meets Constantin Guys, who becomes a friend. Nadar begins planning a *Panthéon* of outstanding contemporaries.
1852	January. Nadar's "Lanterne magique" (caricatures, or *portraits-charges*, of celebrated men) begins appearing in *Le Journal pour rire*. Nadar builds up the store of *portraits-charges* he will use for his *Panthéon*. The first *Nadar-Jury*, caricaturing the Salon, published in *L'Éclair*; it will become a tradition, with installments published in years to come in *Le Tintamarre*, *Le Rabelais*, and *Journal amusant*.
1852–55	Henri Giffard attempts to fly a dirigible.

1853	June. Nadar moves with his mother to 113, rue Saint-Lazare.
1854	Nadar finances Adrien's photography lessons from Gustave Le Gray and arranges the financial backing for Adrien's studio at 11, boulevard des Capucines. Nadar himself learns the technique from Adolphe Bertsch and Camille d'Arnaud, and sets up a studio in his home at 113, rue Saint-Lazare. March. Nadar publishes the *Panthéon Nadar.* He brings out more *portraits-charges* in *Binettes contemporaines.* April. Nadar begins to photograph members of his family, friends, and colleagues. September 11. Nadar marries Ernestine-Constance Lefèvre. Nadar's pantomimes, *Pierrot boursier* and *Pierrot ministre*, are performed at the Théâtre des Funambules by his friend Charles Deburau, and at the Folies-Nouvelles.
1854–55	Adrien's studio is on the brink of financial ruin. From mid-September 1854 to mid-January 1855, Nadar collaborates with him to help save it. The mime Deburau is photographed there. Nadar arranges for the firm to exhibit at the Exposition Universelle of 1855.
1855	January 16. Adrien asks Félix to leave and to relinquish his share in the studio. Adrien wins a gold medal for the *Pierrot* photographs, exhibited under the name "Nadar jeune." Adrien moves his studio to 17, boulevard des Italiens. Nadar returns to 113, rue Saint-Lazare. Thérèse Tournachon moves to the rue de Tivoli. Félix starts legal proceedings against Adrien to force him to stop using the name "Nadar jeune." Adrien becomes a member of the Société Française de Photographie.
1856	January. Philipon creates the *Journal amusant* and soon afterward the *Petit Journal pour rire*, of which Nadar becomes editor-in-chief. Nadar publishes a collection of his stories, *Quand j'étais étudiant.* February 8. Paul Nadar is born to Félix and Ernestine. Adrien wins the first round of the lawsuit filed against him by Félix. Nadar wins a gold medal at the Exposition Photographique in Brussels. Nadar becomes a member of the Société Française de Photographie.

1856–59	Nadar produces reams of caricatures and articles for Philipon's journals. He photographs his friends and eminent figures in literature and the arts; also actresses and singers.
1857	Nadar travels to Brussels, where he exhibits his portraits and wins a medal. December 12. The lawsuit against Adrien is concluded: the judge rules that Félix is "the only, the true Nadar."
1858	February. The *Petit Journal pour rire* ceases publication. April 25. Adrien's boulevard des Italiens studio is declared bankrupt. Nadar takes the first aerial photograph. October 23. Nadar files a patent for aerial photography. He takes the first photograph by artificial light. He publishes a revised *Panthéon Nadar* in the supplement to *Le Figaro*.
1859	March. Nadar is editor of *Journal amusant*. Nadar exhibits a large group of portraits from the *Figures contemporaines* at the Salon of the Société Française de Photographie. June 10. Adrien appeals the decision of December 1857; his appeal is rejected.
1860	February 21. Death of Thérèse Tournachon. Félix pays Adrien's debts. July 12. Nadar establishes the Société Générale de Photographie to provide financial backing for a new studio at 35, boulevard des Capucines; Philipon is president.
1861	February 4. Nadar files a patent for photography by artificial light. April. He tries equestrian photography on the Champs-Élysées. September. Nadar's studio on the boulevard des Capucines opens.
1861–62	Nadar takes photographs in the catacombs.
1862	Death of Henri Murger. Death of Charles Philipon.

1862–64	Adrien sets up a new photographic studio with J.-P. Johannes at 124, avenue des Champs-Élysées; they make equestrian portraits and animal pictures.
1863	Nadar meets Ponton d'Amécourt. July 6. The two men form the Société d'Encouragement pour la Locomotion Aérienne au Moyen d'Appareils Plus Lourds que l'Air. July 31. Nadar's "Manifeste de l'autolocomotion aérienne" appears in *La Presse*. August. The Société founds its own journal, *L'Aéronaute*. October 4. First ascent of the *Géant* at the Champ-de-Mars. Built by Louis and Jules Godard, the balloon can carry twenty-four passengers in its two-story gondola. October 18. On its second ascent, the *Géant* crashes at Hanover; Félix and Ernestine are injured. November 21. Nadar is seriously in debt, according to a police department record.
1864	Nadar publishes *Mémoires du Géant*.
1864–65	Nadar photographs George Sand and Sarah Bernhardt. He photographs the sewers of Paris.
1865	Nadar exhibits his photographs in Berlin, Saint Petersburg, New Orleans, and Amsterdam. He publishes *Le Droit au vol*, with a preface by George Sand. He ascends in the *Géant* at Lyon (July 2) and at Amsterdam (September 11)
1867	June 23. Nadar makes his final ascent in the *Géant*, then sells the balloon. August 31. Death of Baudelaire.
1869	April 13. Adrien creates a firm to make photographic enamels; it will fail in 1872.
1870–71	The Franco–Prussian War and the siege of Paris give Nadar a final opportunity for aeronautics. He creates a military company of balloonists and makes numerous ascents for observation. The beginning of aerial postal service.

1871	Paris Commune. Nadar has difficulties with his health and with his business. He leaves the boulevard des Capucines for the rue d'Anjou.
1873	Nadar and Ernestine retire to the Hermitage in the forest of Sénart.
1874	April 15. The first Impressionist Salon opens in the rooms Nadar still holds on the boulevard des Capucines; exhibitors include Monet, Pissarro, Sisley, Renoir, Guillaumin, Cézanne, and Degas.
1877	Nadar publishes the *Histoires buissonnières*.
1878	Nadar helps to organize an exhibition of Daumier's works. The Nadar Studio wins a gold medal at the Exposition Universelle in Paris.
1879	Death of Daumier. He is buried in Père-Lachaise cemetery.
1880	Nadar publishes *Hôtellerie des Coquecigrues*, filled with remembrances of friends and with a preface by Charles Bataille.
1882	Nadar publishes *Sous l'incendie*, on the war of 1870–71.
1884	Adrien exhibits with the Société des Artistes Français at the salon of 1884.
1886	Nadar and Ernestine travel to Italy. May 18. Nadar is a member of the jury for the first Exhibition of Photography in Florence. August 26. Nadar interviews the chemist Eugène Chevreul on his hundredth birthday. The intended sound-recording of the interview fails, but the text, "L'Art de vivre centenaire," is published with the photographs in *Le Journal illustré* of September 5. Paul Nadar, who has worked with his father for years, is now virtually directing the studio.
1887	Ernestine suffers a stroke. Nadar writes for *Le Temps* and *La Question sociale*.
1889	Photographs by the Nadar Studio (father and son) are shown at the Exposition Universelle and win a grand prize.
1891	Paul Nadar founds the journal *Paris-Photographe*.

1893	Adrien lives at the retirement home at Saint-Perrine, then at the pension Galignani at Neuilly.
1894	January 17. Nadar is made an honorary member of the Société Aérophile de France. Paul's *Paris-Photographe* faces financial disaster. Félix Nadar's financial situation is precarious.
1895	April 1. Félix transfers legal ownership of the Nadar Studio to Paul. June. Nadar travels to Marseille and decides to make a new beginning there. December 5. A sale of lithographs and watercolors from the Nadar collection is held at the Hôtel Drouot, Paris.
1896	Nadar takes part in the publication of the *Tombeau de Baudelaire*, organized by Mallarmé. July. Nadar undergoes surgery.
1897	September. Nadar establishes a new photography studio in Marseille. He writes for the *Petit Provençal.* His collection of balloon-related objects is bought by the City of Paris and placed in the Musée Carnavalet.
1899	Nadar sells his studio in Marseille.
1900	The Exposition Universelle includes a retrospective of Nadar's work. Nadar publishes *Quand j'étais photographe.* June. Nadar again undergoes surgery.
1903	January 24. Adrien dies, after ten years in a mental hospital.
1906	Nadar's health deteriorates: he suffers from congestion of the lungs, recurrences of his asthma, and kidney stones.
1909	January 3. Death of Ernestine. July 25. Louis Blériot flies across the English Channel in a monoplane. Nadar's telegram to him is published in *La Presse.*
1910	March 20. Death of Félix Nadar. He is buried in Père-Lachaise cemetery.
1911	Nadar's *Charles Baudelaire intime* is published.

1939	September 1. Death of Paul Nadar. The studio, which passes to his daughter Marthe, survives only a few years longer.
1950	January. The Caisse Nationale des Monuments Historiques et des Sites acquires from Anne Nadar, Paul's second wife, some 60,000 negatives from the Nadar Studio. The Bibliothèque Nationale acquires the prints (both original and modern), the archives, and the documents pertaining to Félix and Paul Nadar.

Notes

INTRODUCTION: NADAR'S PHOTOGRAPHOPOLIS

1. Siegfried Kracauer, "Photography," in *The Mass Ornament: Weimar Essays*, trans. and ed. Thomas Y. Levin (Cambridge, MA: Harvard University Press, 2005), 59.

2. Walter Benjamin, "Paralipomena to 'On the Concept of History,'" trans. Edmund Jephcott and Howard Eiland, in Benjamin, *Selected Writings*, vol. 4, *1938–1940*, ed. Howard Eiland and Michael W. Jennings (Cambridge, MA: Belknap Press of Harvard University Press, 2003), 405. For the original German, see *Gesammelte Schriften*, 7 vols., ed. Rolf Tiedemann and Hermann Schweppenhäuser (Frankfurt am Main: Suhrkamp Verlag, 1972), I, 1238. The internal quotes within Benjamin's passage are from André Monglond's 1930 *Le Préromantisme français* (Geneva: Slatkine Reprints, 2000), xii; and Hugo von Hofmannsthal's *Der Tor und der Tod* (1894), in *Gesammelte Werke*, ed. Herbert Steiner (Frankfurt am Main: S. Fischer, 1952), III, 220.

3. David Ferris, "The Shortness of History, or Photography *in Nuce*: Benjamin's Attenuation of the Negative," in *Walter Benjamin and History*, ed. Andrew Benjamin (New York: Continuum, 2006), 20.

4. Walter Benjamin, "Convolute N," in *The Arcades Project*, trans. Howard Eiland and Kevin McLaughlin (Cambridge, MA: Belknap Press of Harvard University Press, 1999), 456. Further references to this text will be indicated parenthetically by *AP*, and page number.

5. Walter Benjamin, *The Writer of Modern Life: Essays on Charles Baudelaire*, trans. Howard Eiland et al., ed. Michael W. Jennings (Cambridge, MA: Belknap Press of Harvard University Press, 2006), 27. Further references to this text will be indicated parenthetically by *ML*, and page number.

6. Rosalind Krauss, "Tracing Nadar," *October* 5 (Summer 1978), 29.

7. The one exception is Jérôme Thélot who, in the third chapter of his book *Les inventions littéraires de la photographie*, argues for the theoretical and performative character of Nadar's writings. See "*Photographie homicide*, par Nadar," in *Les inventions littéraires de la photographie* (Paris: Presses Universitaires de France, 2003), 53–69.

8. See "La première épreuve de photographie aérostatique," in *Quand j'étais photographe* (Paris: Seuil, 1994), 104.

9. See Benjamin, "Excavation and Memory," trans. Rodney Livingstone, and *Berlin Chronicle*, trans. Edmund Jephcott, in *Selected Writings*, vol. 2, *1927–1934*, ed. Michael W. Jennings, Howard Eiland, and Gary Smith (Cambridge, MA: Belknap Press of Harvard University Press, 1999), 576 and 611.

10. Cited in Stephen Bann, "'When I Was a Photographer': Nadar and History," *History and Theory*, Theme Issue 48 (December 2009), 97.

11. Ibid.

12. See Nadar, *Quand j'étais étudiant* (Paris: E. Dentu, 1881), 303.

13. Marcel Proust later expands this suggestion by claiming in *Time Regained* that: "A book is a huge cemetery in which on the majority of the tombs the names are effaced and can no longer be read." See Proust, *Time Regained*, vol. VI of *In Search of Lost Time*, trans. Andreas Mayor and Terence Kilmartin (New York: Random House, 1993), 310.

14. The two citations here from "1830 and Thereabouts" can be found on pp. 204 and 224 of the present translation. Further references to this translation will be indicated parenthetically by *W*, and page number. These two citations can be found in Nadar's original French in his *Quand j'étais photographe* (Paris: L'école des lettres, Seuil, 1994), 331 and 367. All subsequent references to this complete French edition of the memoirs will be registered parenthetically by *Q*, and page number, and will follow the English reference.

15. The French original reads: "Quand le bruit se répandit que deux inventeurs venaient de réussir à fixer sur des plaques argentées toute image présentée devant elles, ce fut une universelle stupéfaction dont nous ne saurions nous faire aujourd'hui l'idée, accoutumés que nous sommes depuis nombre d'années à la photographie et blasés par sa vulgarisation" (*Q*, 9).

16. See *Berlin Chronicle*, in Benjamin, *Selected Writings*, vol. 2, 613. There, Benjamin writes "of images that, according to the teachings of Epicurus, constantly detach themselves from things and determine our perception of them."

17. See Lucretius, *De rerum natura: A Poetic Translation*, trans. David R. Slavitt (Berkeley: University of California Press, 2008), 140–141.

18. I am indebted here to Eric Downing's excellent reading of the role and place of Lucretius' discussion of images within Benjamin's photographic reflections. See Downing, "Lucretius at the Camera: Ancient Atomism and Early Photographic Theory in Walter Benjamin's *Berliner Chronik*," *Germanic Review* 81.1 (Winter 2006), 21–36. On the relation between Democritus' theory of the eidola and photography, see Branka Arsic's essay, "The Home of Shame," in *Cities without Citizens*, ed. Eduardo Cadava and Aaron Levy (Philadelphia: Slought Books and Rosenbach Museum & Library, 2003), 36.

19. See Nadar, *Exposé de motifs pour la revendication de la propriété exclusive du pseudonyme Nadar*, et *Supplément au mémoire* (Paris: Dondey-Dupré, 1857), 14–16. On the centrality of the portrait in general for Nadar, see "À la recherche de la 'ressemblance intime,'" in Stéphanie de Saint Marc's recent biography, *Nadar* (Paris: Éditions Gallimard, 2010), 140–166.

20. On the citational character of photography, see my *Words of Light* (Princeton, NJ: Princeton University Press, 1997), xvii.

21. While I wish to take advantage of the allegorical resonance of Hérald de Pages' name, Pages (1815– ?) was indeed a journalist and poet, and one of the founders of *Le Petit Journal*. There is a photograph of him taken by Nadar in the photography collection of the Bibliothèque national de France. See: <http://gallica.bnf.fr/ark:/12148/btv1b530506520>.

22. See Thélot, *Les inventions littéraires de la photographie*, 54. I am indebted to Thélot's summary and analysis of this episode in much of what follows. What interests me most, however, is what the story tells us about the itinerancy of the image in general.

23. Nadar incorporates this earlier version into his memoirs, which itself confirms his sense that the story is linked to the moment "when he was a photographer." In other words, what happens in the story tells us what is true of photography in general.

24. The text even seeks to account for the pharmacist's murderous intentions by recalling that the "avenging trio" comes from a "sinister zone" where violence is the order of the day, and is even inscribed within the very landscape and fauna surrounding them there:

> Let us not forget, in order to understand well and to understand everything, that this avenging trio, from a reality more dramatic in its perfect agreement than that of *Don Juan*, comes directly from the sinister zone whose provinces are tinted totally black on the criminalist maps and on those of public instruction. It is the country where people kill the little old man by dragging him under the nasal sound of the organ, the land of the widow Bancal and of Bastide-le-Gigantesque, where the rocks endlessly return the echo of "the lament of "Fualdès." In this region inherently, naïvely scelerate, the sun, which intoxicates like a strong wine, releases vapors that smell of blood. The viper's bite is more deadly there; the plants with exasperated colors, wolfsbanes or foxgloves, exude more acrid, more subtle poisons. The rattle of the cicada becomes obstinate in order to cover the step of the murderer, and, from the Pyrenees to the Abruzzi, the knife naturally seems to push the fingers, as if to extend and perfect the hand that kills. ...
>
> In a good judicial system, where everything counts, this in its turn will not be forgotten. (*W*, 47; *Q*, 80–81)

25. In a self-portrait that he famously took in the Paris Catacombs, sometime between 1861 and 1862, Nadar appears seated against a wall of bones and surrounded by bottles of photographic chemicals. He has his arms crossed and, next to his head, and parallel with it, is a skull and bones, with its two bones crossed in a kind of visual echo of Nadar's pose. This identification between the photographer, his chemical laboratory, and death also registers the photograph's relation to survival, since the photograph taken at a particular moment, even if we account for the long exposure time necessary to produce it—continues to circulate. This is why every photograph is always about both destruction and survival.

26. On this point, see Thélot, *Les inventions littéraires de la photographie*, 59.

27. Ibid., 61.

28. Ibid.

29. See Roland Barthes, *Camera Lucida: Reflections on Photography*, trans. Richard Howard (New York: Farrar, Straus, and Giroux, 1981), 92.

30. Thélot, *Les inventions littéraires de la photographie*, 65.

31. See Gabriel Tarde, "Preface to the Second Edition," trans. Elsie Clews Parsons (New York: Henry Holt, 1903), xiii–xiv. Tarde's *Lois de l'imitation* was first published in 1890 by the Félix Alcan editorial house in Paris, and reprinted with a new preface in 1895.

32. We could even say that, in a certain way, Nadar is simply following out the consequences of "Gazebon Avenged," which is a story that, among many other things, suggests that we always live "within quotation marks."

33. See Charles Baudelaire, *Les Fleurs du mal*, trans. Richard Howard (Boston: David R. Godine, 1985), 78 (English), 252 (French).

34. I am indebted in this discussion of Paris's catacombs to Christopher Prendergast's *Paris and the Nineteenth Century* (Cambridge, MA: Blackwell Publishers, 1995), especially pp. 74–101; David L. Pike's *Subterranean Cities: The World Beneath Paris and London, 1800–1945* (Ithaca, NY: Cornell University Press, 2005), especially pp. 101–128; Shelley Rice's *Parisian Views* (Cambridge, MA: MIT Press, 1997), especially chapter 5; and Caroline Archer's *Paris Underground* (New York: Mark Batty Publisher, 2005).

35. See Prendergast, *Paris and the Nineteenth Century*, 80–81.

36. On this point, see ibid., 81.

37. For the original French, see *Quand j'étais photographe*, 155–156.

38. Cited in Shelley Rice's *Parisian Views*, 173.

39. Ibid., 177.

40. Baudelaire, *Les Fleurs du mal*, 90–91 and 268–269.

41. See Eric Fournier, *Paris en ruines: Du Paris haussmannien au Paris communard* (Paris: Éditions Imago, 2008), 18.

42. For an excellent and early account of the use of microscopic

photography during the siege, see Galton Tissandier's *A History and Handbook of Photography*, ed. J. Thomson, F. R. G. S. (London: Sampson, Low, Marston, Low, & Searle, 1876), 235–248. There, he writes: "During the war of 1870–71, when Paris was invested by the enemy, photography succeeded in reducing the size of the messages sent by carrier-pigeons, so as to render them almost invisible to the naked eye. No philosopher could have imagined this use of photography, called forth by the dire necessities of war" (235).

43. See Nadar, *Sous l'incendie* (Paris: G. Charpentier, Éditeur, 1882), 11. All further references to the dialogue will be inserted parenthetically in the text by *SI* and page number.

TRANSLATORS' NOTE

1. Stephen Bann, for example, in his essay "'When I Was a Photographer': Nadar and History" [in *History and Theory*, Theme Issue 48 (December 2009), 101], asserts that the memoirs were published in 1899, as does Mia Fineman in her wonderful catalog *Faking It: Manipulated Photography Before Photoshop* (New York: Metropolitan Museum of Art, 2012), 260.

2. See Maria Morris Hambourg, "A Portrait of Nadar," in *Nadar* (New York: The Metropolitan Museum of Art, 1995), 10.

3. See Charles Bataille, "Nadar," *Diogène*, no. 17 (November 30, 1856), 4.

4. See Kiki Dimoula, "Thoughts of an Awkward Immigrant to a Foreign Language," in *The Brazen Plagiarist: Selected Poems*, trans. Cecile Inglessis Margellos and Rika Lesser (New Haven: Yale University Press, 2012), xi.

5. See Benjamin, "The Task of the Translator: An Introduction to the Translation of Baudelaire's *Tableaux parisiens*," trans. Harry Zohn, in *Walter Benjamin: Selected Writings, Volume 1: 1913–1926*, ed. Marcus Bullock and Michael W. Jennings (Cambridge, MA: The Belknap Press of Harvard University Press, 2004), 260. Further references to this essay will be referenced parenthetically by TT, and page number.

6. Dimoula, *The Brazen Plagiarist*, xii.

BALZAC AND THE DAGUERREOTYPE

1. [The two inventors to whom Nadar refers here are Nicéphore Niépce (1765–1833), who discovered photography in 1822, and Louis-Jacques Daguerre (1787–1851); but the invention was not made public until 1839, after its acquisition by the French state.]

2. [George Sand, born Amantine-Lucille-Aurore Dupin (1804–1876), was a French novelist and memoirist and a close friend of Nadar's. He photographed her often during the 1860s.]

3. Charles Baudelaire, *Aesthetic Curiosities* ["The Salon of 1846," in *Baudelaire: Selected Writings on Art and Artists*, trans. P. E. Charvet (Cambridge: Cambridge University Press, 1981), 87; any notes, or even parts of notes, that are not enclosed within brackets are by Nadar].

4. [Nicéphore Niépce is recognized as one of the earliest practitioners of photography. He captured "negatives" using a *camera obscura* and paper sheets coated with silver chloride. In 1829 he associated himself with Louis-Jacques Daguerre, who discovered the process for developing and fixing images in the 1830s, and after whom the first photographic reproductions were named. They were then called "daguerreotypes" despite the fact that—Nadar argues—the very first photographic experiments belonged to Niépce. Nadar here evokes the debate about photography's origins, a debate that remains very much alive today.]

5. [Charles Bourseul (1829–1912) was one of the first experimenters with the telephone. Although no prototype was built then, he had already described the transmission of the human voice by electrical currents in 1854.]

6. [Charles Cros (1842–1888), French poet, inventor of the phonograph, as Nadar notes here, but also the inventor of color photography.]

7. [Jules Antoine Lissajoux (1822–1880), professor of mathematics, was interested in sound waves and developed an optical method for studying vibrations. His experiments were exhibited at the Paris Universal Exhibition in 1867.]

8. [Ferdinand Brunetière (1849–1906), French writer and critic, was known as a rationalist, free-thinking scholar until, in 1895,

he published an article entitled "Après une visite au Vatican," in which he writes of the failure of science to provide a basis for social morals, and declares his return to Catholicism. See *Revue des Deux Mondes*, 4e période, tome 127 (1895), 97–118.]

9. Louis de Lucy ["Le Problème de l'Aéromotion" (*L'Aéronaute*, no. 4), cited in Nadar's *The Right to Fly*, trans. James Spence Harry (London: Cassell, Petter, and Galpin, 1866), 40].

10. [Nadar most likely means to refer to 1822, not to 1842. This could be a typographical mistake; we cannot be certain, however, since he sometimes has a rather playful and even whimsical vision of the history of photography.]

11. [The word "recul" here also can refer to the distance necessary to take a photograph.]

12. [Nadar here refers to Gerolamo Cardano (1501–1576), a physician, mathematician, astrologer, and philosopher who published the solutions of the quartic and cubic equations. He was also an accomplished gambler, and his book on games of chance, *Liber de ludo aleae* (*Book on Games of Chance*), contains the first systematic treatment of probability.]

13. [Paul Gavarni, pseudonym of Hippolyte-Guillaume-Sulpice Chevalier (1804–1866), French lithographer, painter, and illustrator, whose work often appeared in *Le Charivari*. He illustrated, among others, novels by Balzac and Eugène Sue; Camille-Léon-Louis Silvy (1834–1910) was a French photographer who lived in London and photographed many members of the British royal family. According to Nadar, he was one of the "Primitives of Photography"; Charles de Spoelberg de Lovenjoul (1836–1907), great Belgian collector and writer. Heir of an old aristocratic Belgian family, he put together an impressive library of nineteenth-century French writers.]

14. [The two protagonists of Molière's 1659 play *Les Précieuses ridicules*. Having come to Paris in search of love, the two women scorn their first two suitors and then suffer the suitors' revenge. The two characters in this play of hidden identities and mocked pretensions are here evoked by Nadar to impugn the poses taken by Paris's "elite minds."]

15. [Léon Gozlan (1803–1866), French novelist, secretary of Balzac, wrote a biographical essay on him, *Balzac en pantoufles*, 2nd ed. (Paris: Michel Lévy Frères, 1856).]

16. [Théo, abbreviation for Théophile Gautier.]

GAZEBON AVENGED

1. [Sophie Risteau, Mme Cottin (1773–1807), French writer; wrote sentimental romances, one in particular, *Mathilde* (1805), set in the historical period of the Crusades.]

2. [Indented and presented as a citation, Nadar's line here could be referencing any number of biblical passages in which oxen are slaughtered, sacrificially or otherwise, but he is perhaps more directly evoking Jeremiah 11:19: "But I was like a lamb or an ox that is brought to the slaughter." What is interesting here and elsewhere in this vignette is the section's rampant citationality, something that helps Nadar suggest that we never truly speak in our voice and we are, in this way, always divided from ourselves: motifs that are staged throughout this section, as characters continually become someone else.]

3. [Gustave Trouvé (1839–1902), French engineer and inventor, researched various modes of communication, including telegraphy and microphones, and developed different means of transportation, including outboard motorboats and electric cars; Paul-Gustave Froment (1815–1864), inventor and instrument maker; in 1851, he built the pendulum arrangement for Léon Foucault's famous experiment, and was known for developing motors that could wind clocks; Marcel Deprez (1843–1918); French electrical engineer, known for his experiments devoted to the transmission of electrical power across long distances; and Clément Ader (1841–1925), French inventor and engineer; effectively realized the first flying machine thirteen years before the Wright brothers. He also established the first telephone network in Paris in 1880.]

4. [Giovanni Caselli (1815–1891), Italian physicist; the first scientist to solve the problem of autographic telegraphy, which permitted an exact facsimile of a message, drawing, or signature to be reproduced across a distance. An early version of a fax machine, the apparatus is pertinent to the young man's claim of taking photographs of subjects beyond his field of vision.]

5. [François Arago (1786–1853), French mathematician and astronomer; he experimented with the velocity of sound, magnetism, and theories of light. A member of the French legislature, he was among photography's most enthusiastic admirers. He championed Daguerre in the Académie des Sciences and the Chambre des Députés, securing the inventor a lifetime pension in exchange for the rights to his process. On August 19, 1839, he famously introduced the photographic process, step by step, before a joint session of the Académie des Sciences and the Académie des Beaux-Arts.]

6. [William Woodnut Griscom (1851–1897), American inventor, responsible for introducing electric motors into marine propulsion. He invented a motor that, named after him, brought all in one circuit the motor's armature, electro-magnets, and battery.]

7. [Isidore Latour de Saint-Ybars (1810–1891), poet, historian, and dramatic author. Best known for his tragedies, *Virginie* (1845) and *Rosemonde* (1855).]

8. [Carl August von Steinheil (1801–1870), German physicist, engineer, and inventor. Producer of the first daguerreotype in Germany, he famously experimented with ground electricity; M. Bourbouze, French electrician; during the Siege of 1870–1871, he tried to establish telegraphic communication between Paris and the provinces by using the Seine as a conductor and receiving whatever current could be picked up by a metal plate sunk into the river through a galvanometer.]

9. [Nadar here refers to three members of the Royal Society of London who, in July 1747, tried to use the river Thames as a conductor: William Watson (1715–1787), Lord Charles Cavendish (1704–1783), and the then President of the Royal Society, Martin Folkes (1690–1754).]

10. [Jöns Jacob Berzelius (1779–1848), Swedish chemist, one of the founders of modern chemistry; he discovered and isolated several new elements, and helped develop notation for chemical formulas.]

11. [Adolphe-Philippe d'Ennery (1811–1899), French dramatist, a very prolific and popular author. He became famous for, among other works, *Les Deux Orphelines* (co-written with Cormon). François Coppée (1842–1908), French poet, whose works in both verse and prose provoked Rimbaud's irony, due to their intense pathetic tone.]

12. [Jacques Babinet (1794–1872), French physicist and astronomer, well known for his contributions to optics and for his promotion of aerial navigation; Jean-Baptiste Biot (1774–1862), French physicist, astronomer, and mathematician, established the existence of meteorites. Known for his investigations into polarized light and optical rotation, he ascended in the first hot-air balloon ride with Joseph Louis Gay-Lussac in 1804 in order to study the magnetic, electrical, and chemical condition of the atmosphere at various elevations. For a brief discussion of the debate between Babinet and Biot, in which Babinet accuses Biot of superstition, see Abel Hureau de Villeneuve, "Babinet," in *L'Aéronaute, Bulletin mensuel international de la navigation aérienne*, no. 11 (November 1872), 182–183.]

THE BLIND PRINCESS

1. It is truly impossible not to ask a question here: How many years have passed since the day when the balloon of the School of Meudon unexpectedly went, one nice morning, to neighboring Chaville, I think, and returned immediately, profiting in all haste from a brief spell of good weather, that is, gaining the victory over the absent enemy?

It was then that, for the confusion of our country and of human intellect, a Minister of Public Instruction, or rather of Public Ignorance, dared to declare at the very heart of the Institute (Babinet being dead, Barral set aside, and Marey not yet there), these words that remain, scandalous, in the peroration of his report:

"*Glory to the French Army, which has JUST DISCOVERED how to steer balloons! ...*"

Assuredly—and who would contradict this?—assuredly on this most extraordinary discovery, the richest of human findings, never did the predestined, the admirable inventor tire of affirming and reaffirming again the glory of his conquest, of reducing to nothing all incredulity, all doubt, by a continuous succession of aerial voyages, accomplished daily, with days, hours, and itineraries of round trips announced, proclaimed in advance.

Or how many times, after the so solemn affirmation of Minister H. M., has the School of Meudon only repeated its short hop to Chaville and back?

And how much after so many successive years did the unproductive student of these "*flying fish*"—that do not fly and would never be able to fly—cost, how much does he still add every year to our already heavy costs?

2. [Nadar refers here to the eighteenth-century French poet and romance writer Jean-Pierre Claris de Florian (1755–1794), who was best known for his fables, published posthumously in 1802, of which "The Monkey Showing the Magic Lantern" is among the best. In the fable, the monkey, Jacques, convinces himself that, while his master is away, he can demonstrate the workings of the magic lantern, something he has seen his master do innumerable times. Forgetting to light the lantern, however, he is unable to offer a successful performance for his audience. The fable suggests the folly of pretending to be what one is not, of believing that a copy could be as convincing as the original, and, because he convinces himself that he can imitate his master, the folly of believing rhetoric when common sense suggests something else. A story of the failure of imitation that begins in a story about visual presentation, it would offer rich resources for thinking about photography's own capacity for reproduction. See *Fables de Florian* (Paris: Librairie de l'Enfance et de la Jeunesse, 1845), 52–54.]

3. These expenses, like all the others, including the one of the special train provided for us without our asking for it, were paid by us up to the last *Silbergroschen*—something that the King *certainly* did not know. We similarly also paid for medical services, except for those provided by the excellent Dr. Muller, who declined all payment and received some days later, from our government at the time, the ribbon of the Legion of Honor.

I have saved all my receipts, adding up to some six thousand francs (I say: six thousand francs) for our weeklong stay ... transport, indemnities for damages, etc.

This in order to respond on this occasion to the Prussian newspapers, which—spiteful because of my balloon mail services during the siege, and of an article of mine where I displayed no tenderness for Germany—did not hesitate then for a whole week, and in one voice, to accuse me of ingratitude—for me, the most odious of human perversions.

HOMICIDAL PHOTOGRAPHY

1. [Nadar suggests that the architect in question is a pseudo-architect with a nice, sonorous play between "architecte" and "archi*toc*."]

2. [The French here is "La '*spécialité*' est née trop maligne pour, s'étant laisseé faire, se laisser refaire."]

3. [The French here is "l'orbite embitumé." This identification between the woman and bitumen works to suggest a link between persons and the photographic process—something that will occur often in this section of the memoirs—since Niépce famously used a thin coating of the tarlike material on a pewter plate onto which he secured the first camera photograph.]

4. [Nadar here refers to the 1878 "Lebiez-Barré" case, in which two penniless young men, Paul Lebiez and Aimé Barré, murdered an old woman in Paris and, in order to eliminate the evidence of the crime, Lebiez scientifically cut up the body. Soon afterward, Lebiez, one of the most distinguished students of the medical school of Paris, gave a lecture on Darwinism; at his trial, he was also accused of demonstrating the consequences of a theory according to which the strongest always hold sway over the weakest.]

5. *The right to use and abuse.*

6. *All the votes!* [The Latin here means: "On every point," but Nadar translates it as "Tout les suffrages!"]

7. [Nemrod or Nimrod, Noah's grandson: the Bible says of him: "He was a mighty hunter in the face of the Lord" (Genesis 10:9).]

8. [Antoine Fualdès, French judge who in 1827 was murdered at Rodez in the Aveyron department by the stockbroker Jausion and the latter's brother-in-law Bastide. His body was discovered floating in the Aveyron river. The trial of the murderers resonated nationwide, and the accident inspired a popular lullaby of grief.]

9. [Here Nadar exploits the various connotations of *arrêt* in French, which not only include a judicial "judgment" or "sentence" but also "arrest" in a policial sense, and "arrest" as what a photograph does when it captures or freezes its subject.]

10. [This is the first explicit reference in this section to the "Fenayrou Affair," which serves as the basis for Nadar's story here, and is referenced again in his postscript to the section. For a presentation of the details of the case, see Henry Brodribb Irving, "The Fenayrou Case," in *A Book of Remarkable Criminals* (New York: George H. Doran, 1918), 268–285; and Mary S. Hartman, *Victorian Murderesses: A True History of Thirteen Respectable French and English Women Accused of Unspeakable Crimes* (Mineola, NY: Dover

Publications, reprint edition, 2014), 205–214. Nadar's "ex-*m*actotum," of course, brings together "factotum," which recalls the now ex-pharmacist assistant, who filled many roles in the pharmacy, including the role of the wife's lover, and "deux ex-*m*achina," which perfectly evokes the young pharmacist's entrance into the plot of the story as an unexpected, intervening force that moves the story forward and, like God, is "the initial author of so many ills."]

11. [Nadar here references a renowned murderer, Louis Menesclou, who was tried in Paris in 1880 for the rape, murder, and dismemberment of a four-year-old girl.]

12. [Hippolyte Bernheim (1840–1919), French physician and neurologist, widely known for his use of hypnotism in the medical treatment of "organic" diseases of the nervous system, and, according to Freud, one of his strongest early influences; Cesare Lombroso (1835–1909), Italian criminologist and physician who sought to establish the hereditary nature of deviance and to identify such "born criminals" through physical features. In his 1889 *Man of Genius*, he claimed a close link between genius and insanity.]

THE FIRST ATTEMPT AT AEROSTATIC PHOTOGRAPHY

1. [Jacques-Alexandre Charles (1746–1823), French physicist, first used hydrogen to fill aerostats, following the invention by the Montgolfier brothers who, in their experiments, had used hot-air balloons. With the Robert brothers, Anne-Jean and Nicolas-Louis, he launched the first hydrogen-filled balloon in 1783. In regard to the title of this section, "The First Attempt at Aerostatic Photography," the French word "épreuve," which we are translating here as "attempt," also means "test," "trial," and, in a photographic context, "proof" or "print."]

2. The first hemistich of a line of Cicero: *Cedant arma togae: que les armes le cèdent à la toge*; which means that the military government yields to the civil government.

3. [Jacques Cassini (1677–1756), French astronomer of Italian origins, focused his research mostly on the description of the shape of Earth. He became a member of the French Academy at the age of seventeen and was elected to the Royal Society of London in 1696.]

4. [Reference to the family members of Eugène Godard (1827–1890), French aeronaut, who joined Nadar in numerous adventures, such as, among other things, the ascent on the *Géant*. This event is here recollected in the chapter on "The Blind Princess." During the Paris siege (1870–1871) Godard became one of the most prominent organizers of the first "air mail" service. He carried out more than 2500 balloon flights in France and abroad.]

5. [The Pereire brothers were among the most prominent nineteenth-century financiers in Paris, and were rivals of the Rothschilds. They were of Portuguese origin.]

6. An honorable scientific journal—*Les Inventions nouvelles*—was taken by surprise by one of its editors, who affirms flatly that the first aerostatic negative was obtained in 1881—by Mr. Paul Desmarets.

The incontestable notoriety of our experiment, which had figured in several exhibitions *much before* 1881, and the date of our patents responded in advance to this unexpected assertion, without any need to refer to the year of *Charivari* where everyone can find Daumier's lithograph reproduced on the cover of this book.

7. [The Tissandier brothers, Albert (1839–1906) and Gaston (1843–1899), flew the first aerostat with an electric engine in 1883. During the siege of Paris, Albert piloted one of the first mail balloons outside the city, carrying over 1000 lbs. of mail and dispatches from over 100 families. Gaston published the first book on aerial photography, *La photographie en ballon*, in Paris in 1886, with a frontispiece consisting of an original photographic print by Jacques Ducom. Gaston had flown over Paris with Ducom in 1885, and over Auteuil with Paul Nadar in 1886.]

SUBTERRANEAN PARIS

1. [François-Constantin de Chassebœuf, Count of Volney (1757–1820), philosopher, joined the group of the "ideologues," and authored, among other things, the work here cited by Nadar: *The Ruins, or Meditation on the Revolutions of Empires* (1791); Edward Young (1683–1765), English poet, became widely known all over Europe for the poem hereby cited, *Night Thoughts* (1742).]

2. [Charles Pierre Chapsal (1787–1858) was a French grammarian who, with François-Joseph-Michel Noël (1756–1841), wrote the *Nouvelle grammaire française*, which was first published in 1823; Jacques Delille, the ironical transcription of the last name of abbot

Delille (1738–1813), was a fair, but quite impersonal and scholastic versifier.]

3. [The Latin phrases here translate as "In memory of the ancestors" and "Beyond these borders, they rest in the expectation of the hoped-for happiness," respectively.]

4. [Nadar refers here to Jacques-Antoine Dulaure (1755–1835), French archaeologist and historian who wrote extensively on the history of Paris, France, and the French Revolution. The most important of his works is his ten-volume *Histoire physique, civile et morale de Paris depuis 1821 jusqu'à nos jours* (1825); and to Paul Fassy (1833– ?), who published his *Les Catacombes: étude historique* in 1861.]

5. [Luke 1:52: "He hath put down the mighty from their seats, and he hath raised the lowly ones."]

6. ["Our days passed like water."]

7. [Louis Bourdaloue (1632–1704), French Jesuit and court preacher. Well-trained in rhetoric, philosophy, and moral theology, he was known as the "king of preachers and the preacher of kings"; Joseph Prudhomme was a character created by Nadar's friend, the lithographer, caricaturist, actor, and writer Henri Monnier (1799–1877). Prudhomme was the personification of the nineteenth-century Parisian bourgeoisie who, in turn, was modeled in part on Monnier himself. Prudhomme was adopted by Honoré Daumier, who included him in more than sixty caricatures.]

8. 1867. [Although the church opposed the public display of "sacred" human bones, public demand moved the French government to open the Catacombs to the general public in 1867. 1867 was of course also the year of the Universal Exhibition, in which several archaeological displays presented skeletal remains.]

9. [Charles-Julien Lioult de Chênedollé (1769–1833), French poet who published his *Le génie de l'homme* in 1807 and his *Études poétiques* in 1820. He was particularly interested in the relations between man, nature, society, and the world of astronomy.]

10. [Lucien Gaulard (1850–1888), inventor of instruments for the transmission of alternating current electricity. Best known for his development of a power transformer.]

11. [Jean-Jacques Pradier (1792–1852), Swiss-born French sculptor who worked in the neoclassical style and contributed to the Fontaine Molière in Paris. He was friends with several writers, including Victor Hugo, Théophile Gautier, and Gustave Flaubert; Antoine-Augustin Préault (1809–1879), French Romantic sculptor who first exhibited at the Paris Salon in 1833 and whose most famous surviving work is his 1876 relief sculpture of Ophelia, now in the Musée d'Orsay.]

12. Letter from N … (*Paris*), to Louis Blanc (*Versailles*), … May 1871.

13. [Giovanni Battista Piranesi (1720–1778), Italian artist, designer, architect, and theorist; he moved to Rome at the age of twenty and studied the city's ancient monuments. He began etching inventive views of ancient ruins, and later created a series of etchings of fantastic prison interiors. His highly original designs and drawings influenced many artists and literary figures, during his lifetime as well as afterwards.]

14. [The barathrum is the pit in Athens into which criminals were thrown. It also can refer, figuratively, to the pit or chasm of hell.]

15. [Jean-Baptiste Boussingault (1802–1887), French chemist, discovered that nitrogen is essential to plants and animals and conducted several studies of the action and value of manures; Justus von Liebig (1803–1873), German chemist, considered the founder of organic chemistry and the "father of the fertilizer industry" for his discovery of the importance of nitrogen to plants; Louis Grandeau (1834–1911), professor of agriculture, known as the "grand old man of agricultural science in France," studied the nutrition of plants and animals and also the use of fertilizers and manures.]

16. ["Under Jupiter, under the sun"; that is: in the open air, under the sun.]

FEMALE AND MALE CLIENTS

1. [Biblical character. Princess of Phoenician origins, wife of Arbat, king of Israel. Prophet Elijah accused her of despotism, idolatry, and love of luxury, and she became associated with false prophets and, later, with fallen or abandoned women.]

2. ["Petit Bob" is a kind of sunhat.]

DOCTOR VAN MONCKHOVEN

1. [Claude Louis Berthollet (1748–1822), Savoyard-French chemist, who first demonstrated the bleaching action of chlorine gas and soon after revolutionized the bleaching industry. His career was enriched during the Napoleonic era. Napoleon chose Berthollet to accompany him to Egypt as his scientific adviser. Berthollet became an important member of the scientific and archaeological institute that Napoleon established in Cairo, and he became vice president of the French Senate in 1804; Armand Séguin (1767–1835), French chemist who discovered a faster and more inexpensive process for tanning leather.]

2. This observatory, bought by the Belgian government after Monckhoven's death, is today national property.

3. [Félicien Rops (1833–1898), Belgian artist, printmaker, and caricaturist, closely linked with nineteenth-century Symbolism and Decadence, and a friend of Charles Baudelaire.]

4. [Nadar here refers to the protagonist of Walter Scott's 1819 novel *The Bride of Lammermoor*, Edgar Ravenswood. What is interesting is that he states that the motto of the Ravenswood family is "The Open Hand," when in fact that novel says explicitly that it is "I Bide my Time." There are several moments in Scott where the figure of the open hand appears, and perhaps the most salient one can be found in chapter XX of *Waverley, or 'Tis Sixty Years Hence*. There, Scott refers to a Gaelic proverb, "May the open hand be filled the fullest."

Nadar may simply be confused here, but this confusion serves him well when, in his book on Baudelaire, *Charles Baudelaire intime: le poète vierge*, published posthumously in 1911, he writes: "Let us not forget that, as if born under the Ravenswoods' motto, 'The Open Hand!,' Baudelaire had begun by more than liberally dissipating a fortune and, given that, did not avoid pressuring his friends—of whom I was one." See *Charles Baudelaire intime* (Paris: A. Blaizot, 1911), 45. Here, this motto works better for Nadar, since he wishes to suggest the ease with which Baudelaire opened his hand to ask for money whenever he needed it.]

5. [The French here is: "Bon, reprend-il encore, mais rendre boeuf pour oeuf!"]

OBSIDIONAL PHOTOGRAPHY

1. [Gabriel Jean Baptiste Ernest Wilfrid Legouvé (1807–1903), French dramatist, essayist, and poet, known for his support of women's rights and of the progressive education of children. With Eugène Scribe (1791–1861), he wrote the notorious *Bataille de dames* in 1851, and his *Histoire morale des femmes* had appeared three years earlier, in 1848. His *De l'alimentation morale pendant le siège* appeared in 1870.]

2. [Jean-Marie-Joseph Coutelle (1748–1835), French engineer, scientist, and pioneer in the history of ballooning. He was the first officer of the Company of Aeronauts, and he was invited to use his expertise to help Napoleon with his planned invasion of Britain; Nicolas-Jacques Conté (1755–1805), French painter, army officer, balloonist, and the inventor of the modern pencil.]

3. A very special mention is owed to this brave lad, chosen by me before anyone else for this first launch, which had to be entrusted to a very confident and experienced man.

He had already once half-drowned with the same *Neptune*, which we used, for many days, for lack of others, for our ascents in captivity—so ruined, deteriorated, and dried up that it had become so fragile that, at the descent, as Duruof would put it, the fingers entered between every stitch "as in an act of *pleasure*."

Altogether proud and happy to go first, even under these perilous conditions, Duruof sacrificed for this honor, without a second's hesitation, half of his profit from the manufacture of postal balloons, the bargaining for which I had concluded with the government the day before for the benefit of my two aides. This half of the profits was his only payment.

4. There were even double simultaneous departures; this was the case on the day when Gambetta finally decided to let us take him up—since that day was no longer *a Friday*.

THE PRIMITIVES OF PHOTOGRAPHY

1. Bayard was the first photographer to produce photographs (on paper). He presented his research to François Arago in 1839, but the savant, the head of the democratic opposition, a member of the Chamber of Deputies was already protecting Daguerre and had his project approved by the Chamber. Bayard also organized the first world exhibition of photography in 1839; it took place in Paris.

Photography on paper therefore had to wait until 1847, for the Frenchman Blanquart-Évrard to return to the processes of Bayard and of the Englishman Fox Talbot by improving them, and thus enabling photography to be commercialized.

2. Adam Salomon was also famous for his portraits; an old sculptor, he was one of the first to know how to be creative with lighting. He achieved effects of light, a very particular kind of mobility, a certain blurriness, which gave his photographs a singular appearance.

3. [The Latin here means "an excellent flock."]

4. After long years of research, Gustave Le Gray succeeded in inventing the dry collodion process, which plays a decisive role in the history of photography. The fate of Le Gray was that of all the first photographers for whom the commercial part of the profession did not play an important role; almost all got crushed by the industry, which continued to grow; they mostly refused the pose and the process of retouching. Le Gray has left us a portrait of Napoleon III, a real document on the character of the emperor that tells us infinitely more about him than all the innumerable painted and photographed portraits of the period.

5. [Nadar here uses the figure of St. Helena to evoke Napoleon—St. Helena was the island to which Napoleon was exiled after his defeat at Waterloo in 1815—and, in particular, Napoleon's role in creating a Salon des Refusés (Salon of the Refused) in 1863 order to display the works rejected by the Salon de Paris for not following the usual protocols. Works rejected included paintings by Monet, Cézanne, Degas, Renoir, Pissarro, Sisley, and others, many of which were painted in the open air. In April 1874, approximately 30 of these rejected artists put together an exhibition in Nadar's studio.]

6. [Narcisse Virgilio Díaz de la Peña, a French painter of the Barbizon school.]

7. [Disdéri, the official photographer of the emperor, a very skillful merchant, was also, in his time, a serious competitor of Nadar. Curiously, his writings show that his opinions on photography were not that different from those of Nadar.]

8. We will cite here first the charity of Mr. Numa Blanc, Jr., from Cannes.

9. [Here Nadar refers to the sixteenth-century sculptor, draftsman, and goldsmith Benvenuto Cellini.]

10. Mrs. Adam Salomon has left a very small book of a few pages in thirty-twomo, quite a modest format for a real work of art. This booklet, hard to find today, is titled: *Of Education*. In her modesty, the author pretends that she has translated the advice of a Chinese princess to her daughter.

Lamartine wrote in two paragraphs, according to the proportions of this cute little book, a preface which ends with this surprising phrase: "... Finally we can say of this little book that it is *The Imitation of the Mothers of the Family*" (? ...). And that Karr who could never understand my distrust of his Lamartine!

11. [Louis de Bourbon, Prince of Condé (1621–1686), French general and the most famous member of the Condé part of the House of Bourbon. He was known as *le Grand Condé* for his military skills.]

12. [La Villette, touted in the late 1860s as the greatest market and slaughterhouse area in all of Europe. One of the poorest areas of Paris, and home to a great number of factories and industrial warehouses, La Villette was widely known as an area of high crime; Cannebière, the historic high street in the old quarter of Marseille, full of cafés and shops.]

13. [Kermesse, a Mass performed on the anniversary of a church's founding and in honor of the church's patron, and accompanied by feasts and dancing.]

14. Among some very curious canvases issuing from the sale of this Exhibition, I possess a fake Meissonier, which never fails to hypnotize every visitor. Very eminent amateurs, the most expert of experts (I don't want to name anyone), there is not one—I'm saying: *not even one*; the effect is certain!—who, guided by mere intuition, does not remain fixed on it with an admiring stare ...

It is just simply a small photograph of a man in Louis XIII costume, rubbed with some red paint à la Meissonier—in order to make innocents and other signatories measure the genius of the capillary painter.

15. [Gotha almanac, a directory of Europe's nobility, first published in Germany in 1763 and then published annually from 1785.]

16. [Stanislaw Julian Ostroróg (1830–1890), an early portrait photographer, whose pseudonym, Walery, was taken from his wife's name, Waleria.]

17. [Louis Veuillot (1813–1883), French journalist and writer who notoriously supported papal authority. He wrote over fifty books, many of which describe the beauty of Christian doctrine.]

18. [Paul Scarron (1610–1660), French poet, dramatist, and novelist, mostly known for his burlesques and comedies. He often borrowed from Spanish sources; his most enduring work, *Roman comique* (1651–1657), adapts materials from Cervantes' *Don Quixote*; Jacques Offenbach (1819–1880), German-born French composer and cellist. He is best known for his unfinished opera *The Tales of Hoffmann* and the nearly 100 operettas he wrote between the 1850s and 1870s. Napoleon granted him French citizenship.]

19. [Jean Leblond de Branville (1502–1553), French poet and translator, well known for his translations of ancient and modern Latin texts into French, including Thomas More's *Utopia* in 1550.]

20. [Hippogriff, a legendary, magical creature that resembles a winged horse with the head and upper body of an eagle, first appearing in Virgil's *Eclogues*. Born of a horse and a griffin (its birth is described in canto IV of Ludovico Ariosto's *Orlando Furioso*), the hippogriff was presumably able to fly around the world, and to the moon. Since griffins and horses were supposed to be mortal enemies, the hippogriff appears as a figure of love, and of the impossible; Chimera, in Greek mythology, a fire-breathing female monster having a lion's head, a goat's body, and a serpent's tail. Like the hippogriff, the chimera, composed of incongruous parts, suggests an illusion or invention of the mind, that is, something impossible.]

THE NEW PRESIDENT OF THE FRENCH SOCIETY OF PHOTOGRAPHY

1. [Théodore de Banville (1823–1891), French poet, theorized the necessity of formal perfection and the autonomy of art, one of the major contributors to "Parnasse contemporain." He and Nadar were lifelong friends from 1843 onward.]

2. [Michel-Eugène Chevreul (1786–1889), French chemist, became a member of the Academy of Sciences in 1826. He focused his research on fatty substances, and was the first scientist to isolate

stearic acid. Nadar and his son Paul interviewed Chevreul on the occasion of his 100th birthday, and photographed him during the interview; this interview became the first illustrated interview. The interview and photographs are now available in *Paul Nadar, premier interview photographique* (Lausanne: Éditions Ides et Calendes, 2000).]

3. [Jean Bouillaud (1796–1881), physician, conducted research on cardiovascular diseases and was an early advocate of localizing cerebral functions.]

4. 1885, second edition. [See *La Méthode graphique dans les sciences expérimentales et principalement en physiologie et en médicine, deuxième tirage* (Paris: G. Masson, Éditeur, 1885).]

5. Third year, no. 3, of *Paris-Photographe*. See also, in the next number, the very interesting account of similar results obtained by Viscount Ponton d'Amécourt.

THE BEE TAMER

1. [Pays d'Oc and Pays d'Oil are two areas in southern France where the two principal dialects in medieval France are still spoken. *Oc* means "yes" in Provençal; *oil* means "yes" in Old French. Nadar also plays here on the echolalia between *oil* and *ail*, which means "garlic," since the food in southern France uses a great deal of garlic.]

2. [Nadar here uses the Italian *tutti*.]

3. [Louis-Auguste Commerson (1802–1879), French journalist, founder of *Tam-Tam*, which later became *Le Tintamarre*, a polemical, satirical, burlesque magazine.]

1830 AND THEREABOUTS

1. I refer here to the Teste affair and General Despans-Cubière. [Jean-Baptiste Teste (1780–1852) was a French politician, Chief of Police during Napoleon's Hundred Days, later a minister of Louis Philippe from 1830 to 1843. In 1847 he was accused, along with General Cubière, of facilitating a state concession for a salt mine in exchange for the payment of a huge bribe. It was one of the major scandals of that time.]

2. [See Victor Hugo, *Les Misérables*, trans. Isabel F. Hapgood (New York: Thomas Y. Orowell, 1887), 114.]

3. [Adolphe Thiers (1797–1877), French statesman, journalist, and historian. He was Minister of the Interior in 1832 and from 1834 to 1836, and Minister of Trade from 1833 to 1834. He became President of the Republic in 1871, after ruthlessly using troops to defeat the Paris insurrection.]

4. [Benôit-Constant Coquelin (1841–1909), French actor, one of the most famous theatrical figures of the nineteenth century, and a member of the Comédie-Française for more than twenty-five years, playing the lead role in nearly fifty productions, including plays by Molière, Théodore de Banville, and Paul Ferrier. After resigning from the group in 1886, he successfully toured Europe and America, often with Sarah Bernhardt; L'Abbé François-Ferdinand Châtel (1795–1857), founder of the French Catholic Church. He was the first abbot to conduct the Mass in French, not in Latin. He was against the celibacy of priests and for the emancipation of women; Jacques de Molay (c. 1243–1314), the last Grand Master of the Knights Templar and the most famous representative of the Order. He was condemned to death by King Philip IV after a conflict for power between Philip and Pope Clement V, and after the Knights Templar were abolished by papal decree.]

5. [Barthélemy Prosper Enfantin (1796–1864), French social, political, and economic theorist, a founder of Saint-Simonianism, often referred to as "Père Enfantin." Enfantin and his followers formed a communal group in Ménilmontant, He also had imagined a Suez Canal that would serve as a bridge between the East and the West.]

6. Élie Reclus, *Les Primitifs d'Australie*. [See Élie Reclus, *Le Primitif d'Australie ou les non-non et les oui-oui* (Paris: E. Dentu, 1894), 22. Reclus (1827–1904) was an ethnographer in the classical sense, but also, and far more radically than his colleagues and contemporaries, a critic of bourgeois life and an anarchist (he is at the beginning of the tradition that links anarchism to primitive "gift" systems).]

7. [Étienne Cabet (1788–1856), in his novel *Travels to Icaria* (1840), described the utopia of a communist society which, after the failure of the 1848 revolutionary uprising in Europe, was later attempted

with dubious results in America: first in Texas, and subsequently in Illinois and St. Louis.]

8. [Constant Cheneau established a Reformist Christian cult that baptized adults, conceived of confession as a conversation, and believed in the primordial unity of humanity in Eve-Adam. The cult was referred to as the religion of Evadism (a name formed by putting together the names of the first man and the first woman) or of *Ma-Pa*, from *mater* and *pater*; Émile de Girardin (1806–1881), French journalist and publicist, called the Napoleon of the press for his ability to publish inexpensive newspapers with wide circulations.]

9. [Hyacinthe-Louis de Quélen (1778–1839) was the 125th Archbishop of Paris from 1821 to 1839. Following the violence of the July Revolution of 1830, he was driven twice from his palace. Later, during the epidemic of 1832, he turned his seminaries into hospitals and cared for the sick at the Hôtel-Dieu.]

10. [Emmanuel-Augustin-Dieudonné-Joseph, comte de Las Cases (1766–1842) was a French atlas maker and author, most famous for his *Memorial of Saint Helena*, which presumably consists of notes taken from his conversations with Napoleon. He was expelled in 1816 by the governor of Saint Helena, Sir Hudson Lowe, for infringing British regulations, and for criticizing Lowe for his treatment of Napoleon.]

11. [Jean-Barthélemy Hauréau (1812–1896), French historian, journalist, and writer. In 1848 he was appointed Director of Manuscripts in the Bibliothèque nationale in Paris, but he resigned from the position in 1851, in protest against Napoleon's *coup d'état* in December of that year. His best-known work was his *Histoire de la philosophie scolastique* (1872–1880).]

12. [TF and TP are the initials, respectively, of *travaux forcés* and *travaux à perpétuité*.]

13. [*Bousingot* or *Bousingo* is an offensive word, used after the July 1830 revolution to refer to a group of young political and literary rebels who flaunted their shabby clothing, and expressed advanced democratic ideas.]

14. [Nadar here refers to the Luxor obelisk, a 75-foot-high Egyptian obelisk which was transported in 1833 from the entrance to the

Luxor Temple in Egypt to the Place de la Concorde in Paris. It was shipped on the barge *Louqsor* and was installed in the center of the Place de la Concorde by King Louis-Philippe. The obelisk is over 3,000 years old, and is inscribed with hieroglyphics depicting the pharaohs Ramses II and Ramses III.]

15. [Pierre Lescot (1515–1578), one of the great French architects of the mid-sixteenth century, most famous for his rebuilding of the Louvre, which he started in 1546 as a commission from King Francis I. The style and design of Lescot's work on the Louvre reflect a revolution in French architecture that incorporated classical elements into more traditional French design, and thereby created a unique style of French classicism, which Nadar references here.]

16. [Doyenné was the name of a building located on a namesake pathway across the area which is nowadays occupied by Carrousel Square. Nerval, Rogier and Moussaye, and later Petrus Borel, Gautier, and other writers and artists who belonged to the Romantic groups called "Jeune-France" and "Bousingot" lived in a nine-bedroom apartment inside this building.]

17. [*Schapska* or *chapska*, flat-topped cavalry helmet of Polish origins, which was later adopted by several military corps of the French Army.]

18. [An old two-wheeled public carriage.]

19. [François-Joseph-Victor Broussais (1772–1838), French physician, theorist of "physiological medicine," believer in the physiological interdependence of the various organs, considered inflammation of the tissues the very cause of all diseases, which he treated with diet and phlebotomy. Such treatments were extended also to mental illnesses, as in the situation described here by Nadar.]

20. [Mathieu Orfila (1787–1853), French physician of Spanish origins, often called the "father of toxicology," was the first great nineteenth-century exponent of forensic medicine.]

21. [François-Vincent Raspail (1794–1878), French chemist, naturalist, and physician, became well known in the 1830s as one of the most prominent exponents of the Republican Party. He was a scientist, and studied chemistry and biology. His work anticipated important elements of cell theory. Here, Nadar alludes to this aspect of his legacy. His name rhymes with *ail*, that is, with *garlic*.]

22. [Brid'oison is the character of the foolish and empty-headed judge in Pierre Beaumarchais's *The Marriage of Figaro* (1778).]

23. [Here "Je-les-serre" is a wordplay based on the phonetic mix-up of the Police Chief's last name, *Delessert*, and the sentence *Je les serre*, I lock them (implicitly, with handcuffs).]

24. Today the rue d'Amsterdam, rue de Berlin, rue de Rome, etc., the neighborhood Malesherbes, Saint-Augustine Church, etc.

25. [Arbela, name of the ancient Assyrian city of Erbil and of the namesake battle in which Alexander the Great defeated Darius III of Persia in 331 BC.]

26. [Gabriel Davioud (1823–1881), architect, exponent of architectural eclecticism; during the Second Empire he collaborated with Haussmann in the project for the demolition and renovation of Paris's old neighborhoods.]

27. [Charles-Victor Prévot d'Arlincourt (1788–1856), poet and novelist, author of epic narratives (on Charlemagne) during the First Empire, wrote mediocre and unrealistic novels, of which the most famous is *Le Solitaire* (1821).]

28. [Nadar suggests that Balzac here speaks like a Celt. The Celts were people in early Europe who spoke Celtic languages, and generally occupied lands stretching from the British Isles to Galatia.]

29. Charles Baudelaire, *Aesthetic Curiosities* ["The Salon of 1846," in *Baudelaire: Selected Writings on Art and Artists*, 93].

30. [Jean-Joseph Vadé (1719–1757), French singer, playwright, and poet, known for his use of the *genre poissard*, a theatrical and poetic genre that plays with the language and mores of the lower classes. It was often deployed in informal "parades" or pantomimes organized for private aristocratic entertainments, but it infiltrated the repertory of the Parisian fairs and inspired vaudevilles and burlesques. Vadé was best known for his capacity to re-create the authentic jargon of fishwives and street vendors.]

Index

Abdullah Frères, 141, 164
Ader, Clément, 2, 14, 245
aerial navigation, xii, xxxiv–xxxix, xlii, xlv, l–li, 22, 29–34, 57–72, 181–182, 231, 247, 250–251
  the *Géant*, xxxix, 32–33, 232, 251
Aguado, Olympe, 141, 143
Aguado, Onésyme, 141, 143
Alaux, Jean, 144
Alessandri, Antonio, 141, 164
Alophe (called "Menut"), Marie-Alexandre, 147, 151–152
Andraud, Antoine, 69, 70, 71
Arago, François, xxiv, 15, 245–246, 255
Ariosto, Ludovico, 258
Arlincourt, Charles-Victor Prévot, 220, 263
Auber, Gabriel, 211
Aubert, Louis, xxviii

Babinet, Jacques, 25, 182, 247
Bal[l]ard, Antoine Jérôme, 190
Ballue, Hippolyte Omer, 141, 146
Baltard, Victor, 207
Balzac, Honoré de, xvii–xviii, 4–5, 171, 221, 244–245, 263
Bann, Stephen, xiv
Banville, Théodore de, xlv, 181, 194, 228, 258, 260
Bareswill (of Lerebours and Bareswill), 141, 143
Barral, Jean-Augustin, 91, 247
Barré, Aimé, 249
Barthes, Roland, xxxii
Bataille, Charles, l, 233
Baudelaire, Charles, x–xi, xxxvi, xli, lii, 149, 176, 228, 232, 234, 237–238, 242–243, 254–255, 263
  Benjamin on, x–xi
  on the erasure of Paris, xli
  "The Salon of 1846," 243
  "Spleen II," xxxvi
  "The Swan," xli
  "Tableaux parisiens" ("Parisian Scenes"), lii
Baudrand, Mr., 157
Bayard, Hippolyte, 141–142, 174, 255–256
Beaumarchais, Pierre, 263
Becquerel, Edmond, 141, 143, 157
Béguin, Antoine, 174
Belgrand, Eugène, 94
Bell, Alexander Graham, 15
Benjamin, Walter, ix, x–xi, xiii, xvii–xix, xxxvi, xxxviii, xlii, xliv, lii–lv
  Arcades Project, x, xi, xvii–xix, xxxviii, xliv, 238
  on Baudelaire, x–xi, lii
  "Berlin Chronicle," xviii, 239
  on Nadar, xi, xiii, xvii–xviii, xxxviii
  "On the Concept of History," ix
  "Task of the Translator," lii–lv, 237

Beraud, Anthony, 212
Berlioz, Hector, 219
Berne-Bellecour[t], Étienne-Prosper, 141, 147
Bernhardt, Sarah, 232, 260
Bernheim, Hippolyte, xxxi, 54, 250
Bertall, Charles-Albert d'Arnoux, 141, 147
Berthollet, Claude Louis, 122, 254
Bertsch, Adolphe, 62–63, 141–143, 176, 230
Berzelius, Jöns Jacob, 21, 246
Beyle, Marie-Henri (known as Stendhal), 221
Biot, Jean-Baptiste, 25–26, 62, 247
Bisson, brothers, 62, 141, 147–152, 155
Blanc, Louis, 253
Blanc, Numa, 141, 147
Blanc, Numa, Jr., 256
Blanquart-Évrard, 256
Borel, Petrus (Joseph-Pierre Borel d'Hauterive), 262
Bossut, Charles, 122
Bouillaud, Jean, 184, 259
Bourbouze, Jean-Gustave, 21, 246
Bourdaloue, Louis, 81, 252
Bourseul, Charles, 2, 243
Boussingault, Jean-Baptiste, 92, 253
Branicki, Constantin, 86
Branville, Jean Leblond de, 175, 258
Braun, Adolphe, 164
Briges, Count of, 147
Broussais, François-Joseph-Victor, 212, 262
Brunetière, Ferdinand, 2, 243

Cabet, Étienne, 205, 260–261
Cardano (Cardan), Gerolamo, 4, 244
caricature, 156–157, 220, 229, 231, 252
Carjat, Étienne, 141, 147, 157
Caselli, Giovanni, 14, 245
Cassini, Jacques, 60, 79, 250
catacombs, xii, xxxvi–xxxviii, 75–84, 86, 94
  egalitarian confusion of death in, 78–80
Cavendish, Lord Charles, 21, 246
Cellini, Benvenuto, 13, 143, 156, 257
Cervantes, Miguel de, 258
Cézanne, Paul, 233, 256
Champfleury (Jules François Felix Fleury-Husson), 175
Chandelier, Charles, 154
Chappe, Claude, 2, 220
Chapsal, Charles Pierre, 76, 251
Chaptal, Jean-Antoine, 122
Charcot, Jean-Martin, 2
Charivari, 156, 220, 229, 244, 251
Charles, Jacques Alexandre, 57, 250
Chassériau, Théodore, 149
Châtel, François-Ferdinand, 205, 260
Chauveau, Jean-Baptiste Auguste, 189

Cheneau, Constant, 205, 261
Chênedollé, Charles-Julien Lioult de, 83, 252
Chevalier, Charles, 142
Chevreul, Michel-Eugène, 183, 233, 258
Cicero, Marcus Tullius, 250
citation, xxi, xxvii, xxxiv–xxxv
Claudet, Antoine, 164
Coëtlogon, C. E. de, 223
Commerson, Louis-Auguste, 199, 259
Comte, Auguste, 221
Condé, Louis de Bourbon, Prince of, 160, 257
Condorcet, Marie Jean Antoine Nicolas de Caritat, marquis de, 122
Conté, Nicolas-Jacques, 2, 120, 122, 132, 255
Cooper, James Fenimore, 207
Coppée, François, 24, 246
Coquelin, Benôit-Constant, 205, 260
Cormenin, Louis, 149
Cottin, Sophie Risteau, 10, 245
Couder, Auguste, 221
Courbet, Gustave, 167
Coutelle, Jean-Marie-Joseph, 132, 255
Couture, Thomas, 174
Cros, Charles, 2, 243
Cuvier, Georges, 204

Dagron, René, xliv, 137–138
Daguerre, Louis-Jacques, xviii, 1, 3–4, 6, 142, 228, 243, 246, 255
Dallemagne, Adolphe-Jean-François-Marin, 141, 159–161
D'Amécourt, Viscount Ponton, 31, 232, 259
Darcet, Jean, 122
Darjou, Henri Alfred, 174
D'Arlincourt, Charles-Victor Prévot, viscount, 220, 263
D'Arnaud, Camille, 62, 141, 143, 176, 230
Darwin, Charles, 175, 249
Daudet, Léon, xlix
Daumier, Honoré, 156, 233, 251–252
Davanne, Louis Alphonse, 143
David, Jacques-Louis, 144
Davioud, Gabriel, 218, 263
Daziaro, J., 164
death, xiii–xv, xl–xli, xliv–xlvii
  and photography, xxxii–xxxiii, xxxv, 51–53, 78–80, 111–117
Deburau, Jean-Gaspard, 157
Degas, Edgar, 233, 256
Delaage, Henri, 86
Delacroix, Eugène, 144, 149, 221
Delaroche, Paul, 144, 164, 221
Delessert, Benjamin, 143
Delessert, Édouard, 143
Delessert, Gabriel, 213, 263
Delille, Jacques, 76, 80, 251
De Lucy, Louis, 141, 147, 164, 244
Demény, Georges, 189
D'Ennery, Adolphe-Philippe, 23–24

De Pages, Hérald, 12, 16–17, 19–20, 22, 23–25
Deprez, Marcel, 14, 245
Déroche, Mathieu, 141
Desmarets, Paul, 251
Despans-Cubière, General, 260
De Vigny, Alfred Victor, 221
Díaz de la Peña, Narcisse Virgilio, 146, 166, 256
Diderot, Denis, 179
Dimoula, Kiki, lii, lv
Disdéri, André-Adolphe-Eugène, 141, 151–155, 256
  and the carte de visite, 151
  fortune of, 153, 155
Dolfus de Mulhouse, 148
Doré, Gustave, 1, 86, 167
doubling, xxiii, xxvi–xxvii, xxx, 20
Downing, Eric, 239
Ducis, Jean-François, 80
Ducom, Jacques, 72, 251
Dugué, Ferdinand, 217
Dulaure, Jacques-Antoine, 79, 252
Dumas, Alexandre (père), 175, 212
Duprez, Gilbert-Louis, 219
Duruof, Jules, 132, 255
Du Sommerard [Dusommerard], Alexandre, 211

Edison, Thomas A., 2, 70
Enfantin, Barthélemy Prosper, 205, 260

fashion, xvi, 5, 120, 154, 158–159, 207, 209, 219
Fassy, Paul, 79, 252
Fenayrou, Marin, xxviii–xxix, 53–54
Ferris, David, ix–x
Fineman, Mia, 242
Flaubert, Gustave, 253
Florian, Jean-Pierre Claris de, 32, 248
Folkes, Martin, 21, 246
Fortier, Alphonse, 143
Foucault, Léon, 245
Foulquier, Joseph François, 174
Fourcroy, Antoine François, comte de, 2, 119, 121–122
Fourier, Charles, 205
Freud, Sigmund, 250
Froment, Paul-Gustave, 14, 245
Fualdès, Antoine, 47, 240, 249

Gambetta, Léon, 255
Gaulard, Lucien, 84, 252
Gautier, Théophile, 5, 149, 175, 221, 245, 253, 262
Gavarni, Paul, 5, 154, 171, 174, 244
Gay-Lussac, Joseph Louis, 247
Gellain, Françoise (Madame Legros), 82
Gérard, François, 144
Géricault, Théodore, 144, 167, 221
Ghémar, Louis, 126, 141, 164 168
ghosts, xiv, xvii–xviii, xx, xxvi, 3–6, 20
Gille, Philippe, 98
Girardin, Émile de, 205, 220, 261
Girodet-Trioson, Anne-Louis, 144

Godard, Eugène, 63, 65, 250–251
Gozlan, Léon, 5, 149, 245
Grancher, Jacques-Joseph, 213
Grandeau, Louis, 92, 253
Griscom, William Woodnut, 16, 246
Guizot, François, 219–220, 222, 224

Halphen, Louis, 86
Hambourg, Maria Morris, 1
Hampsteingl, Franz, 141, 143, 158
Hauréau, Jean-Barthélemy, 207, 261
Haussmann, Georges-Eugène, xl–xli, 263
Heim, François Joseph, 221
Heine, Heinrich, 132
Henry, brothers, 122
Hess, Karl, 221
Hoffmann, E. T. A., 159
Houssaye, Arsène, 143, 176, 217
Hugo, Victor, 91, 203, 221, 253, 260

Ingres, Jean-Auguste-Dominique, 144, 221
Isambert, François-André, 223

Janin, Jules, 149, 175
Janssen, Jules, 122, 190

Karr, Alphonse, 194, 257
Kracauer, Siegfried, ix, 237
Krauss, Rosalind E., xi, 237

La Blanchère, Pierre Moulin du Coudray de, 157
Lafon de Camarsac, Pierre Michel Marie Alcide, 164
Lalande, Jérôme, 122
La Landelle, Guillaume Joseph Gabriel de, 86
Lamartine, Alphonse de, 257
Laplace, Pierre-Simon, 2
Las Cases, Emmanuel-Augustin-Dieudonné-Joseph, comte de, 206, 261
Latour de Saint-Ybars, Isidore, 19, 246
Laussedat, Colonel Aimé, 71
Lavoisier, Antoine, 2, 122
Lazerge, Hippolyte, 141, 159–161
Lebiez, Paul, 41, 54, 249
Leclanché, Léopold, 13, 143
Legouvé, Gabriel Jean Baptiste Ernest Wilfrid, 131, 138, 255
Le Gray, Gustave, 62, 143–152, 256
  and painting, 143, 145, 152
Legros, Alphonse, 141–142
La Landelle, Gabriel de, 31
Leleux, Adolphe and Armand, 149
Lemaître, Frédérick, 157
Lemercier, Joseph, 141, 157
  and lithography, 157
Lemierre, Antoine-Marin, 80
Le Pic, Ludovic, 150
Lerebours, Noël Marie Paymal, 141–142
Lescot, Pierre, 211, 262
Lewitzki, Count Sergei Lvovich, 141, 164

Liebig, Justus von, 92, 253
Liesegang, Dr. Eduard, 26
Lireux, Auguste, 221, 228
Lissajoux, Jules Antoine, 2, 243
lithography, 156, 217, 234, 244
and Alophe, 151
and Daumier, 251
Lombroso, Cesare, 54, 250
Lorain, Paul Joseph, 189
Louis-Philippe, King, 147, 262
Lowe, Sir Hudson, 206
Luckhardt, Fritz, 164
Lucretius, xviii, xx, 239
Lucy, Louis de, 141, 164, 244
Lumière, Auguste and Louis, 93
Lyon, Thierry de, 141

Mach, Ernst, 188
Manet, Édouard, 144
Marconi, Guglielmo, 26
Marey, Étienne-Jules, li, 2, 62, 122, 126, 179–189, 247
and chronophotography, 188–189
medical studies, 183
and Muybridge, 188
and Presidency of the French Society of Photography, 179–189
Marmand, Jean, 141, 149
Marnhyac, Mr. de, 148
Marochetti, Carlo, 170, 172
Martinet-Hautecœur (publisher), 211
Marville, Charles, 141, 148
Mathieu-Deroche, Jean Louis Albert, 164
Maunier de Flore, Mr., 193–200
Mayer, Léopold Ernest and Louis Frederic, 141, 145–146
Meissonier, Jean-Louis-Ernest, 159–160, 257
Menesclou, Louis, 250
Mercadier, Ernest, 136–137
Méry, Joseph, 149, 219
Mesmer, Franz Anton, 2
Mignard, Pierre, 160
Millet, Jean-François, 167
Mirès, Jules, 86
Moitessier, Albert, 141, 143, 157
Molay, Jacques de, 205, 260
Molière (Jean-Baptiste Poquelin), 244
Monckhoven, Desiré Charles Emanuel van, 122–129, 141, 161–162, 165
friendship with Marey, 126
generosity, 127–128
love of astronomy, 125–126
treatises on photography, 123–124
Monet, Claude, 256
Monge, Gaspard, 120, 122
Monglond, André, ix, 237
Monnier, Henri, 252
Montgolfier, Joseph-Michel and Jacques-Étienne, 2, 30, 61, 250
More, Thomas, 258
Moussaye, Count Gustave de la, 262
Muller, Johannes, 248
music, 132, 172, 198, 207, 214–215, 219, 221
Musset, Alfred de, 221
Muybridge, Eadweard, 188

Nadar (Gaspard Félix Tournachon)
and aerial mail service, xliii–xliv, 132–138, 233, 255
and aerostatic experiments, 57–72, 181–182
and artificial lighting, xvi, 22, 84–86, 157, 231
À terre et en l'air, xxxix
and Baudelaire, 254
Le Droit au vol (The Right to Fly), 244
existing between life and death, xiii–xvi
and lithography, xiv
and *Panthéon Nadar*, 174–176, 229–231
photographs of the Parisian Catacombs, 75–84
photographs of the Parisian sewers, 87–94
practice of portraiture, xix–xxi, 9, 11, 85, 97–108
Quand j'étais étudiant (When I Was a Student), xiv–xv, 230, 239
relation to brother Adrien, xxviii, xxx–xxxi
Sous l'incendie (Under Fire), xlv, 233, 242
Nadar, Paul, 72, 230, 233–235, 251, 259
Nanteuil, Célestin, 149, 174
Napoleon I, 254–256, 261
Napoleon III, 154, 256, 258, 261
Nègre, Charles, 157
Nerval, Gérard de, 5, 219, 262
Niépce, Nicéphore, 1, 3, 99, 123, 142, 145, 242–243, 249
Nodier, Charles, 210
Noël, François-Joseph-Michel, 76, 251
Nourritt, Adolphe, 219

Offenbach, Jacques, 175, 258
Offret, Dr., 53–54
opera, xxxvii, 34, 132, 219, 258
Orfila, Mathieu, 212, 263
Ouvrard, Gabriel-Julien, 222

painting, 187, 221, 256
relation to photography, 146, 159–160, 163, 166
Paris, xii, xl–xlvii, 203–224
Catacombs, 75–94
Haussmannian destruction of, xl–xlii
markets, 80, 103, 207, 213, 223, 257
as necropolis, xxxvi, 83
as photographopolis, 62
sewers, 87–94
Siege of, xli–xliv, xlv, 131–138
Universal Exhibition (1855), xiv, 156–157
Universal Exhibition (1867), 252
Paris-Photographe, 187, 233–234, 259
Pasteur, Louis, 2, 213
Paxton, Joseph, 207
Péligot, Eugène, 190
Penguilly, Octave, 149
Pereire, brothers, 204, 251
Pereire, Émile, 86, 159
Pereire, Isaac, 159
Perier, Paul, 142

Peyronnet, Pierre-Denis, comte de, 215
Philipon, Charles, 211, 220
photography, 63, 93, 113, 124, 135, 148, 179, 221, 228
aerial, 57–72
business of, 61, 68, 107–108, 168, 171
collodion process, xxxviii, xliii–xliv
contested origins, 1
daguerreotype, xvii–xviii, xx, 1, 3, 5, 69–70, 142, 171–172, 228, 243, 246
and death, xxxii–xxxiii, xxxv, 51–53, 111–117
and dissolution of the self, xiv–xv, xix, xxiii, xxvi–xxvii, 19–20
early pioneers of, 141–176
manipulation of, 143, 157–158, 256
and painting, 146, 159–160, 163, 166
and violence, xxviii–xxix, xxxii–xxxiii, 51–53
Pichot, Amédée, 210
Picot, François-Édouard, 144, 221
Pierson, Pierre-Louis, 141, 145, 146
Pingret, Édouard-Henri-Théophile, 221
Piranesi, Giovanni Battista, 90, 253
Pissarro, Camille, 256
Poe, Edgar Allan, 50
Poitevin, Alphonse Louis, 123, 141, 143, 145, 157, 163
Pontécoulant, Louis Gustave le Doulcet, comte de, 218
Porché, François, xxxvi
Pradier, Jean-Jacques, 85, 253
Préault, Antoine-Augustin, 85, 144, 149, 253
Prendergast, Christopher, xxxvii, 241
Prevost, Jean-Louis, 174
Proust, Marcel, 238
Prudhomme, 81, 252
Puteaux, Lucien, 134

Quélen, Hyacinthe-Louis de, 206, 261

Rabelais, François, 79, 183
Raisson, Horace, 220
Randon, Gilbert, 142
Raspail, François-Vincent, 2, 212, 262
Reclus, Élie, 260
Regnault, Henri-Victor, 190
Rémusat, Charles François Marie, comte de, 215
Renoir, Pierre-Auguste, 233, 256
retouching photographs, 157, 256
Hampsteingl's practice, 143, 158
Le Gray's refusal of, 256
Salomon's practice, 143, 158
Rice, Shelley, xl, 241
Richebourg, Pierre-Ambrose, 142
Richelieu, Duke de, 218
Rimbaud, Arthur, 246
Robert, Anne-Jean and Nicolas-Louis, 250

Rogier, Camille, 262
Rops, Félicien, 127, 254
Rossini, Gioachino Antonio, 219
Rothschild, James Mayer, Baron de, 149
Roux, Émile, 213
Royer-Collard, Pierre-Paul, 215

Saint-Victor, Niépce de, 149
Salomon, Adam, 141, 143, 147, 158–159, 256–257
Sand, George, 1, 232, 243
Sarony, brothers, 141, 164–165, 173
Sauvageot, Louis, 211
Scarron, Paul, 175, 258
Scheffer, brothers, 221
Scott, Sir Walter, 254
Scribe, Eugène, 255
Second, Albéric, 86
Séguin, Armand, 119, 122, 254
Séraphin, Dominique, 207
Séverin, Robert, 141, 164
Seymour, Lord, 223
Silvy, Camille-Léon-Louis, 5, 164, 168–173, 244
Sisley, Alfred, 256
Solms, princess of, 34–36
Soulié, Frédéric, 212
Spoelberg de Lovenjoul, Charles de, 5, 244
Staël, Madame de (Anne Louise Germaine de Staël-Holstein), 216
Steinheil, Carl August von, 21, 124, 246
Stephenson, Robert, 17, 204
Steuben, Charles Auguste Guillaume, 144
Sue, Eugène, 244
Swift, Jonathan, 58

Taglioni, Marie, 219
Tainter, Summer, 15
Talbot, William Henry Fox, 123, 256
Tarde, Gabriel, xxxiv–xxxv
Taupenot, Jean-Marie, 143, 157
Taylor, Baron Isidore, 163, 205
Teste, Jean-Baptiste, 259
theater, xiii, xvi–xvii, xxxvii, xlvi, 219, 221
Thélot, Jérôme, xxviii, xxxii, xxxiv, 237, 239
Thierry, Jean-Pierre, 142
Thiers, Adolphe, 204, 220, 222–224, 260
Tissandier, Albert and Gaston, 72, 251
Tissandier, Galton, 242
Tournachon, Adrien, xxviii, xxx–xxxi, 141, 147, 227, 229–234
  and Deburau, 157
Tripier, Louis, 143
Trousseau, Armand, 86
Trouvé, Gustave, 14, 245

Vadé, Jean-Joseph, 223, 263
Vaillat, Eduard, 141–142
Van Loo, Carle, 160
Vauquelin, Louis Nicolas, 122
Venette, Nicolas, 217
Vernet, Horace, 144, 221
Veuillot, Louis, 160, 173, 258
Vidal, Léon, 141, 161–164
  books on photographic techniques, 163

Vigneron, Pierre Roch, 151
Villemain, Abel-François, 215
Virgil (Publius Vergilius Maro), 258
visibility/invisibility, xvii, xxiv–xxv, 3, 9–10, 17–18, 245
Voillemot, André-Charles, 174
Volney, François-Constantin de Chasseboeuf, Count of, 76, 251

Wagner, Richard, 132
Walery (Stanislaw Julian Ostroróg), 141, 172–173, 258
Wallon, Jean, 205
Warnod, Jean Victor, 141, 157
Watson, William, 21, 246
Wedel, Count of, 34–36
Wright, Wilbur and Orville, 245

Young, Edward, 76, 251